Sarah Kessler
Competing Climate Cultures in Germany

Sociology of Sustainability | Volume 4

The series is edited by Arbeitskreis SONA Soziologie der Nachhaltigkeit.

Sarah Kessler (Dr.) is a social scientist at the Institute for Social Change and Sustainability at Wirtschaftsuniversität Wien. She obtained her doctoral degree at the Department of Geography, Ludwig-Maximilians-Universität (LMU) Munich, Germany. She works on topics spanning environmental sociology, sustainability research, practice theory, science communication and digital ethnography. Currently, she investigates group-specific societal receptions of climate change, climate-cultural diversity and issues of responsibility, efficacy and knowledge regarding climate protection.

Sarah Kessler

Competing Climate Cultures in Germany

Variations in the Collective Denying of Responsibility and Efficacy

[transcript]

The text and wording of this book almost exactly correspond to my doctoral thesis that was supervised by Henrike Rau at the Department of Geography at the LMU München. It was defended and published in the summer of 2022. Only minor revisions were undertaken for this book publication.

This publication has been funded by the Bavarian network for climate research (bayklif).

Bibliographic information published by the Deutsche Nationalbibliothek
The Deutsche Nationalbibliothek lists this publication in the Deutsche Nationalbibliografie; detailed bibliographic data are available in the Internet at https://dnb.dnb.de/

First published in 2024 by transcript Verlag, Bielefeld

Cover layout: Maria Arndt, Bielefeld
Printed by: Majuskel Medienproduktion GmbH, Wetzlar
https://doi.org/10.14361/9783839471432
Print-ISBN: 978-3-8376-7143-8
PDF-ISBN: 978-3-8394-7143-2
ISSN of series: 2748-7598
eISSN of series: 2749-2044

Printed on permanent acid-free text paper.

For Oskar, Ruby, and the currently banana-seized baby.
May the world realise ***soon*** *what's at stake for your lives.*

Contents

Part I – Introduction

Part II – Theoretical and methodological framework

Part III – Empirical findings

Part IV – Discussion, recommendations and outlook

List of figures

List of abbreviations

AfD	Alternative für Deutschland (Alternative for Germany)
bayklif	Bayerisches Klimaforschungsnetzwerk (Bavarian network for climate research)
BAYSICS	Bayerisches Synthese-Informations-Citizen Science Portal für Klimaforschung und Wissenschaftskommunikation (Bavarian synthesis information citizen science portal for climate change research and science communication)
BMEL	Bundesministerium für Ernährung und Landwirtschaft (Federal Ministry of Food and Agriculture)
CDU	Christlich Demokratische Union Deutschlands (Christian Democratic Union of Germany)
CSU	Christlich-Soziale Union Bayern (Christian Social Union of Bavaria)
cf.	compare to
CO_2	Carbon dioxide (Kohlenstoffdioxid)
e.g.	for example
FDP	Freie Demokratische Partei (Free Democratic Party)
Freie Wähler	Free Voters of Bavaria
i.a.	among other things
ibid.	in the same place
IFEU	Institut für Energie- und Umweltforschung (Institute of Energy and Environmental Research)
IPCC	Intergovernmental Panel on Climate Change (Weltklimarat)
LMU	Ludwig-Maximilians-Universität (LMU Munich)
OPAC	Online public access catalogue
NGO	Non-governmental organisation
SPD	Sozialdemokratische Partei Deutschlands (Social Democratic Party of Germany)
UBA	Umweltbundesamt (federal environmental agency)
UN	United Nations
USP	Unique selling point
vs.	versus

List of tables

Preface & Acknowledgements

> I denied climate change for longer than I care to admit. I knew it was happening, sure. Not like Donald Trump and the Tea Partiers going on about how the continued existence of winter proves it's all a hoax. But I stayed pretty hazy on the details and only skimmed most of the news stories, especially the really scary ones. I told myself the science was too complicated and that the environmentalists were dealing with it. And I continued to behave as if there was nothing wrong with the shiny card in my wallet attesting to my 'elite' frequent flyer status. A great many of us engage in this kind of climate change denial. We look for a split second and then we look away. Or we look but then turn it into a joke ('more signs of the Apocalypse!'). […] Or […] we tell ourselves comforting stories about how humans […] will come up with a technological miracle that will safely suck the carbon out of the skies […]. Which […] is yet another way of looking away. Or we look but try to be hyper-rational about it […]. Or we look but tell ourselves we are too busy to care about something so distant and abstract […]. Or we look but tell ourselves that all we can do is focus on ourselves. Meditate and shop at farmers' markets and stop driving, but forget trying to actually change the systems that are making the crisis inevitable […]. Or maybe we do look – really look – but then, inevitably, we seem to forget. […] We engage in this odd form of on-again-off-again ecological amnesia for perfectly rational reasons. We deny because we fear that letting in the full reality of this crisis will change everything. And we are right.

Naomi Klein – This changes everything, 2015, p. 3ff.

Just like Naomi Klein is describing in this paragraph, I too experienced a lingering and increasingly nagging feeling that climate change should be playing a much greater role in the way we go about our lives, given the extent of the threat posed by it. And here I was particularly puzzled by why some people took the issue much more to heart than others. I could not trace the reasons back to education, political stances or socio-economics. I was especially phased by these different leanings also existing in my parents' generation. More baffling still, eco-conscious baby-boomers did not seem to necessarily have raised eco-conscious millennials but some indifferent baby-boomers had. Why was that? Why was it that some people felt compelled to protect the climate – felt it was their responsibility to do something, while others either blended it out or fatalistically accepted that the planet would eventually just heat like crazy?

Puzzling over philosophical and ethical questions had been a passion of mine at school already, certainly during my masters' course when I wrote my thesis on philosophical issues in development. The prospect of deeply grappling once again with moral concepts got me very excited. And the topic of climate-cultural differences in society gave me a lot of them: responsibility, climate justice, intergenerational justice, global justice, social fairness and so on...

When I started my doctoral research in September 2018 as part of the BAYSICS[1] project, these were the questions that I brought with me. Quickly it became clear to me that it was a very apt time to be researching these issues: what I had not known when I started, of course, was that a mere two weeks before I began my work at the LMU Geography department, on August 20th 2018 in fact, Greta Thunberg had not gone to school for the first time for reasons very much related to my questions. In the rest of that year, *Fridays for Future* was rapidly developing into a large movement and by the time I held my first interviews, climate change had become a much more fiercely debated public issue. So much so that it was one of the key topics in the 2019 European Election, where only a couple of days prior, the German YouTuber *Rezo* released his infamous video in which he fatefully bashed a number of established parties, and most of all the CDU, Germany's leading governing party at the time. Some of my interviews directly relate to this event. For example, on the Monday after the election results had come in, I spoke to a CDU politician and member of the Bundestag who was also part of the party's environmental committee.

Increasingly, I realised that the debate had a whole series of different layers – there were young YouTubers responsibilising established political actors, yet there were also voices in the public that replied that it was outrageous that immature young protestors were telling hard-working managers what to do. What a time to be researching this topic!

The election results revealed the public's desire for climate action, which political leadership answered with a climate cabinet that was to come up with legislation in the summer of 2019. This 'climate package' became however subject to heaps of criticism that often rendered it no more than a 'climate parcel' in public perception. When 2020 came around, I was finishing up my data collection and I distinctly remember doing my last group interview with the mobility provider on a Tuesday in February as it was Pancake Day (*Faschingsdienstag*). That week was when the Covid

1 BAYSICS (Bayerisches Synthese-Informations-Citizen Science Portal für Klimaforschung und Wissenschaftskommunikation) is part of the Bavarian climate change research network bayklif, funded by the Bavarian State Ministry of Science and Art (Bayerisches Staatsministerium für Wissenschaft und Kunst).

action committee was established by the German federal government. On March 10th, I travelled to Berlin for the first meeting of the scientific advisory board for the environmental awareness study and people were already greeting each other awkwardly by bumping their fists or feet. Only ten more days later, Germany went into full lockdown for the first time.

How lucky was I that I had just finished collecting my data and I could continue to work from home analysing my materials and sorting what they revealed to me? This was of course interspersed with several zoom calls with Henrike, my supervisor, who really did a lot of sorting of my thoughts and gave me the most valuable prompts and inputs of her own. I want to take this opportunity to say the biggest thankyou to you, Henrike! Without your warm guidance and valuable feedback, I would absolutely not have gotten on the way I did. And we always had a good laugh or two as well. Without Henrike, you also would not hold this book in your hands – so thank you so much once again for your initiative also in this vein!

In the course of writing a book chapter with Henrike on the media analysis that is covered by chapter 5 in this thesis, the concept of climate cultures emerged as a very useful conceptual tool for this research. I then applied the concept to the focus group discussions to see what insights it yielded in relation to professional work environments. At that time, in autumn 2020, I also had my second baby, my Ruby. So I often sat there, researching and writing my stuff and nursing her at the same time. My husband Kevin would bring her to me when she was hungry and hold her over the top of the door, so I could only see her head and then he would say things he thought she'd want to say in a high voice. I went back to work in April 2021 and now, a year later, I am finally handing in this thesis. I immensely enjoyed working on it.

Writing it would however not at all have been possible without the enormous and continuous support of my parents, especially my Mum, who so often took Oskar and now also Ruby and entertained them with all sorts of wonderful activities. And my Dad would take Oskar to kindergarten on his way to work or pick him up when I was in meetings. I will forever be grateful for the amount of help I got during these past 3,5 years from the two of them and the big part they played in me being able to finish this work.

I also want to thank everyone who gave me their time and valuable input in the interviews. Without them, this research would obviously not have been possible. I am also very grateful for having been part of the Bavarian climate research network (bayklif) and in it the BAYSICS consortium. Extensive exchanges with colleagues from BAYSICS subproject 8 led by Prof. Dr. Ulrike Ohl (University of Augsburg) and subproject 9 led by Prof. Dr. Arne Dittmer (University of Regensburg) were always particularly agreeable and fruitful.

It was also the bayklif consortium that granted me the publication support for this book project – I am immensely grateful for this extremely valuable opportunity.

Thank you also to my close friends who talked things through with me and kept me going. Thank you Nina, Isabelle, Annika and Laura for being there for me during this exciting, fulfilling but also challenging time in my life.

And finally, thank you Kevin! For giving me the space and time to do this work and understanding how important this is for me. For being the best Dad to our kids, so I didn't have to feel so torn between them and working. For keeping the house standing when I'd be so exhausted and so pregnant. For coming along on every dream I come up with and grinning in the face of antiquated family roles with me.

Summary

The question of how to deal with impending climate change is arguably the greatest societal challenge of today. However, effective climate action will only occur on the scale that is needed if broad sections of society participate. Different societal actors have to contribute, including politicians, businesses, civil society groups and individual citizens. In other words, responsibility for climate action must be taken by everybody.

This said, accepting responsibility is not enough to initiate effective climate action. Instead, responsibility is closely intertwined with the (perceived) level of efficacy an agent holds: not everyone has the same power over climate-related outcomes or equal access to participate in climate action initiatives. Moreover, this sense of efficacy strongly relates to an agent's level of climate knowledge. These three concepts – responsibility attributions, efficacy expectations and climate-related knowing – constitute the conceptual cornerstones of this study. More precisely, the study revolves around one particular question: how do particular constellations of responsibility, efficacy and knowing among different social groups shape their members' (lack of) engagement in climate action? To answer this question, the present investigation fuses state-of-the-art research from across a range of social science disciplines such as human geography, environmental sociology, psychology and the environmental humanities.

Based on this conceptual framework, this study generated rich empirical evidence from Germany through a multi-method approach to social research. In the initial part, expert interviews with politicians, government officials, NGO executives and academics captured 'official' opinions on climate change and climate action. Experts' views on issues of responsibility, efficacy and knowledge in relation to climate action received particular attention. Not only was the narrative here quite congruent, the public was also mostly thought of as homogenous. This assumed uniformity of public opinion seemed somewhat limited, initiating a second empirical step involving an in-depth analysis of conventional and social media content. This analysis yielded a much more diverse picture that challenged elite[1] notions of a public consensus regarding climate change and the need for action. In fact, a substantial gap emerged between groups in society whose members receive, acknowledge and internalise 'official' messages regarding climate change and climate action, and those with whom these messages do not (at all) resonate. It is shown that mainstream calls for climate action generally reflect the language and mind-set of those holding larger shares of (particularly cultural) capital, thereby eclipsing the everyday realities of large parts of the population. Observing these divergences and tensions inspired the development of a typology of climate cultures, defined as dynamic variants of social organisation that provide a framework for recognizing culturally relevant information regarding climate change and that are (re-)produced through climate-relevant everyday practices that reveal diverse forms of 'lived' responsibility and actual experiences of (in)efficacy. The latter includes responses to more abstract attributions of responsibility and efficacy in 'official' climate change discourses that may or may not clash with people's everyday experiences.

Through this typology of climate cultures, three key areas of discrepancy concerning responsibility, efficacy and knowledge were identified. First, a major gap exists between official attributions of responsibility and efficacy (often reflected in 'elite' discourses) and experiences of (ir)responsibility and (in)efficacy that people make in their everyday lives. Here, the responsibilisation of individual consumer-citizens appeared to be particularly problematic, given their limited efficacy. Second, attributions of responsibility to different societal actors and related expectations regarding their efficacy can diverge significantly. Successful climate action is unlikely when people experience these divergences. For example, individual consumers often voice demoralisation when they witness practices taking place in the realm of work that have particularly large climate impacts but are out of these individuals' control. Then, being responsibilised in numerous incremental ways in the private sphere is experienced as especially futile.

In cases where these divergences are particularly pronounced, the resulting implementation deficit can sometimes even turn into active disengagement or resistance. For instance, farmers who were interviewed felt particularly disadvantaged and unheard by current politics. They reacted almost allergically to current calls for more climate action since in their perception, the agricultural industry was being

1 It is important to highlight from the very beginning, that in this study, the labels 'elite' and 'privileged' refer to Bourdieu's understanding of those rich in cultural capital and those groups in society that hold considerably more power (e.g., in terms of education levels). It is vital to note here, that I scrutinise differences and conflicts *within* the German population (between those more and less rich in this capital). I *explicitly do not* use these terms as the opposites of 'the elites' and 'the population' as the rhetoric of the political far right frames it.

made the scapegoat (responsibility attributed) for climate issues they did not acknowledge or necessarily see as being related to farming (efficacy negated).

More of the public could be reached if research and policy recognised these substantial discrepancies. Third, it is possible to identify different types of knowledge about climate change that extend well beyond cognition to include visceral and affective aspects. This encompasses not only what is being said to a person but crucially also what swings along with messages, often on an emotional level, and is then, often subconsciously, interpreted and kept. Dropping the conception of the individual as cognitive rational entity and considering practitioners in context instead would be much more conducive to climate action.

Interestingly, different constellations of responsibility, efficacy and ways knowing do not only help to distinguish between climate cultures, they also translate into different forms of socially negotiated denial of (the urgency of) climate action. Two points stand out as particularly unexpected: first, a host of voices exists that engage in explicit denial[2], ranging from moderate climate-scepticism to outright renunciation. These have hitherto not been well-researched, especially in Germany. Second, it is possible to identify a more subtle form of implicit denial that manifests itself through a gap between climate concern and climate action. Here, high levels of societal awareness of the challenge of climate change are neither reflected in shifts in everyday practices nor in changing voting patterns. Perhaps surprisingly, implicit denial is also evident among the 'elite' parts of society, indicating that higher socio-economic status does not necessarily imply less denial. It is thus absolutely vital to accept these divergent forms of denial as a major source of climate inaction among both capital rich and -poorer groups in German society. This study clearly contributes to furthering scientific knowledge on this important issue.

Material emerging from the third empirical step, a series of focus group discussions, confirmed that notions of responsibility, efficacy and ways of knowing also carry different meanings in different occupational settings, highlighting the salience of organisational (climate) cultures in shaping the views and practices of their workforce. Employees of the NGO, the green startup and the (strategic sustainability division of the) mobility provider were all professionally closely connected to climate matters, yet their notions of responsibility for climate action still varied considerably: whilst the concept of climate responsibility endorsed by NGO employees was very comprehensive and included one's own everyday behaviour, other corporate cultural factors (i.e., a deep value of technological progress and travelling to see the world) stalled climate responsibility within the group of the mobility provider and the green startup.

---

2 Here, it should be noted that the data for this study was collected before the Covid-19 pandemic when as a society, we were much less used to people outrightly questioning scientific conclusions.

Finally, the relevance of this study for climate policy and action cannot be overestimated. Profound differences in how climate change is viewed and (not) acted upon are not yet reflected in research or policy. This is deeply problematic, as it renders climate action largely irrelevant to less privileged sections of society, perpetuating their sense of marginality and inefficacy. Moreover, the necessity to link both cognitive and emotional aspects of knowing in the context of climate debates and action also presents a key challenge to those interested in advancing climate action. Reflecting on these challenges, the study concludes with some concrete recommendations for designing climate policy and action programmes that address and involve the whole of society.

Part I – Introduction

1 Introduction

1.1 Lack of consensus on the IPCC consensus[1]

This study seeks to answer how climate action[2] (that must be an integral element of any sustainability transition) can be successfully fostered and implemented in a society that is in fact in deep cultural disagreement over how to approach the issue of climate change. These profound cultural differences – German society's divergent **climate cultures** – build its focus.

The main interest lies in the differences between social groups concerning how climate change is seen and (not) acted upon. In 'official'[3] discourses, it is generally assumed that climate action should be conceived of and implemented as an inclusive project involving the whole of society[4], as only then will it succeed on the scale that is needed. This means that different societal actors have to contribute, including political, corporate, civil and individual agents. In other words, it is considered to be everybody's **responsibility** to participate in climate action. Such societal responsibility is however intimately intertwined with the (perceived) level of **efficacy** an agent holds: if those who are endowed with substantial efficacy, i.e., high levels of resources and thus power over outcomes, were attributed a special responsibility, the positive climate impact may be particularly large. However, substantial societal resistance exists towards the majority of initiatives that disproportionately strain higher income groups. Election outcomes repeatedly confirm the unpopularity of

1 See for instance Cook et al., 2013, p. 3: "Among abstracts that expressed a position on AGW [anthropogenic global warming], 97.1 % endorsed the scientific consensus. Among scientists who expressed a position on AGW in their abstract, 98.4 % endorsed the consensus".

2 In this study, climate action is considered an integral part of any wider sustainability initiative and comprehensively refers to anything related to climate protection (mitigation but also potentially adaptation measures).

3 In this study, 'official discourses' refers to discourses practiced by those who hold considerable (mainly *political*) power and decision-making capacities.

4 See for instance German National Climate Protection Initiative (by the Federal Environmental Ministry): https://www.klimaschutz.de/de/ueber-die-initiative/ziele-und-aufgaben (accessed 31/10/2023).

redistributive measures like increased carbon taxation. Immediately, one sees the differences at play: not everyone in society has the same level of power over climate-related outcomes or similar access to participate in climate action. Thus, arguably, there are also variations in the amount of responsibility to be attributed. Both aspects, in turn, also strongly relate to an agent's level of climate **knowledge**[5] and thus, at least to an extent, his or her education. Therefore, these three concepts, responsibility attributions, efficacy expectations and climate-related knowing, lie at the heart of this study. More precisely, the investigation centres on the different constellations of these three key notions that reflect certain cultural leanings that exist in particular segments of society.

For decades, there have been suggestions on how to grasp and sort such cultural differences. Nevertheless, they are still (or maybe again) being ignored by the decision-makers sending out (official) messages on climate change. Research mirrors this absence of cultural sensitivity:

> Rather than attending to the culturally specific ways in which people make sense of and respond to climate change, most social scientific research on climate response has measured subjects' relationships to researcher-identified units of meaning, such as beliefs, attitudes, concerns, and behaviors, often without accounting for the researchers' own subjectivities, and the ways that those shape the questions being asked.
>
> Ford and Norgaard, 2020, p. 45

This has significantly contributed to the lack of progress up to this point. To ameliorate this, this study builds upon ideas by Pierre Bourdieu and scholars who have followed into his footsteps. He has written extensively not only on cultural difference but also about societal power relations (Bourdieu, 1984/1998). The present study's explicit focus on diversity challenges dominant views of the population as one unified entity that will readily respond to official unequivocal messages of climate politics (Klimapolitik) sent out by the government along the lines of: 'Everyone must do their bit to save the climate!'.

Bourdieu writes for instance: "Apparent, directly visible beings, whether individuals or groups, exist and subsist in and through *difference*" (1998, p. 31, orig. emph.). In his view, those with less power strive to express similarities with those at the top, whilst those at the top aim to distinguish themselves from those with less influence. For the advancement of climate action, "it is necessary to locate the source of power in order to challenge it and make changes" (Goldblatt, 2004, p. 126, paraphr. Fox-

5 Importantly, the present study conceptualises this as embodied and rooted in practice, which goes beyond knowing in the merely cognitive sense of the term.

Keller, 1985). It is therefore argued that understanding power relations in society and their links with questions of responsibility, efficacy and knowledge is an essential precondition for more effective climate action. This is precisely what the analysis of climate-cultural differences is particularly well suited to, because it sheds light on the variations in access to different behaviours: if you have to shop for groceries with your children when you live in the countryside and have a bus run only once every hour, will you really be convinced to "leave your car! [And think:] Let's go by bike instead"[6,7]?

Acknowledging societal difference goes hand in hand with the realisation that people make meaning not primarily in the absolute. The relative is what counts the most, as Richard Wilkinson and Kate Pickett have written:

> What matters is where we stand in relation to others in our own society. [...] We should perhaps regard the scale of material inequalities in a society as providing the skeleton, or framework, round which class and cultural differences are formed. Over time, crude differences in wealth gradually become overlaid by differences in clothing, aesthetic taste, education, sense of self and all the other markers of class identity.
>
> Wilkinson and Pickett, 2010, p. 25ff.

The need to include inequality

The Covid-19 pandemic has exacerbated inequality in Germany, not only economically, but also in terms of education, housing and health provision (Butterwegge, 2020; Statista Research Department, 2021). Since then, socio-economic inequality remains high because levels of redistribution are not sufficient to ameliorate this (see also i.e., Kenner, 2015, p. 02f.). Consequently, increasing shares of wealth are concentrated at the top which has profound implications for carbon emissions. Climate-relevant practices therefore must urgently be considered in concordance with inequality (Laurent, 2014, cited in Kenner, 2015, p. 03). People who are financially well-off often behave in ways particularly harmful to the climate, since they are the ones who can afford periodic vacation flights and fuel-intensive off-road vehicles (Bilharz, 2007, p. 116; Wahnbaeck, 2018). As 'conspicuous consumption' (Veblen, 1899) like driving SUVs, travelling to exotic destinations by airplane, or barbecuing one's Kobe steak has served as means for distinction for those at the top, highlighting the negative climate impact of these practices is particularly

---

6 See for instance this article on initiatives to increase urban cycling: https://www.ruhrnachrichten.de/nordkirchen/nordkirchen-macht-auch-2021-wieder-mit-bei-der-aktion-stadtradeln-w1625025-2000217608/ (accessed 17/09/2022).

7 All translations were carried out by the author.

problematic for those societal segments who have meaningfully incorporated them into their everyday lives. Emerging resistance to climate action measures is thus unsurprising. Therefore, it must urgently be recognised that "if we do not deal with these twin challenges [of climate action and inequality] together our society could face collapse" (Motesharrei et al., 2014, cited in Kenner, 2015, p. 03). In Motesharrei et al.'s analysis, the authors investigated the historical conditions under which pioneering cultures (like the Romans and Mayans and in China and India) most often disintegrated. They found this repeatedly to have been "the stretching of resources due to strain placed on the ecological carrying capacity, and the division of society into Elites (rich) and Commoners (poor)" (Motesharrei et al., 2014, cited in ibid). These cultural mechanisms that serve to subtly maintain climate-relevant divisions and existing power relations thus build the study's core focus.

An investigation that recognises the centrality of climate-cultural diversity is therefore of principal importance, because the way the topic of climate change has been approached thus far, scientifically as well as politically, springs predominantly from 'elite'[8] logics that the practitioners of these circles (naturally and habitually) employ. This insinuates that the whole of society could just practice climate action according to these particular logics, when actually only a fraction can, as the actual life realities of the majority of the public unfold in fact in markedly different ways. In this study, the term 'elites' denotes groups in society that are socio-economically privileged, influential and highly visible, partly because they enjoy easy access to key communication channels (TV, social media, scientific community, political decision spaces). As a result of this access to (cultural) capital, they significantly shape public debates, including those concerning climate change and action. They generally view themselves as leaders and influencers who can form public opinion and debate in key areas of social and cultural life. In the wake of the aforementioned official agenda-setting of climate action as an inclusive project, this elitist und undifferentiated type of communication is becoming increasingly irrelevant to growing segments of the population. Yet, paradoxically, "[...] it is the members of oppressed, objectified groups who are expected to stretch out and bridge the gap between the actualities of our lives and the consciousness of our oppressor" (Lorde, 1884, p. 854, cited in Ford and Norgaard, 2020, p. 59). Recognising this facilitates a better understanding of why some groups in German society are so 'allergic' to official calls for more climate action.

---

8 It is important to highlight from the very beginning, that in this study, the labels 'elite' and 'privileged' refer to Bourdieu's understanding of those rich in cultural capital and those groups in society that hold considerably more power (e.g., in terms of education levels). It is vital note here, that I scrutinise differences and conflicts *within* the German population (between those more and less rich in this capital). I *explicitly do not* use these terms as the opposites of 'the elites' and 'the population' as the rhetoric of the political far right frames it.

What has thus far dominated most thinking and scientific approaches have been economic logics that focus on individuals and consider what 'factors' or 'drivers' 'cause' them to make (generally self-interested) decisions that harm the climate. For example, cultural or social factors are largely excluded from these dominant approaches and treated as 'externality' or 'context'. However, cultural and social factors are not simply an add-on that can be left out, they are key to understanding why people do what they do. Economic theories focus on (average) individuals and are thus ill-equipped to handle actually existing differences within society.

In relation to this, Di Muzio writes that the common application of aggregate national indicators like GDP per capita in fact conceals the relative inequalities that exist within societies (cf. 2015, p. 27, cited in Kenner, 2015, p. 03). Here, Kenner argues that "the same could be said to apply to the ecological footprint" (2015, p. 03). As privileged and influential sections of society have the greatest incentive to maintain the status quo, questions of power and its distribution in society become central. This also reflects Meadows' (1998, p. 4) observation that "indicators arise from values (we measure what we care about), and they create values (we care about what we measure)". Therefore, the persistent marginalisation in climate debates and sustainability assessment of non-technical, non-quantifiable solutions such as the transformation of people's everyday practices have greatly reduced the mobilising momentum of climate action (cf. Rau, 2018).

Existing approaches that at least attempt to account for differences in society, such as lifestyle- or milieu models like those suggested by the German Sinus Institute (as discussed in detail in chapter 7), have shed some of their explanatory power as traditional ways of assessing people's socio-economic status are starting to become obsolete. Here, a 2016 study conducted by the German Federal Environment Agency (UBA) confirms that higher economic status does not automatically lead to people taking more responsibility for climate action, in fact quite the opposite is the case:

> People with higher incomes usually consume more energy and resources – regardless of whether they perceive themselves to be environmentally aware or not. [...] 'The surplus income is all too often spent on large cars, larger homes and more frequent air travel, even despite otherwise environmentally conscious behaviour. But it is precisely these 'big points' which have the largest human carbon footprint. The purchase of organic foods or a high level of waste separation do not offset this'.
>
> Maria Krautzberger, UBA President, press release, 2016

This was recently confirmed by a 2020 rerun of the survey and subsequent publication of results:

> A higher income leads to an increase in environmental impact in all areas of consumption. [...] There was no indication of any stabilisation or even decoupling of income and environmental damage. Particularly large are the increases [with income] in carbon emissions in the mobility sector. The impact of flying and driving in high-income households is over three times as high as in low-income households.
>
> UBA, supplementary brochure, Oehlmann et al., 2021, p. 14

This implies that conventional socio-economic variables have somewhat ceased to explain the real societal differences that exist in Germany today. With respect to this, a member of the scientific committee of the 2020 study comments:

> The new issue [of the study] presents some good news for us as well as a productive puzzle: the good news is that the pandemic has not led to people in Germany forgetting about the ecological crisis or considering it less important. The puzzle is that the differences in individual (environmentally) relevant readiness to change seem to be distributed in the population in a way that can only very marginally still be explained through the conventional variables of education, income, place of living, etc. In this way, the study encourages politics to become more ambitious and challenges the social sciences to continue working on their understanding of the potentially 'transformative' groups within society.
>
> Manuel Rivera, (IASS), Potsdam, in UBA, 2021, p. 6

What is lacking, therefore, is a social-scientific perspective that prioritises the social, embodied, tacit and implicit components of mundane everyday sense-making about climate change that unfolds differently depending on social positioning. The aim of the present study is thus to counteract this repeatedly bemoaned "absence of the social" (Henkel et al., 2018, p. 11) in relation to climate debates.

Hence, the present study is located at the interface of human geography, environmental sociology, psychology, and the environmental humanities. As Overland and Sovacool argue, world-wide allocation of funding resources has been severely skewed towards the natural sciences (refer to figure 1 below), which is deeply problematic: "Although the natural and technical sciences often generate results that are, or are perceived to be, clearer and more concrete than the social sciences, they cannot handle issue areas – such as attitudes, norms, incentives, and politics – that are intrinsically social" (2020, p. 4). More funding streams must be steered into these directions and more social scientists have to urgently enter the picture and dedicate their energy and expertise to the climate crisis.

Figure 1: Funding for climate research in the natural and technical sciences versus the social sciences and humanities (USD, [global])

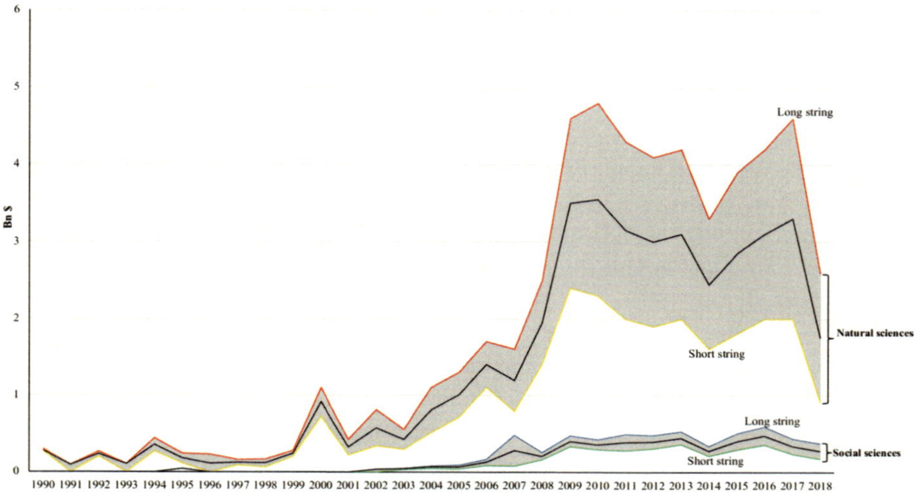

The grey areas represent ranges of estimates derived from short and long search strings; (taken from Overland and Sovacool, 2020, p. 3)

Sverker Sörlin reiterates this: "These [social-scientific] scholars sit on reservoirs of knowledge that must not remain untapped as we take on the immensity of the future of global change (2013, p. 22). Here, Norgaard writes: "[...] the question becomes not how do we better educate and inform the public, but under what circumstances are people able to move beyond a sense of helplessness, guilt or fear of the future and take actions that are in their collective, long term survival interest?" (2018, p. 4). This is the job of social science, a job that this study's culturally sensitive analysis substantially contributes to.

It therefore presents an inquiry into what role climate action plays in people's lives (if any) and how progress can be achieved by asking how measures fit into people's everyday realities. Studies (cf. e.g., Nerlich et al., 2010) show that climate change is mainly perceived by the public as a scientific topic. However, overlooking its economic and political relevance results in "climate becoming the all-determining factor and climate science, more precisely: medially visible climate scientists become the guardians of truth and the prophets of the future" (Neverla et al., 2019, p. 64f.), rendering political negotiations largely redundant. Yet this disregards the crucial role of cultural and socio-economic aspects in climate related decision-making (cf. ibid.) that then unfold their full force in political debate. This is also stressed by Nerlich et al. in relation to climate change being a so-called 'unobtrusive issue': "'People are thus liberated to argue from, and act upon, pre-established beliefs, convictions, prejudices and superstitions' (Adams, 2007). This turns climate change from a purely scientific phenomenon into a cultural one" (Nerlich et al., 2010, p. 2). Consequently, it pays to also become aware of the inertia of climate-relevant lifestyles and cultural traditions. The reason we are so attached to our habits lies in us carrying them out subconsciously, i.e., without any kind of mental exertion (Ernst, 2010, p. 135). Therefore, this study's consideration of cultural practices elucidates us to the dynamic "meanings of normal and the patterns of consumption associated with them [that] require constant reproduction" (Shove, 2010, p. 1279). The way climate action has however been tackled thus far, being spoken about mainly in only one and a quite exclusive language of science and privilege, thus fails to address and include those segments of society that actually represent its largest share.

It is therefore necessary to pay attention to the "complex subuniversa, within which people organise their knowledge, experience changes in their life realities, practice different forms of acquisition or avoidance and search for and find frequently competing explanations" (Welzer et al., 2010, p. 16). Yet, clearly, these subuniversa "are in no way ascertainable by natural science or technology" (ibid.). Furthermore, the panaceas of technological innovation and continued economic growth collide with the urgent need to reduce carbon emissions caused by both production and consumption: in the eyes of many, a possible solution today may be what is understood by geo-engineering – "the deliberate large-scale intervention in the Earth's natural systems to counteract climate change" (Oxford Geoengineering Programme, 2018). Here, in 2011 the influential British Royal Society declared that in the case of climate emergency, interventions on a planetary level that partially seal off sunrays potentially embody the only way to reduce global temperatures fast enough (Klein, 2015, p. 256). Not to mention that intervening into global climate throws up questions of jurisdiction and democratic authority that have remained unanswered to date, but "whatever the scheme, relying on [such] a technological miracle carries tremendous, reckless risk" (ibid.).

It must thus be investigated instead how people actually live and how climate action can potentially be meaningfully integrated into their different everyday life realities. Here, the social environments in which practitioners operate on a daily basis should receive particular attention. These surroundings fundamentally shape internalised propensities that then collectively yield the respective stances with which they approach, in turn, their surroundings and life in general. This also includes which thoughts even occur to people in the first place. How these thoughts on the topic of climate change are then verbalised, presented and potentially defended in certain social settings lies at the core of this investigation.

So what exactly is meant by 'climate-cultural difference'?

In this study, differences between climate cultures revolve around the three central concepts of responsibility, efficacy and different types of knowledge. This answers Welzer et al.'s call to involve the social sciences because the examination of climate change "also concerns the cultural practices and contexts of meaning that have caused climate change, thereby challenging human interpreting and sense-making and the philosophical consideration of aspects of justice and responsibility [...] as well as the knowledge-sociological analysis of collective interpretative patterns (Welzer et al., 2010, p. 13). Taking seriously the everyday practices and realities of ordinary citizens highlights the limited efficacy of the individual and challenges the extensive overemphasis on individual responsibility that characterises approaches to climate action that privilege knowledge and information. Such particular discrepancies between attributed responsibility and perceived or real efficacy embody a further key aspect of the investigation. As Dubois et al. point out, "there is a gap between how households perceive their responsibility and ability to mitigate climate change and the responsibilities and roles communicated by climate policies" (2019, p. 152).

Besides pointing to these incongruences between the notions of responsibility and efficacy, this study also asks for a substantially broadened conceptualisation of knowledge. It is argued that questioning the unchallenged hegemony of conventional, cognitivist knowledge needs to be a central element of any future climate change debate, policy and action. This requires a new concept of (climate) culture that moves beyond mainly knowledge-oriented definitions that have established themselves in recent times (Heimann, 2016, p. 25). This study deliberately deviates from these narrow conceptualisations, offering instead a much more comprehensive notion of knowledge as being embodied and rooted in everyday practices. This is particularly pertinent as the existing literature, however, still defines climate cultures *in terms of* (cognitive) knowing (cf. e.g., Heimann and Mallick, 2016). Yet ever more precise scientific information on the changing climate fails to convey what this actually means in terms of practical consequences for people's everyday lives (see e.g., Welzer et al., 2010, p. 15). Advice based on such information must inevitably remain scientifically underdetermined with regard to the relevance of cultural aspects (cf. ibid.). Thus, one needs to consider instead "the ideas, practices, ways of thinking and doing in more or less organized forms that range from sophisticated academic knowledge embodied in highly regarded texts [...] to the common sense, routine practices of our daily lives, such as looking after ourselves and our children" (Goldblatt, 2004, p. 122).

Considering the role of emotions and how they might prevent people from acting in ways conducive to climate action therefore presents a further promising avenue for shedding light on climate inaction. Andreas Ernst suggests here "to consider how environmentally conducive behaviour can be integrated into the existing social, institutional and material infrastructures, since this is where the powerful levers related to significant behavioural change can be found" (2010, p. 129). It is thus theorised that some segments of society can potentially be better reached emotionally than through inflating their informational base.

This is also reflected in Kari Mari Norgaard's ground-breaking research on *the social organisation of denial*. She, amongst others, enlightens us to the following: "The notion that well-educated, wealthy people in the Northern hemisphere do not respond to climate change because they are poorly informed not only appears inadequate [...] but also fails to capture how in the present global context *knowing* or *not knowing* is itself a political act (2006, p. 365). With this, Norgaard highlights the need to investigate how people organise themselves to handle the existential crisis of climate change. She theorises that climate inaction may result from feeling intensely overwhelmed by this tremendous threat. In this study, it is investigated how this is approached differently by each of the social groups analysed. Here, one of Norgaard's key contributions is the realisation that this denying of climate change happens on the collective level. Thus, the conventional focusing on individuals leaves central processes obscured: depending on the climate-cultural constitution of each group, existing knowledge about climate is being pushed away, responsibility is denied or diffused or one's own influence is negated, which yields group-specific denial tendencies that embody valuable insights for policymakers who wish to understand why their messages have thus far fallen on deaf ears.

Filling in these blind spots by recognising the need to go beyond an exclusive focus on the individual and integrating the analysis of (discursive) practices into the conceptual frame is precisely the path that needs to be taken to counterbalance the current overemphasis on cognitive forms of knowing with respect to climate change. This perspective recognises that

> [...] education and knowledge are not the only aspects missing. [...] Behaviour does not stand alone, solipsistically in space, instead it is always embedded into a behavioural context that also contains social aspects. [...] In everyday life we routinely overestimate how much of our behaviour we actually determine ourselves. [...] (Therefore,) what is required is a co-evolution of behaviour and its material, social and institutional surroundings.
>
> Ernst, 2010, p. 137

Hence in this study the climate cultures starring in media samples and focus group discussions are distinguished by certain clusters or sets of key discursive practices. From these emerge both – different concepts and constellations – of the three key notions of responsibility, efficacy and knowing. If we remain blind to how this differs in society between capital rich climate cultures and those whose members are underprivileged, climate action will remain no more than an *elite project*.

This study thus addresses the following research questions:

- Which societal actors are held responsible for climate action by the public?
- Which societal actors are perceived as efficacious when it comes to climate action?
- Is there a discrepancy between this attribution of responsibility and the expectation of power/influence/efficacy?
- How could this discrepancy be decreased? What is the potential role of information in reducing observable gaps between responsibility and efficacy?

1.2 Structure of study

After this introductory chapter (**chapter 1**), a critical review of leading literature is presented to identify gaps regarding the treatment of cultural phenomena in the context of climate change and climate action (**chapter 2**). This starts with a detailed examination of different scholars' takes on the three central notions of responsibility, efficacy and knowing. For the synthetisation of an alternative, more comprehensive knowledge concept, it draws on Bourdieu's *habitus* and subsequent thinking on *embodied knowledge*. Staying true to Bourdieu's tradition, Kari Mari Norgaard's revolutionary research on the social organisation of denial is then attended to and subsequently built upon, yielding this study's own definition of climate cultures that makes a clear distinction between attributions of responsibility and efficacy and their actual manifestations in people's everyday lives.

Chapter 3 presents the study's research design and methodological framework. These rest on the conviction that a social-scientific enquiry of collective societal patterns requires a particular (relational) mode of investigation. As a result, two out of the three empirical steps focus on what was being said *between* people and how they react and relate to each other. The other previous empirical step consisted in semi-structured (individual) expert interviews.

Chapter 4 is the first empirical chapter. Here, with these initial expert interviews, the objective was to investigate the current state of (official) knowledge. This was approached through semi-structured interviews with scientists, politicians, government- or NGO executives and one teacher. The chapter describes these experts' thoughts on responsibility, efficacy and knowing related to climate action.

In a conscious effort to move beyond elite perceptions, a second empirical step (media analysis) captured views of the public on social media (in addition to a second set of elite discourses). This is covered by **chapter 5**. As Udo Kuckartz writes, it is clear to see that knowledge about climate change stems from mass media (2010, p. 147).

Here, the climate cultures are however not merely differentiated by climate-related knowing in terms of content but instead on how this is employed and applied in practice in German media discourses.

Media attention to climate change, including its consideration on social media (Schäfer, 2012), is strongly event-related (Neverla et al., 2019, p. 23; Schäfer and Bonfadelli, 2017, p. 11; Schmidt et al., 2013) – either being triggered by meteorological or even more significantly by (supranational) political events. Hence in this study, the time surrounding the 2019 European election is taken as temporal focus. To determine which competing climate cultures coined public discourse at that time, an innovative mode of investigation (flow model) was employed to observe the climate-cultural standpoints and (discursive) practices of different public actors linked to climate (in)action, like politicians, scientific experts, prominent public figures and the public themselves.

Schäfer and Bonfadelli find fault with the fact that "the social context, within which the user concerns themselves with climate related media content, as well as their motivation and their interpretations of said content have not been investigated sufficiently" (2017, p. 12). This is precisely what this study aims to address. As "culture, just like climate, is hard to see and harder to measure" (Hulme, 2015, p. 2), focusing on the media landscape provides a promising way to make the cultural variations linked to climate change visible.

As a manifestation of conventional media reporting, climate cultures featuring in three political talk shows in German prime-time television, print- and online news-reports linked to these same TV-programmes were considered. Secondly, the social media engagement corresponding to these talk shows on Twitter and Facebook as well as videos by YouTubers like Rezo and Mai Thi Nguyen-Kim were examined to see how the public was habitually reacting to these elite discourses. The latter were included because they embody new forms of science communication and suggest that it may be becoming somewhat *cool* in youth culture to talk and be concerned about climate change (cf. Lüdke, 2015).

That these debates and views (i.e., 'non-elite' climate cultures, including sceptical and even denialist voices) were so thoroughly invisible in everyday life presented a major puzzle. Hence, in a third empirical step (**chapter 6**), it was investigated how climate debates unfolded in a professional context. Here it was of particular interest whether (and how) the occupational field had an influence on collective interpretation and handling of the current societal imperative to protect the climate. Another motivation for this step was to find out whether the sceptical statements encountered in the social media discourses also existed in the public beyond social media.

The preparation, implementation and analysis of these focus group discussions followed Kari Marie Norgaard's (2011) design that she developed and tested in her social-scientific research on climate perception in Norway (and the US). Through the deliberate deployment of focus groups, this approach goes beyond the limiting aspects of conventional science previously mentioned. By analysing social factors like group dynamics and internally harboured conflict potential, new insights were won that go beyond the mere responsibilisation of the individual consumer. Corner and Randall emphasise in this context that "the efficacy of group-based programmes for promoting durable pro-environmental behaviour change has been demonstrated on numerous occasions" (2011, p. 1011; see also Sahakian et al., 2021) which shows that more attention must urgently be paid to these mechanisms since they embody a potentially fruitful future avenue for effective climate action.

Chapter 7 then offers an in-depth discussion of the empirical findings. Here, a series of discrepancies are identified. One type of these divergences consists in the gap between official attributions of responsibility and efficacy (often seen in elite discourses) and the lived responsibility and actual efficacy that people experience in their everyday lives. The other type of discrepancy consists in the often encountered divergence between the two notions of responsibility and efficacy that different societal agents are either attributed or endowed with. It is shown that more of the public could be reached if these significant discrepancies were recognised. The necessity to link both cognitive and emotional aspects of knowing in the context of climate debates and action also emerges as a key challenge to those interested in advancing climate action.

Chapter 8 then provides some concluding remarks and a future outlook.

Part II – Theoretical and methodological framework

2 Literature review and theoretical foundations

2.1 Introduction

It is often implicitly assumed that climate action has to be undertaken as an inclusive project involving the whole of society. Yet it is argued that, first and foremost, societal responsibility for climate action has to be contemplated in terms of the actual power an agent holds. Here, power is conceptualised in terms of efficacy – i.e., control or influence over outcomes. The amount of (different types, as will be explained later) of knowledge and information at an agent's disposal also shapes their power over outcomes.

Since responsibility is such a deeply relational concept, it cannot be contemplated in an individual sense or at the individual level. Impacts of information campaigns that seek to motivate individuals to act 'climate responsibly' by increasing knowledge about the threat of climate change thus mostly remain below expectations (the notorious *value-action gap*). Here, meaningful climate action requires attention to societal attributions of responsibility and experiences of efficacy, to avoid an over-emphasis on factual scientific knowledge and a widespread blindness to people's everyday experiences and practices.

The questions asked are therefore: who in society is given responsibility for climate action? Who in society holds the power to really make a difference in this respect (= efficacy)? Is there a discrepancy between these two attributions? And, lastly, what role do information and knowledge play in achieving efficacious climate action?

The next section begins by grappling with the study's three core concepts: responsibility, efficacy and knowing, and, importantly, their concatenation, which served as point of departure for an extensive literature review. Thereafter and building on Kari Marie Norgaard's ground-breaking inquiry into the links between climate change, emotions, and everyday life, it is argued for a culturally sensitive social-scientific analysis of climate action. This fuses the concepts together in a novel, original conceptualisation of climate cultures and their variations in German society.

2.2 Responsibility

Everywhere on advertising posters and shopping bags, one is asked today to take responsibility for the climate, to choose the climate-friendly product and consume in a climate-friendly way. Referring to the broader subject of sustainability[1], Buschmann and Sulmowski state that "responsibility plays a central role for sustainability discourses" (2011, p. 283). Declarations and calls to action from the German federal government in relation to climate change responsibilise the public in questionable ways. For example, in 2019, German agricultural minister Julia Klöckner introduced a campaign at schools asking students to consider farming's climate impact. In a press release[2], Klöckner stated: "Only together we will manage to arrest climate change – here, agriculture is a solution bringer. But also each and every single one can have an impact. And this is the case because be it vegetables, fruit or meat – *we* decide what lands on the plate and thus on the field. [This campaign] wants to motivate children and adolescents to discover and conquer the scope of influence of agriculture and also of one's own consumption for more climate action" (BMEL, 2019, orig. emph.). This puts the lion's share of climate responsibility not only onto individual consumers but specifically children (of all people). Such responsibilisation of the public is also accentuated by the role the topic of climate action plays in the run-up to elections and other political contestations. This omnipresent call to climate action, framed through the angle of responsibility, is amongst what Ludger Heidbrink refers to when he speaks of a boom the concept of responsibility has experienced in recent decades. For Heidbrink, who has occupied himself extensively with the concept, responsibility in its traditional sense is characterised as follows:

> Paramount is determining who is responsible for whom (or what) according to which criteria (or who can be attributed such a responsibility).
>
> Heidbrink, 2003, p. 21f.

Other definitions of the concept echo this multidimensionality, indicating that responsibility is never absolute but always dependent: someone is being held responsible by somebody else according to some form of regulation or authority. In referring

---

1 Relevant citations that refer to the broader subject of sustainability are included in this thesis because climate action is seen as an integral part of sustainability efforts.

2 By the German agricultural ministry: https://www.bmel.de/SharedDocs/Pressemitteilungen/DE/2019/225-echt-kuh-l.html, (accessed 17/09/2022); the name 'Echt kuh-l!' is a wordplay on the words 'cool' and 'cow'; the German word 'Kuh' [spoken '*ku*] means 'cow'.

to a particular 'authority of responsibility', Heidbrink also points towards responsibility attribution being situational and context-specific. The philosopher Hans Lenk defines the concept similarly:

> To be responsible, or to take responsibility for something (or someone), means that somebody is obliged to (against) an addressee for actions, results of actions, tasks and states of affairs, and that he or she has to justify these actions and results before (or in the face of) a judgement, according to standards, criteria, or norms.
>
> Lenk, 2006, p. 2/5

Accordingly, Heidbrink proposes to distinguish further between different forms of responsibility, "be it the event related causal responsibility, the social role- or function related responsibility, the ability related competence responsibility and the legal responsibility in the sense of liability" (2003, p. 7). Yet this, in turn, brings its own problematic as "these differentiations quickly reach a point where they produce more ambiguities than clarities" (ibid.).

Despite this limitation, Heidbrink nevertheless attributes significant conceptual value to the notion of responsibility, as it goes beyond linear and unequivocal moral concepts and even withstands incalculable, uncertain and surprising events: "Since it is not based upon categorical but hypothetical imperatives, it is particularly suited to be applied in **normative grey areas** and to prove itself amongst the turbulences of complex contexts" (2003, p. 19, my emph.). Clearly, the challenge posed to humanity by climate change is one of the factors that bestow this point in human history with an extent of complexity that is unprecedented: "Climate change is unlike any other environmental problem, really unlike any other public policy problem. It's almost uniquely global, uniquely long-term, uniquely irreversible and uniquely uncertain – certainly unique in the combination of all four" (Wagner and Weitzman, 2015, p. 8).

More traditional conceptions of responsibility that stress linearity and causality have been increasingly challenged, since this logic that is based upon "(causality, blame, knowledge) [...] is limited and limiting in the context of contemporary hazards like climate change" (Adam and Groves, 2007, cited in Butler, 2010, p. 176). Therefore, climate change represents one of these contemporary grey areas in which responsibility can unfold its full conceptual potential. However, there is a host of further complicating factors at play, for example that a national focus remains inadequate, because the atmosphere is unbothered by country borders. Yet, the true crux lies in aspects related to societal treatment of climate change:

> The success of the responsibility principle embodies a direct reaction to the increase in complexity in the modern world. Its task lies in providing adequate crite-

> ria for assessing dynamic processes increasingly acquiring a momentum of their own [...] which guarantee the integration of social action even where insecurity and uncertainty dominate.
>
> Heidbrink, 2003, p. 19

This resonates with what the influential philosopher Hans Jonas noted in his 1979 magnum opus *The responsibility principle*[3], in which he almost prophetically characterised current social realities. Whilst he proclaims that:

> the old prescriptions of the 'neighbour' ethics – of justice, charity, honesty, and so on – still hold in their intimate immediacy for the nearest, day-by-day sphere of human interaction, this sphere is [however] overshadowed by a growing realm of collective action where doer, deed, and effect are no longer the same as they were in the proximate sphere, and which by the enormity of its powers forces upon ethics a **new dimension of responsibility never dreamed of before**.
>
> Jonas, 1985, p. 6, my emph.

When thinking about responsibility, one obviously enters the realm of morality. This fact alone accentuates the concept's relational and social nature, as it does not make sense to conceive of either, responsibility or morality, as distinct from human interaction: "What makes moral thinking moral thinking is the function that it plays in society" (Greene, 2016). As mentioned, one is not endowed with certain amounts of responsibility by nature, instead responsibility is negotiated and attributed socially (cf. Grunwald, 1999, cited in Grunwald, 2018, p. 423). Two conclusions can thus be drawn so far: first, responsibility as a concept is itself deeply complex and at the same time equipped to deal with profound complexity, at least to an extent. It is deeply dependent, thus multidimensional, however there comes a point where further differentiations and specifications do more harm than good – they cause more confusion than they manage to lift – a classical Kuznets curve. Secondly, its multidimensionality renders the notion of responsibility an idea uniquely equipped to be applied in the social, relational and collective realm.

Cumulative responsibility

Lenk points towards responsibility attributions becoming even more complicated in situations characterised by cumulative responsibility. He refers to the dying forests,

3 English version: 1985.

but his words seem almost better suited for the attribution of responsibility in relation to the climate crisis:

> Here, many different little harms well below a threshold accumulate to create a total damage which as such cannot be accounted to each individual. Thus there is a problem of the attribution of responsibility here. Everybody who takes part (e.g., runs a car or uses coal or oil heating systems) contributes, but any individual contribution is not as such already really harmful. To whom can we attribute responsibility for the total damage?
>
> Lenk, 2006, p. 3/5

Jonas also points to the challenge ethics faces today, that it has to be able to deal with such cumulative consequences of action because of the explosive proliferation of technology:

> The cumulative self-propagation of the technological change of the world constantly overtakes the conditions of its contributing acts and moves through none but unprecedented situations, for which the lessons of experience are powerless. [...] All this would have to be co-intended in the will of the single action if this is to be a morally responsible one.
>
> Jonas, 1985, p. 7

Attributing responsibility in situations distinguished by cumulative harm or collective action thus presents particularly puzzling challenges: a characteristic obstacle in such situations (in the economic sense) lies in the occurrence of collective decision dilemmas like free-rider dynamics or the so-called "tragedy of the commons" (Hardin, 1968). Therefore, these are also typical for climate change (climate as commons): "The earth's climate system offers a rare example of a pure public good" (Vanderheiden, 2016, p. 2). In economic theories this is conceived of as follows: "[...] *free riding* refers to the absence of contribution towards the provision of a public good by an individual, even though he or she will not be excluded from benefiting from that good" (Marwell and Ames, 1981). Here, Heidbrink stresses "how difficult it is to impinge upon economic processes with moral standards or to trace back collective damage progressions to unequivocally identifiable causes and originators" (2003, p. 17). The concept of free riding rests upon the logic "that under such conditions it is irrational for an individual to voluntarily contribute" (Marwell and Ames, 1981, p. 296). This situation characterises climate change, where agents often claim a disproportionate portion of common goods for themselves whilst not contributing accordingly (and sometimes not at all) to the maintenance of the goods – one only has to think of the recent *Dieselgate* scandal caused by German automotive managers. This illustrates that the rationality paradigm is obsolete (a point that will be returned to below), because especially in relation to climate change this attitude leads directly into the abyss: if everybody thinks only of himself, then it is absolutely not taken care of everyone. Also, in matters that are not illegal (as the manipulation of motor vehicles was, of course), an agent weighs the comparatively large effort to (voluntarily) adapt their life to climate action vis-à-vis the crushingly small value they will incur through their contribution. Therefore, the incentive to free ride is not only particularly large, it is also rational in the strict economic sense. Stephen Gardiner (2001) further writes that the free rider mechanism becomes exacerbated with climate change being an intergenerational issue: as humans, we are wired to seek instant gratification: "With intertemporal public goods like climatic stability, free riding becomes especially tempting, as cooperation costs are borne immediately but its benefits primarily accrue in the future" (cited in Vanderheiden, 2016, p. 3). Mike Hulme (2009/10) also points to this psychological phenomenon and argues that one solution may be to shift the focus towards the local, where improvements can be grasped more directly. Once again the inadequacy of theories built on rationality, self-interest and individualism arises because if everybody free rides (which would be 'rational'), then the world will end sooner or later together with these theories.

Critique of the responsibilisation of the individual

Against this backdrop, Heidbrink ultimately voices a deep ambivalence towards the notion of responsibility in his book *A critique of responsibility*. Besides recognising its conceptual value, especially in complex situations (as discussed), he nevertheless takes considerable issue with it: he finds it to be substantially overused, in particular with regard to the increasing autonomy and personal responsibility that is expected from single citizen consumers: "All the more urgently it has to be determined which individual burdens are caused by the dominance of personal responsibility and where the limits of impertinence – and this also always refers to social fairness – lie" (Heidbrink and Hirsch, 2006, p. 14).

Famous philosopher Sigmund Bauman thus demands a new form of ethics that has at its core a "*moral responsibility* which (re)enables citizens to manage **common** affairs" (Bauman, 1995, p. 284, my emph.). This badly needed new ethics is however acutely incompatible with omnipresent calls for autonomy and individual responsibility "observed as a characteristic of contemporary politics" (Butler, 2010, p. 176). In this context, Heidbrink foresees that in this century, industrial societies will "develop into comprehensive responsibility societies" (2006, p. 13) with a continuously increasing share of aspects and tasks becoming attributed to personal responsibility (ibid.). Often this results in paralysing overstrain of individual citizens, not least because practical skills and competencies conducive to climate action (e.g., sewing, repairing, preparing food with seasonal and regional ingredients) have become ousted by economic rationales like progress and efficiency.

What is of special interest to this study is this particular tension between individual and collective responsibility. When turning to the literature on responsibility and climate action, it becomes immediately apparent that the single consumer, or in the words of Elisabeth Shove, "the individual CO_2 addict" (2010, p. 1280), is given excessive attention. However, this "prevailing fixation on individual behaviour within mainstream policy and some areas of research tends to decontextualize consumption, dislocating its effects from its drivers and constraints and ignoring the wealth of innovative collaborative, citizen and entrepreneurial activity emerging internationally" (Rau et al., 2014, p. 193). Nico Lüdtke defines *responsibilisation*, as "the process in which power structures influence processes of self-discovery, thereby transferring the responsibility to the citizenry that actually belongs to the state" (2018, p. 113). Thus, the current focus on individual responsibility deflects away from collective responsibility that can only be initiated by elected political representatives in democratic systems. In this respect, Bauman and Beck speak of institutions "for overcoming problems [that] are transformed into institutions for causing problems; [that] you are, on the one hand, made responsible for yourself, but on the other hand are dependent on conditions which completely elude your grasp (and in most cases your knowledge)" (Beck, 1992/1998, cited in Bauman, 2001, p. 5, cited in Butler, 2010, p. 175).

Moving beyond conceptual and methodological individualism

According to Buschmann and Sulmowski, the consumer is imagined as autonomously choosing between clearly selectable options "in the sense of an imagined average standard person held together by some fictional unity" (2018, p. 290). In their eyes, this springs from the dominant neoliberal paradigm characterising our system: a prime component of this is "the therein contained relocation of the focus of responsibility onto the individual and the concomitant incentive to adopt individual responsibility" that are to be understood as "a symptom of the programme of the withdrawal of the state" (Krasmann, 2003, p. 183, cited in Buschmann and Sulmowski, 2018, p. 286).

Armin Grunwald conceptualises that the individual actually holds two types of responsibility: "We carry this responsibility as individual people on two different shoulders so to speak" (2018, p. 432). On the one hand, there is an individual responsibility that stems from an acutely overrated consumer power and on the other hand a rather collective responsibility as member of the citizenry to take part in political processes and make one's voice heard. Rau et al. write that therefore, "individual citizen consumers alone cannot, and should not, be expected to shoulder the material and social burdens of a transition towards greater sustainability" (2014, p. 203).

Ulrich Beck also criticises that, in combination with neoliberalism, the individual is made to become their own *moral entrepreneur*, supposedly holding the entirety of humanity's fate in their hands. From this, there results a new *categorical imperative* that demands: behave as if the survival of the world depended on your actions! Eat less meat, forego flights, switch to green energy! "The key contradiction here is that the individual is condemned to individualisation and self-responsibility, even vis-à-vis global threats, despite the fact that he is severed from the decision contexts which escape his influence" (2009, p. 170). Buschmann and Sulmowski also believe that "the boom of responsibility attributions in relation to sustainability can be understood as *mode of governing* of neoliberally organised societies. Practices that once were born out of an emancipatory impetus, today contribute to an individualisation of structurally conditioned problems" (2018, p. 291). Thomas Alkemeyer similarly notes an *inner conflict* that surfaces when the current situation is examined from both sides: on the one hand we accept a political situation, "that passes on the public and legal responsibility *of society* for the citizenry onto the subjects themselves" (2018, p. 417), yet at the same time this state of affairs also mirrors "*the basic promise of modernity*, to lead an autonomous and self-determined life" (Rosa, 2007, p. 17, cited in ibid.). Several scholars thus deem this individualisation of responsibility with respect to climate action inadequate, not least because this allows politics to escape its responsibility and delegate this disproportionately to the citizenry: "There must be binding rules for sustainability instead of a paternalistic influencing of private consumption" (Grunwald, 2018, p. 433). This influencing includes what has come to be understood as *nudging*.

Critique of nudging

Nudging refers to nonbinding and sanction-free (as opposed to prohibiting or monetarily incentivising) steering of current behavioural patterns in favour of desired alternative behaviour (see e.g., behavioural economists Richard Thaler and Cass Sunstein, 2008). "Consumers are to be merely gently *nudged* in the desired direction" (Paech, 2018, p. 442). While in recent years some proponents of nudging theory (e.g., Stern, 2020) have conceded that this view of human behaviour is inadequate as it is limited by "multiple contextual factors" (p. 2), this does in no way go far enough, as here, the individual is still thought to be merely surrounded by social context, demoting the social environment to at best playing second fiddle. In the few cases where contextual factors are deemed central, the relationship is conceived of as ingenuously one-way with these external and largely stable social, historical, political and cultural circumstances only bearing upon and affecting the individual (cf. Burke et al., 2009, p. 56S). However, the social environment is not to be thought of as simply being "a fixed entity that inevitably impinges upon individuals" (Bandura, 1994, p. 49) – instead, the influence needs to be perceived of as critically bidirectional, integral and dynamic. A more holistic perspective is desperately needed that takes seriously the multidirectional, co-constitutive, constantly-in-formation and often not cognitively processed relationship between individual and social context (cf. Burke et al., 2009). This relationship is expressed in daily practices that therefore encompass the appropriate focus of investigation. Considering these "social rules that govern etiquette and morality [which] comprise examples of [such] naturalised predispositions" (ibid.) allows for making visible the omnipresent and counterproductive over-responsibilisation of the individual citizen.

Denial of political responsibility for climate action

It is thus necessary to shed the current focus on individual behaviour, including the widespread accusation of eco-hypocrisy and "to be explicit about the extent to which state and other actors configure the fabric and the texture of daily life" (Shove, 2010, p. 1281).

In the eyes of Beck, contemporary political systems are partially characterised by governing through a risk discourse that allows the normalisation of threats that the reigning growth-oriented system necessarily brings with it (cited in Butler, 2010, p. 171). Beck terms this for late capitalist governments typical situation "organised irresponsibility" (Beck, 1995; 1997). In the face of currently swelling ecological dangers, Catherine Butler finds these risk discourses to proliferate in the current political present as they "involv[e] attributions of causes, blame, and accountability [which] could be seen to more closely resemble part of the processes of organised irresponsiblity as it guarantees precisely the non-attributability of systemic hazards (2010, p. 188f.). This had the paradoxical consequence that climate action efforts in the global North have led to more environmental destruction in the global South: "As so often in the past, we see how scientific and technical ingenuity are being integrated into patterns of global inequality" (Guha, 2000, cited in Jamison, p. 20). Continued liberalisation of global markets is not actually causing more liberty, by contrast: it threatens to destroy the basis of human existence, because risks, for example those caused by climate change, do not feature in these discourses that rest upon freedom, free markets and free individuals. "Beck's concept of organised irresponsibility focuses upon the discrepancy between contemporary knowledges of causes of harm and the continuation of the very systems of action which create them" (Butler, 2010, p. 174). In many ways political realities steer people into directions that oppose climate action – a fact that by itself proves the inadequacy of individual responsibility attributions. Besides, "when market dynamics come to be seen as the most suitable path towards a better future, democracy and the opportunities for meaningful civic participation become eroded" (Dahlgren, 2012, p. 3).

To mobilise consumers for climate action, political structures need to reflect these intentions. Instead, politics is denying its responsibility by sending mixed messages:

> Examples of the perverse effect of dominant structures are legion: private transport is incentivized over public transport; motorists are prioritised over pedestrians; energy supply is subsidised and protected, while demand management is often chaotic and expensive; waste disposal is cheap, economically and behaviourally.
>
> Jackson, 2009, p. 151

Many climate-relevant political decisions still unfold in a way that is far from responsible and consistent (cf. Nerlich et al., 2010, p. 7). "Such contradictions can result in a loss of trust in government and a form of denial of personal responsibility for [...] environmental impacts [...]" (Kroesen, 2013, Hares et al., 2010, cited in Westlake, 2017, p. 10). The default argument here is that the voter would not accept political decisions that prohibit certain taken-for-granted liberties: "Of course then it is no wonder that Uncle Sam[4] himself not only protects at all costs the worst climate killers from any form of taxation, but also subsidises unprofitable airports if need be" (Paech, 2012, p. 22). We find ourselves in the absurd situation where it is against our own interest to act in a climate-friendly manner, either because we have to give up things we want or because we have to pay a premium.

Butler reports that in her group discussions, a clear discrepancy emerged in the responses of the participants between "the characterisation of climate change as a collective, interconnected, pervasive and societally endemic problem and the political description of a (non)society comprised of free individuals that can act upon climate change through their individualised self-responsible choices" (2010, p. 189). This indicates that "governance for prosperity must engage actively with citizens both in establishing the mandate and delivering the change" (Jackson, 2009, p. 168). Politics should thus also question its perception of citizens and begin to see them as part of a society that is capable of voicing an interest for more than oneself: "There often exists an implicit model of the audience which may not be subject to empirical scrutiny and which may assume from the outset a degree of ignorance or deficit which is itself not a good perspective from which to begin dialogue" (Nerlich et al., 2010, p. 11). Perhaps there is not only a lack of trust in politics amongst the citizenry. In turn, government also displays a lack of faith that voters are willing to favour courses of action conducive to the common good. Julian Nida-Rümelin says in this respect: "It appears strange that the theory of human motivation that is dominant

---

4 Original in German: *Vater Staat.*

today considers the exception of the amoralist as being the rule" (2011, p. 37). Therefore, an interpretation that sees responsibility of the individual as a mature citizen in a collective setting and not only as a remote-controlled consumer is urgently needed.

Bauman thus attributes an agency gap to the policies of contemporary industrial societies caused by this political responsibility vacuum (Bauman, 2001, p. 188, cited in Butler, 2010, p. 188): "Paradoxically, research suggests that people see governments as responsible for addressing environmental problems, yet have little faith that they will" (Nerlich et al., 2010, p. 7). James Blake views this similarly: "The irony is, of course, that although governmental institutions are trusted least, they are seen as most responsible for causing, and therefore solving, environmental problems" (1999, p. 268). A paradoxical divergence thus exists between the potential or power or *efficacy* of the state over climate-related outcomes and the amount of responsibility it is willing to employ. This stands in sharp contrast to the disproportionate over-responsibilisation of individuals. We are hence confronted with a decoupling of responsibility and efficacy because in relation to climate change, the causes are portrayed as endemic whilst the suggested solutions are framed as individual actions that require clear choices between different options (cf. Butler, 2010). The efficacy political and also corporate decision-makers actually hold strongly contradicts their concomitant portrayal as being too profit-driven to act responsibly. **Thus what is of particular interest to this study is this profound discrepancy between the level of responsibility that is being ascribed to societal actors and the actual true power, influence or *efficacy* they hold over the outcome.**

The discrepancy between responsibility and efficacy

Thus, I hold that individual responsibility is overemphasised because firstly, this overstrains the consumer, secondly, it affords a deflection away from the responsibility of politics and thirdly, the inconsistent political status quo prevents consumers from acting consistently in a climate-friendly manner. Even more persuasive from a climate perspective is that the difference the individual is able to make is actually no more than negligible:

> As Cambridge physics professor David MacKay claims: obsessively switching off the phone-charger is like bailing the Titanic with a teaspoon. Do switch it off, but please be aware how tiny a gesture it is. All the energy saved in switching off your charger for one day is used up in one second of car-driving.
>
> Nerlich et al., 2010, p. 7

This is deeply problematic because not only "has this focus on the individual so far obviously not led to more sustainability" (Henkel and Lindemann, 2018, p. 271), it also deflects attention away from the responsibility for instigating climate action that is in fact afforded by the efficacy of truly influential societal actors. Both, influential agents' high efficacy and individuals' miniscule efficacy, by comparison, are denied in this instance. Yet, this almost non-existent efficacy of the individual is also often cited as justification for not acting: what difference does it make in a world with 7,7 billion carbon-emitting individuals if I leave my car today and cycle to work? "There is the problem that some people [...] feel powerless as they are such a tiny cog in a big wheel" (Blake, 1999, p. 266). Messages that appeal to the morality or 'green conscience' (cf. e.g., Geo Magazin, 2000; Jonas, 2018) of individuals can cause frustration as the effect of foregoing consumption will remain unnoticeable. "Reducing your own carbon footprint to zero is a noble gesture, but it's less than a drop in the bucket" (Wagner and Weitzman, 2015, p. 130f.). This results in the paradox that "any individual act of responsibility can feel *ir*responsible, an act of complicity in a collective dance of self-delusion" (Szerszynski, 2007, p. 338, orig. emph.).

2.3 Efficacy

Renowned social psychologist Albert Bandura defines *self-efficacy* as "the belief in one's capabilities to organise and execute the causes of action required to manage prospective situations" (1977, p. 2). Feelings of helplessness or powerlessness also play a particularly decisive role in the realm of climate action:

> People's beliefs about their capabilities affect what they choose to do, how much effort they mobilize, how long they will persevere in the face of difficulties, whether they engage in self-debilitating or self-encouraging thought patterns, and the amount of stress and depression they experience in taxing situations.
>
> Bandura, 1994, p. 2

Heidbrink also underscores the need to consider responsibility *together with* efficacy in his demand for a substantial re-examination of the notion of responsibility according to the practical efficacy agents hold (2003).

Efficacy denied by corporate agents

When wondering who else in society holds the power to truly make a difference for climate action one necessarily arrives at the group of corporate agents, as they significantly contribute to greenhouse gas emissions (and if they changed their ways, society would achieve considerable progress): "The relationship between the industrial corporation and the earth is almost purely exploitative" (Ikerd, 2005, p. 55).

Here, too, blatant decoupling between responsibility and efficacy unfolds: corporate decision-makers carry a lot of responsibility due to the power they hold, yet they are almost unequivocally portrayed as being too self-interested to meet this responsibility.

Jamison here refers to Andrew Rowell who speaks of a so-called *green backlash*, where the powerful players within global processes of institutionalisation have had enough of environmental matters, as they "are unconvinced that ecology will ever be particularly profitable" (Rowell, 1996, cited in Jamison, 2001, p. 20; see also Beder, 2001). Opponents of more climate action exploit climate change's complexity and concomitant indeterminability, for working against an ecologically conscious culture: "The aggressive resistance to increased taxes on diesel fuel that spread across Europe in the summer of 2000 is only the most visible sign of this tendency" (Jamison, 2001, p. 20f.).

However, there is currently growing awareness that climate action must become an inclusive project involving the whole of society, including the corporate sector: "Due to companies' increased scope of action and design potential, societal actors demand stricter (moral) means of controlling corporate behaviour" (Hardtke and Kleinfeld, 2010, p. 78). Ongoing globalisation renders economic interactions increasingly complex. If you turn one screw in this deeply intertwined global system, this can send out shock waves in multiple directions, the extent of which is impossible to predict beforehand: "This is the downside of a highly collaborative economy, whose operational performance results from everything being connected to everything" (Paech, 2012, p. 21). Economic processes have also become much more closely intertwined with societal structures, because the control authority of politics has been dismantled. Arnd Hardtke and Annette Kleinfeld conceptualise that multinational corporations are attested a special responsibility when they operate in less economically developed regions as the public is becoming increasingly aware of this institutional vacuum. Thus, "increasingly, it is being asked **how** companies are making their profits" (2010, p. 160, my emph.).

However, John Ikerd deems it unlikely that companies will meet this increasing public call for responsibility due to limited investor tolerance for profit impinging environmental matters, especially in those sectors that rely heavily on extractive resources. Hence, he concludes that "the only effective constraint to corporate environmental exploitation is for people to act collectively, though laws and government regulations designed to protect the environment" (2005, p. 56). Achieving more climate action therefore depends on the emergence of a new culture that is "committed to caring for each other and caring for the Earth" (ibid.). Also needed is an evolution in our perception of corporate entities (and our demands thereof) "from an exclusively profit-oriented organisation to a socio-economically motivated institution of society" (Brown, 1979, p. 6, cited in Hardtke and Kleinfeld, 2010, p. 160).

NGOs, responsibility and efficacy

One further disparity between responsibility and efficacy surfaces in relation to non-governmental organisations (NGOs). This directly contrasts the situation in the corporate sector just described: compared to corporations as well as politically legitimised institutions, NGOs carry much less responsibility; their efficacy is however often substantial (see also, Dryzek et al., 2003, p. 154):

> The fact that volunteer organisations are controlled by neither the state nor the market makes them potentially important sites where people can get together, share their experiences, and from this sharing develop their own narratives about the causes, consequences, and potential solutions to problems in their lives.
>
> Habermas, 1984, cited in Norgaard, 2011, p. 44

Since the 1990s, Michael Aßländer has observed the formation of global interest groups parallel to multinational corporations, that harbour the aim of responsibilising the latter and demonstrating to them how they can operate in more moral ways. Here, Aßländer (2011, p. 69) builds on what Beck (1998, p. 39f.) called a *non-politics politics*, namely that NGOs which have transnational scope but no political legitimisation are disproportionately involved in decisions:

> They are all seen as apolitical, but act in a new central sense politically, since they profoundly help shape power relations, legal norms, lifestyles, ways of work and imaginary worlds of the global societal landscape – and with it also those of the national societies.
>
> Beck, 1998, p. 39f., cited in Aßländer, 2011, p. 31

Because of increased global political deregulation, NGOs hold transnationally operating companies responsible as politics is failing to do so and regulate for climate action. Consequently, Aßländer terms NGOs "the new authorities for responsibility" (2011, p. 60), as they point to companies' misdemeanours and make use of their way of sanctioning them by calling out *buy-cott* or instigating bashing campaigns. "At the same time, NGOs have a legitimacy surplus within public perception" (ibid., p. 61), which ultimately does endow them with considerable efficacy.

Responsibility according to efficacy

Having shown the stark discrepancy between responsibility attributions and efficacy considerations in the cases of the individual, the state, the corporation and the NGO, it is now turned to approaches that already consider responsibility in connection with efficacy. For example, Michael Bilharz suggests classifying recommended climate actions according to their respective efficacy level. In his view, it comes down to "highlighting those tips for consuming sustainably that *really* make a difference with respect to conventional, non-sustainable consumption. To do so, a strategic priorisation is indispensable" (2007, p. 131, orig. emph.). In his theory, he speaks of actions that have proven to be *hot potatoes* in climate change communications as the observed consumer aversion vis-à-vis the accompanying behaviour changes makes these changes particularly unlikely. Bilharz deems it improbable that there will be willingness in society to, for example, forego flying since this carries such high significance in terms of realising a cosmopolitan way of life. Consequently, Bilharz makes responsibility attributions dependent on efficacy: where the potential for behaviour change remains low, in his view politics is responsible to "provide the collective framework conditions to make unsustainable consumption less resource-heavy" (ibid., p. 132).

Yet, where the potential for behaviour change is already high, the consumer can willingly be attributed responsibility. Here, "the current framework conditions [...] allow already sensibilised consumers to reap personal advantages through such consumption that can also be perceived as such by third parties" (ibid.). In Bilharz's theory, these are the types of consumption that display the highest efficacy, which is why he argues for their priorisation as *key points* of climate action. Whilst acknowledging the role of social valuation and integrating responsibility with efficacy are certainly steps in the right direction, this approach however still falls short on two accounts: first, it continues to mainly hold individual consumers responsible and second, they are expected to attain the necessary information to determine what the key points are, which may simply be impractical in everyday life. Even people who already practice various forms of climate action are not immune to being limited by dominant neoliberal cultural worldviews:

> Even as they saw climate change and other environmental risks as symptoms of immoral systems, the cultural frames in which they were embedded made it difficult for them to move beyond centring on a free, rational autonomous individual as the solution to the very problems this worldview is implicated in creating. [...] the fact that individualism remained the guiding community value limited the collective political potency of the movement.

Ford and Norgaard (in reference to the community within their own investigation), 2019, p. 232

'Perceived' versus 'lived' responsibility and efficacy

Divergences also exist between official attributions of responsibility that are often abstract, and people's lived (experiences of) responsibility, as well as between expectations of efficacy and actual experiences of influence. For example, the idea that individuals can make a difference by 'consuming differently', that is, by buying 'green' products (as opposed to consuming less) may fly in the face of those who are struggling to make ends meet and for whom shopping is mostly about extending already limited financial resources[5]. Similarly, appeals to individual consumers to 'read the labels' and 'make the right choices' may prove to be utterly impossible for people who are time-poor and who may feel squeezed between precarious work, unpaid domestic duties and responsibilities to care for others.

Considering climate action practices in the daily lives of ordinary citizens also highlights the limitations of individual-level efficacy. Here it must be differentiated between the efficacy we attribute to ourselves (self-efficacy), the efficacy we attribute to others and lastly the actual power someone holds over something, i.e., their actual efficacy. This latter type can be determined through an investigation of material practices and how they manifest collectively within one climate culture as opposed to another.

Self-efficacy, the attitude towards one's own competency to manage prospective situations, is a wholly individual concept. This study however also focuses on the difference between ascribed efficacy (to different societal groups) and actual power. Pointing to the link between responsibility and efficacy, Jonas proclaims: "The nature of human action has de facto changed, and [...] an object of an entirely new order – no less than the whole biosphere of the planet – has been added to what we must be responsible for because of our power over it" (1985, p. 7). Here, he does not refer to attributed, expected efficacy but to actual 'lived' efficacy.

Yet, it must still be recognised that a perceived lack of self-efficacy is often experienced as particularly demoralising. Important for this study is the realisation that collective action can present an effective antidote to this: "People who have a sense of collective efficacy will mobilise their efforts and resources to cope with external obstacles to the changes they seek" (Bandura, 1982, p. 143f.). In contrast to most conceptual considerations so far, this study therefore crucially conceives of efficacy in

5 This is a different divergence to the aforementioned discrepancy between responsibility and efficacy (e.g., of consumers). Here, official attributions of responsibility and lived responsibility diverge, because in this instance consumers actually do **not** see themselves responsible for acting in a climate-friendly manner. Here, their (extremely limited) efficacy plays a contributing (to an extent they are inefficacious because the pressures of daily life are not recognised), but secondary role (the main reason lies in them not realistically and adequately being addressed by these responsibility attributions).

its collective sense. "A strong sense of starting together instead of waiting for others to act first will reduce the fear of individual sacrifices" (Stoll-Kleemann and O'Riordan, 2020, p. 12). People often consider themselves more influential and efficacious when deliberating what they can achieve collectively with the like-minded members of their climate culture than when contemplating their individual-level efficacy. When *united by a common cause*, groups of people have been found to gain an impetus that is much more powerful than the sum of their individual efforts. A collective approach that is delimited by shared cultural aspects may prevent us from arriving at what Norgaard (2011) cautions against when speaking of feelings of powerlessness, denial and resignation, when pondering how to make a difference as only one out of seven billion people on the planet. Shared ideas, conventions and interests, and their translation into collective action, can protect people against these negative feelings and experiences. "In getting things done collectively, perceived efficacy is concerned with people's beliefs in their joint capabilities to make [*a certain matter, e.g., climate change*] a national priority" (Bandura, 1997, p. 33).

2.4 Ways of knowing

As shown, responsibility should be considered in connection with efficacy. Importantly, however, both of these notions must also be contemplated in relation to knowing: Jonas writes that as human beings and because of the freedom we are endowed with through consciousness, we are able to take responsibility. Therefore, we also have a duty to educate ourselves. It is our knowledge about the impending catastrophe that obligates us to conserve the planet for future generations. Or in other words: "The responsibility weighs on those who know" (Tammer, 2009), and, by contrast: feliciter ignoravit – *ignorance is bliss*. And blissful it must indeed be to board a flight for a short trip and not find anything wrong with it today. An agent's efficacy is also influenced by their knowledge: "Is there anything science should not try to explain? Science is knowledge and knowledge is power – power to do good or evil" (Davies, 2012). Thus we see an *intertwining* or *concatenation* between the three concepts of responsibility, efficacy and knowledge, the last of which is attended to now.

In *The imperative of responsibility*, Jonas ascribes knowledge quintessential importance for moral considerations (1979, p. 28): "Power can only accrue when the options for action are distributed unequally, which in turn results from differentially distributed stocks of knowledge" (Tammer, 2009). Those who know carry a special integrative responsibility as it is their duty to involve all citizens in decisions concerning future courses of action (ibid.). However, in Jonas' view, this relation between responsibility and knowledge is bidirectional: knowledge is an obligation and Jonas holds the public responsible to inform itself about technological innovation's potentially detrimental consequences because in his eyes it is increasingly escaping society's control. At the same time, "the recognition of ignorance ought to reflectively remind us that our power over the world is too large in order to adequately handle it" (Tammer, 2009). Thus Jonas stresses concomitantly that not everything can be known or foreseen.

Information deficit?

Nevertheless, much existing social-scientific literature on climate action emphasises the role of information provision in instigating climate action. This rests upon the idea of lay people lacking adequate knowledge to recognise the urgency of climate action. Ultimately, however, it has been shown that knowledge alone does not ignite responsible action (cf. Moser, 2006, p. 3). This is also confirmed by the often-cited *value-action gap* (mind-behaviour gap, attitude-behaviour gap): paradoxically, people who voice that they care about climate action and green values, often do not act accordingly at all (cf. Blake, 1999, p. 262ff.) – they thus somehow deny their knowledge about impending climate change. "Overall, there is no direct correlation between communication and behaviour change" (Nerlich et al., 2010, p. 5). Yet, this omnipresently propagated theory, the information deficit model, still assumes that the crux is presented by knowledge about climate change as an inherently complex issue remaining too cryptic for a passive and uninformed public: "The unspoken underlying assumptions typically are that people do not act because they either do not understand or do not care about the issue" (Moser, 2006, p. 5).

This is illustrated by target 12.8 of the Sustainable Development Goals on sustainable consumption (and production) which states: "[B]y 2030 [it counts to] ensure that people everywhere have the relevant information and awareness for sustainable development, and lifestyles in harmony with nature" (UN environment programme, 2015). Although admittedly there have previously been some attempts to include "people's values and circumstances (e.g., Peattie and Peattie, 2009; Seyfang and Paavola, 2008; Jackson, 2005), the provision of information is still a key focus" (Kenner, 2015, p. 10). Better informing the public has hitherto been an integral element of almost any climate action initiative: "What is distinctive about the ways in which some of these changes (towards unprecedented levels of consumption) have been characterised is the emphasis that is given to knowledge in the economic changes" (Goldblatt, 2004, p. 129).

There is evidence of a substantial and widening (cf. Miléř et al., 2012, p. 1438) rift between the knowledge of scientific experts on the one hand and the general public on the other, which in this view must be reduced as rapidly and efficiently as possible. Assuming that one does have responsibility to inform oneself about climate change, some argue that science also must better do its job to shed light on the issue. This type of 'deficit thinking' has been subject to growing criticism, and rightly so. For instance, "presenting evidence contrary to prior beliefs can have the opposite effect and result in a strengthening of previously held beliefs, a phenomenon known as biased assimilation or a backfire effect" as Sauer et al. have shown (2021). Importantly, information deficit thinking also reduces people's responses to climate change to cognitive processes that revolve around factual knowledge, assuming "that the public are empty vessels waiting to be filled with useful information upon which they will then rationally act" (Nerlich et al., 2010, p. 4). Yet as Lidskog et al. write:

> [...] for science to promote action, it is not sufficient that scientific advice is seen as competent and trustworthy. Such advice must also be perceived as meaningful and important, showing the need and urgency of taking action.
>
> Lidskog et al., 2020, p. 118; see also Davidson, 2012

This is mirrored in Welzer et al.'s critique of narrowly cognitivist approaches to climate policy whereby "information such as the predicted 2020 level of CO_2 in the atmosphere at 400 parts per million [...] almost entirely overlooks what this means for the everyday reality of humankind, globally as well as regionally" (2010, p. 15). As they argue, there already exists an abundance of information, research and scientific work that amounts to an "explosion of information around climate change. Advice on how to reduce one's carbon footprint is provided almost daily in newspapers, adverts, books, and on websites" (2010, p. 10).

Alternative approaches that focus on desires and attitudes as determinants of human action do not fare much better, as they still focus on the cognitive in an assumed pre-determined static state of knowing that it counts to uncover. Therefore, it becomes "impossible to see how the contours and environmental costs of daily life evolve" (Shove, 2010, p. 1279). Instead, the focus must be shifted "away from the behaviour, action and motives of monological individuals" in viewing them instead as "members of groups and communities that constitute the context of their mundane activities" (Savolainen, 2007, p. 120, cited in ibid., p. 2).

Critique of rationality

Information deficit discourses are based on the assumption that people generally act by making informed, rational decisions. This discourse on rationality features frequently in the political and public sphere, as exemplified by the following statement made by the FDP (German liberal party) politician Christian Lindner: "To insist on meeting the Paris climate treaty is legitimate. [...] However, we have to make sure that in implementing these targets, we do not only listen to our gut, but also to our head" (2019). This way of thinking has emerged from positivist, substantialist schools of thought such as behavioural psychology and (neo)classical economics. It suggests that the solution is to simply install the right monetary incentives (Shove, 2010, p. 1276f.). The majority of contemporary political decisions are based on this logic, which by nature has to concentrate on the individual:

> The application of policies underpinned by notions of rational individuals, free in their choices (but also implicitly morally governed to make the correct choice) airbrush from view the complexities involved in addressing climate change in a context where the causes are endemic to industrial, capitalist societies.
>
> Butler, 2010, p. 184

Such misleading and wrongful initial assumptions unsurprisingly result in equally wrong but far-reaching consequences: the creed of rationality insinuates that citizens have the free choice to act in a climate-friendly manner. The fact that alternative climate-friendly products are much more expensive alone shows that this excludes some segments of society from the get-go. With this approach, society runs the risk of rendering climate action an elite project. Here, Beck poignantly points out that:

> … without a majority that consists of very diverse people who not only talk about climate policy but also act and vote accordingly, often against their own personal interests, climate policy is doomed to fail. It will only ever cease to be an elitist cloud-cuckoo-land if we find answers to an urgent and still largely taboo question: where is the support for ecological changes supposed to come from that in many cases undermine the lifestyles and consumption habits, the social status and the living conditions of the supporters and that in a time that is already shaped by uncertainty?
>
> Beck, 2010, p. 32

Today a chaotic jungle of information surrounds one's every day, which confirms that making straightforward rational choices remains an illusion. Repeatedly, supposedly climate-friendly and responsible choices have actually turned out to be even counterproductive. A new study by the institute of energy and environmental research in Heidelberg (IFEU) shows that the assumption that buying milk in glass bottles is an ecologically sound alternative is actually a misconception. One of the authors states that "for the time being, we cannot attest the glass recycling system for milk bottles a favourable eco-balance" (Dierig, 2019), as there are so few bottlers that on average one bottle travels a distance of 721 kilometres.

John Maynard Keynes (1937) extensively occupied himself with the recognition that the rationality principle was profoundly overrated, as he was convinced that omnipresent insecurity keeps people from rationally predicting the future – the standard procedure in conventional behavioural theories. Keynes here follows David Hume who realised already in 1738 that since we cannot deductively determine what we are not experiencing, we have to resort back to "custom or a certain instinct of our nature [...] – custom [...] is the great guide of human life" (p. 16). These phenomena, social proof and the reliance on habits or custom, show that rationality is far away from always reflecting people's principal motive. Therefore, increasingly, the focus on the inherently exclusive expert-based rational knowledge and its superiority is being criticised:

> Rejecting these simplistic views of audiences, critics argue for an approach based on a better understanding of how to engage people [...]: for example, through exploration of bottom-up, non-expert climate perceptions rather than top-down, expert understandings.
>
> Nerlich et al., 2010, p. 4

Jamison here finds it paradoxical that "the more expert knowledge we have, and the more use we make of it, the more calamitous the ensuing problems seem to be" (2001, p. 23). Accordingly, I argue that society does not have a climate-related deficit in conventional types of scientific 'rational' knowledge. Therefore, it must be looked for alternative conceptions to achieve meaningful climate action.

Alternative conceptions of linking knowledge with action

People in fact often act entirely *irrationally*. The conventional conception completely overlooks this reality that stems from societal dynamics and interpersonal motives: "Individuals determine appropriate behaviour for themselves [by] examin[ing] behaviour of others there, especially similar others" (Cialdini, 1993, cited in Cialdini et al., 1999, p. 1243) – a phenomenon that has been termed 'social proof' (cf. Cialdini et al., 1999, p. 1242). Thus, the realisation is long overdue that in most cases in modern society consuming has very little to do with the functionality of the product and everything to do with social valuation: "[...] people do not just act out of their self-interest as they also have social, moral and altruistic motivations like e.g., caring for strangers; people do not always base decisions on information – e.g., because some of it is not available and it is impossible to process all information before taking a decision; and also they act based on emotions" (Jackson, 2005, Orrell, 2012, both cited in Kenner, 2015, p. 09). Therefore, it counts to consider which material and social inequalities lie at the bottom of consumption practices, but the extreme responsibilisation of the individual leads to the complete neglect of such relational and relative aspects:

> Apparent, directly visible beings, whether individuals or groups, exist and subsist in and through difference; that is, they occupy relative positions in a space of relations which, although invisible and always difficult to show empirically, is the most real reality (the ens realissimum, as scholasticism would say) and the real principle of the behaviour of individuals and groups.
>
> Bourdieu, 1998, p. 31

One must thus urgently recognise the profound cultural difference that exists in relation to the perception of climate change in Germany. It is essential to finally take seriously the everyday life experiences (cf. Rau, 2018) of those social groups that do not usually speak out on or concern themselves with climate matters. As Bourdieu has argued in his magnum opus *Distinction*, human social behaviour is determined by one's (largely subconscious) perception of others in relation to oneself, as being either similar or different. In his eyes, all human action serves the purpose of expressing either belonging or distinction in relation to a particular societal subgroup.

Bourdieu goes on to say that those at the top practice distinction by consuming to stage their wealth and to set themselves apart from societal groups lower in status as this grants the security of maintaining their elite positions: "The leisure class, at the summit, cuts itself off from society and this is possible because the group of the wealthiest has grown sufficiently large that the richest no longer need to interact with the rest of the population" (Kempf, 2008, p. 65, cited in Kenner, 2015, p. 06). What they aspire to and thus consume is determined by their cultural preferences that due to the luxury of being detached (at least to an extent) from financial limitations follow what Bourdieu calls *a pure gaze*: "The pure gaze implies a break with the ordinary attitude towards the world, which, given the conditions in which it is performed, is also a social separation" (1984, p. 5). This 'pure gaze' and the types of consumption practices it steers practitioners towards are, according to Bourdieu, deeply internalised (beyond consciousness) from an early age onwards. In the upper classes these are detached from mundane everyday necessities: "The eye is a product of history reproduced by education" (Bourdieu, 1984, p. 3). Here, Kenner points out that "in a context of extreme inequality [...] [rich people] may be disconnected from the reality of the ecological crisis" (2015, p. 10), which may lead to them responding even less well to information campaigns. These schemes of classification:

> ... make distinctions between what is good and what is bad, between what is right and what is wrong, between what is distinguished and what is vulgar, and so forth, but the distinctions are not identical. Thus, for instance, the same behaviour or

> even the same good can appear distinguished to one person, pretentious to someone else, and cheap or showy to yet another.
>
> Bourdieu, 1998, p. 8

For the climate activist, the V-label (for *vegan*) on medicine packaging may be the reason to reach for this and not another product. By contrast, the reader of the German meat-lover magazine BEEF may ridicule this labelling for it making zero sense to him. He finds *this stupid vegan hype completely ludicrous! What's not going to be vegan in a tablet?*. Some existing literature is already concerned with societal difference: similar to the Six Americas Study (Leiserowitz et al., 2009), Metag et al. (2015) distinguish five different groups within the German population in terms of their perceptions of climate change urgency. These groups also differ significantly according to how they access information on climate change – i.e., their media consumption and communication patterns. This gives insight in how to tailor climate change communication campaigns to specific audiences: members of 'the doubtful', for instance, do not actively seek out information on climate change. Here an indirect campaign that acts "as 'by-catch' whilst watching something else" (p. 15) is potentially more effective than direct climate change communication. "Until green consumption is automatic (embedded in the daily practices of all actors in society), the complexity of developing new meanings, materials and skills will continue to prevent truly sustainable consumption" (Boström and Davidson, 2018, p. 201, see also Huddart-Kennedy, 2018, p. 16).

Compatibility with the everyday

One avenue to consider here may thus be that the results presented by climate science are just too far away from the average person's daily life. So far, the appeals to the individual to consume greener have hardly been successful, since they have not been equipped to reach people *emotionally* – a requirement that the guild of the marketeers has recognised and used to its advantage for decades. "Emotion serves as the glue that binds us to norms, the performance of socially sanctioned roles and the maintenance of status hierarchies" (Ford and Norgaard, 2019, p. 221). Perhaps the lack of progress in climate action can be much better explained by *not-feeling* instead of *not-knowing*, as the deficit model completely ignores the significance of affective, emotional and bodily aspects of knowing (e.g., Lidskog et al. 2020). This also includes people's engagement in everyday practices that shape their experiences of being in the world (Rau, Davies, and Fahy, 2014; Greene, 2018). Underlying values, emotions and ways of life do not play a role in the messages sent out today when people are rationally asked to, for example, save energy and therefore money (cf. Nerlich et al., 2010). Hulme points out that in contrast to the IPCC-consensus on the anthropogenic contribution to climate change, there is no consensus in sight concerning what the average person ought to do about all this in their everyday lives (2009/10, p. 41). As he goes on: "… by understanding the ways climate change connects with foundational human instincts of nostalgia, fear, pride and justice we open up a way of resituating culture and the human spirit at the centre of our understanding of climate" (ibid., p. 42). Thus, the assumption that consensus must be established on what climate change means[6] should be left behind. Instead, it counts to foster an atmosphere of diverse interpretations as such heterogeneity gives rise to multifaceted "creative applications of the idea of climate change" (ibid., p. 43), in which Hulme sees real opportunity. "We should be using the idea of climate change to reveal, animate and mobilise the latent human values of temperance, compassion and justice" (ibid.).

As the threat posed by climate change is generally perceived as abstract as well as spatially and temporally distant (Moser, 2010, p. 43), it is easily overshadowed by other personal challenges in people's everyday lives (ibid., p. 36). The lack of urgency is further fuelled by the fact that urbanisation leads to increasing numbers of people being shielded from actually experiencing the dynamics of nature:

> Living, working, learning, and playing most hours of the day in climate-controlled buildings, moving in protective vehicles through vastly human-altered landscapes, and spending relatively little time in attentive, observing, or interactive modes in nature makes it difficult to notice subtle, incremental environmental changes.
>
> Moser, 2010, p. 34; see also Glantz, 1999, cited in ibid., p. 34

All this renders climate change complex beyond human cognitive understanding. Here it helps to consider knowing together with efficacy.

Knowledge and efficacy

According to Bandura, "people select, construct, and negotiate environments partly on the basis of their self-beliefs of efficacy" (1994, p. 49). Albeit at least considering the role of environments, this conception that choices are bounded by beliefs in one's own self-efficacy is again profoundly cognitivist and individualistic: people do not arrive at self-efficacy beliefs by actively negotiating with themselves in their own heads about what is best to believe. What is missing here is the is the critical role

6 As Mike Hulme points out, in contrast to the scientific consensus on the anthropogenic contribution to climate change, there is "no comparable consensus – no single perspective or vantage point – that allows us to understand what this kaleidoscopic idea of climate change **means** for us and our descendants" (Hulme, 2009, p. 41, my emph.).

of efficacy-attributions endorsed by others. This encompasses not only what is being said to a person but crucially also what swings along with messages, often on an emotional level, and is then, often subconsciously, interpreted and kept. Therefore, it is entirely inconceivable that we can pinpoint to the origin of our beliefs as much of the time, the process never even surfaces on cognitive levels. It would be much more conducive for climate action to drop the conception of the individual as cognitive rational entity and consider *practitioners in context* instead. The way people choose to act is the result of manifold hopes, pressures and fears as well as material situations and practiced lifestyles that are both constituted by and actively constitute the social context in which people dwell. Therefore, the assumption that our behaviour lies solely in our own hands signifies a fatal, since potentially even paralysing, farce.

Bourdieu: Alternative to cognitivism

In a poignant attack against "what the philosophers of the Cambridge School called morbus mathematicus [that] wreaks havoc even in areas far removed from economics" (1990, p. 47), Bourdieu revolts against the hegemonic paradigm of *normal science* (cf. Kuhn, 1962) that takes the hard sciences to be the gold standard and rests upon mathematic models, deduction, rational action theory and methodological individualism:

> The people who construct them [mathematic models] often abandon themselves to the dogmatic temptation that Kant was already denouncing in mathematicians, and which means you move from the model of reality to the reality of the model.
>
> Bourdieu, 1990, p. 47f.

Bourdieu asks us to overcome this perspective, and to examine practices: "The principle of practices has to be sought instead in the relationship between external constraints which leave a very variable margin for choice, and dispositions[7] which are the product of economic and social processes that are more or less completely reducible to these constraints, as defined at a particular moment" (Bourdieu, [1977] 1990, p. 50). This is because the connection between social context and individual is crucially multidirectional, fluid and co-constitutive. Bourdieu had observed that

---

7 Burke et al. describe these dispositions as "unconscious internalisations of social constraints that are naturalised, comprise common sense, are so obvious, and feel so right and proper within a given cultural or social context that members of the group cannot further explain them – the just are" (2009, p. 64S).

agents express the same kinds of behaviour, especially when they belong to the same social group and that this is even the case when they are unfamiliar with each other:

> The conditionings associated with a particular class of conditions of existence produce habitus, systems of durable, transposable dispositions, structured structures predisposed to function as structuring structures, that is, as principles which generate and organise practices and representations that can be objectively adapted to their outcomes without presupposing a conscious aiming at ends or an expressed mastery of the operations necessary in order to attain them.
>
> Bourdieu, [1977] 1990, p. 53

For this reason, in this study it is argued for "choosing practices as socio-material units of analysis [as this] promotes forms of inquiry that challenge the dominance of conceptual and methodological individualism in research on environmental attitudes and behavior (Shove 2010; Shove et al. 2012; Rau, Davies, and Fahy, 2014)" (Rau, 2018, p. 218). Single and stable actions or behaviours cannot simply be selectively and separately targeted by nudges, as this is not how people in society actually operate: "Social context encompasses multiple realms including both cultural and social domains of influence, as illustrated in Bourdieu's concept of habitus (embodied history, presence of the past)" (Burke et al., 2009, p. 66S), and also importantly involves subconscious processes (cf. ibid.):

> Because the habitus is an infinite capacity for generating products – thoughts, perceptions, expressions and actions – whose limits are set by the historically and socially situated conditions of its production, the conditioned and conditional freedom it provides is as remote from creation of unpredictable novelty as it is from simple mechanical reproduction of the original conditioning.
>
> Bourdieu, [1977] 1990, p. 55

Bourdieu's habitus can therefore be interpreted as the union between structure and agency, so between the positions that agents occupy in a social space and the types of behaviour that are commonplace in it. As an inherently cultural concept it rests upon people's everyday practices: "Habitus exists only in and through the practices of individuals and their interaction with each other and their environment; thus habitus is not just *manifest* in behaviour, it is an integral *part* of it (and vice versa)" (Jenkins, 2002, p. 75, orig. emph.). Bourdieu conceives of the social milieu as springing from processes of adaptation to the social groups' living conditions, where resources are divided unequally (cf. Lutz, 2016). Social milieus thus aid the largely subconscious formation of group specific forms of *habitus*, or *climate habitus* in this study. Bourdieu sees differences in society to not only occur along socio-economic variables (vertical differentiation) but also along cultural factors (horizontal differentiation), which is why his concept is so uniquely equipped to be applied in the present study of climate cultures. This renders milieus in his definition no longer closed but dynamic. Here, habitus builds the nexus between people's practices and their social surroundings.

This is precisely why it makes sense to apply Bourdieu's concept of habitus to an investigation of responses to climate change: if it is the incorporated social structures that have become "second nature" (Jurt, 2010, p. 8) and not the cognitive individual structures that initiate acting, then it is essential to shift the focus from knowing onto what people actually do. Habitus is expressed through action, not through knowing. "In everyday practice it is principally the various life spheres that are important – work, leisure, family, neighbourhood etc. These have to be 'handled' by people, by steering and meaningfully integrating their interests, ideals, actions and emotions" (Bremer, 2004, p. 44). Thus, behaviour in each of these social areas is only one of the diverse elements of the everyday practice of an agent. It is the habitus that provides them with some form of regularity or logic, so that "in all areas of life there is, so to speak, the same handwriting of an actor discernible" (Bremer, 2004, p. 47).

Actions carry various, potentially opposing meanings in different social spaces. "As an acquired system of generative schemes, the habitus makes possible the production of all the thoughts, perceptions and actions inherent in the particular conditions of its production and only those" (Bourdieu, [1977] 1990, p. 55). Accordingly, habitus yields distinct modes of meaning and connotation in each of them: habitus thus

> … ensures the active presence of past experiences, which, deposited in each organism in the form of schemes of perception, thought and action, tend to guarantee the 'correctness' of practices and their constancy over time, more reliably than all formal rules and explicit norms.
>
> Bourdieu, [1977] 1990, p. 54

A praxeological perspective in the tradition of Bourdieu therefore allows overcoming the blatant deficits of current information-centrist, fact-idolising, individualist theories by permitting the recognition of the importance of emotional messages, feelings and relational knowledge. Authors of this multifariously shaped, dynamic and fluid school of thought that Andreas Reckwitz has referred to as "fertile pool of ideas" (2003, p. 112) are, amongst others, Anthony Giddens (see e.g., 1979), Theodore Schatzki (see e.g., 2016) and Ludwig Wittgenstein (see e.g., 1953) who have dealt with alternative forms of knowing like tacit knowledge or implicit knowledge that are of particular interest to this study. Practice theory's "two most central claims can be taken as the materiality of the social and cultural and the implicit, informal logic of social life that oppose the rationalisms and intellectualisms of other social and cultural theories" (Reckwitz, 2003, p. 113). Such an analysis manages to read between the lines and thus come a little closer to reality. Melanie Jaeger-Erben (2017, p. 135ff.) also follows this tradition and shows that two completely different motives can be at play in the carrying out of a particular consumption practice (buying organic food) by two agents: for one person, the climate aspect is central, whilst for the other, the consumption decision is made based on other relevant practices (related to parenting) in the same realm. In an analysis that merely looks at individuals' rational decisions, this insight would remain entirely hidden.

Of course, in this study, it is not argued for a reduction of knowledge, but definitely for a more serious and intensive consideration of other types of knowledge, in particular relational, emotional and affective knowledge. Knowledge itself should be thought of as less cerebral or cognitive and instead as more emotional and embodied. Grappling with this alternative form of knowledge rests on the conviction that "individual persons, whether strategic or norm following, are inseparable from the transactional contexts within which they are embedded" (Emirbayer, 1997, p. 287). These contexts include not only the practices the agents perform but also the sometimes subconscious dispositions that spark their execution and that rest on societal regularities. Such relational approaches further stress the role of the historical and the material.

As shown so far, this study's core concepts, responsibility, efficacy and knowing have been extensively contemplated by various scholars. However, traditional perspectives like those that focus on the individual, information deficits and rationality theory approach these issues quite crudely. They have largely ceased to add value, which is not least verified by the fact that with them, meaningful climate action still leaves much to be desired. In some instances, relations between (two of) the core concepts have been discussed and the concatenation between them has been considered. However, a conception that truly integrates these three ideas is missing to this day. There is a clear need for an alternative approach that does justice to the dynamic of social structures and that recognises the importance of societal influences (cf. Rau, 2018, p. 209). Building on Kari Marie Norgaard's ground-breaking work on the connection between climate change, emotions, and everyday life that she developed in her book *Living in denial* (2011) and several other of her texts, this study contributes to closing this research gap.

2.5 The social organisation of denial

Norgaard's culturally sensitive approach reveals the inherently social nature of denial that affects her respondents' reactions to the threat of climate change: "[...] in wealthy nations, the key questions related to climate change have to do with denial"

(2011, p. 216). She defines her concept as follows: "By socially organized denial I mean that ignoring information about global warming takes place in response to social circumstances and is carried out through a process of social interaction" (2006, p. 352). She speaks of different *cultures of denial* (Sutton and Norgaard, 2013; Norgaard, 2019) and in doing so moves beyond prevailing individualistic psychological conceptions of denial. Norgaard takes issue with the fact that many debates about climate change are dominated by insights from the quantitatively oriented disciplines such as economics and psychology, "where only individual action and not social structures are understood as shaping outcomes" (2018, p. 4). Just like information deficit thinking, psychology, that has historically been investigating denial, focuses on the individual without adequately taking into consideration the social dynamics influencing them. Yet, as has been argued and as also Eviatar Zerubavel, amongst others, vehemently underscores, "society organizes patterns of perception, memory, and organizational aspects of thinking" (1997, cited in Norgaard, 2006, p. 352).

Importantly, Norgaard points to people denying not only their responsibility to protect the climate but them also basing this on their own experienced lack of self-efficacy: "We need democratic engagement and response, yet individuals retreat out of a sense of helplessness" (2018, p. 4). She also observes that people collectively turn a blind eye to more news on the threat posed by climate change by falling back on habitual conversation, attention and emotional response that represent specific cultural strategies of dealing with the issue (2011, p. 9). She shows that conventional individualist explanations of denial fail to grasp shared decisions within a community to ignore a particular threat (here: climate change and its wide-ranging impacts on local livelihoods). "Local feeling rules may diminish or magnify the intensity of response, which, combined with available alternatives that are not incompatible with existing worldviews, render some responses to climate change more viable than others" (Ford and Norgaard, 2019, p. 224).

Thus, her work presents convincing arguments and evidence for denial operating "as a key mechanism in the reproduction of power" (Sutton and Norgaard, 2013, p. 498). As discussed, conventional economic theory conceals power structures and questions of collective responsibility. Bourdieu writes that this is because elite groups successfully exert power on those who are underprivileged by unknowingly receiving their consent. He goes on to say that this consent is not of the enlightened and conscious kind but emerges instead as a form of submission of their bodies being socialised in the way that they were (cf. Bourdieu, 1997, p. 165). "Often missing from the discourse about climate action is consideration of how our ties to histories of colonialism, racial domination, as well as hetero-patriarchal social systems might influence the adoption of new practices" (Ford and Norgaard, 2019, p. 234). So, we see that obscuring diverging distributions of power is itself a means to exert power on those less powerful as this "manages to impose meanings and to impose them as legitimate by concealing the power relations which are the basis of its force" (Bourdieu and Passeron, 1973, p. 12).

Explicit versus implicit denial

Importantly, in this study's conception, different types of denial belong to two broad categories, either explicit or implicit denial. Explicit denial is performed by those sceptical of climate change even occurring whilst implicit denial refers to people that acknowledge the issue but push away the imperative to act accordingly. The latter kind is dealt with in detail by Norgaard and described below. The former kind, explicit denial, refers to climate sceptical views that outright negate the IPCC-consensus. Some people even believe that corporate, scientific and political elites have conspired to further restrict the public's freedoms with the help of climate narratives. The outlook of people who endorse such conspiracy theories[8] is particularly difficult to argue with or alter as "then any additional evidence supporting the consensus will just be seen as *more proof* of the conspiracy" (Hart and Nisbet, 2012, p. 4) – the so-called backfire or boomerang effect: "A boomerang effect occurs when a message is strategically constructed with a specific intent but produces a result that is the opposite of that intent [...]. Furthermore, boomerang effects may be specific to only certain segments of an audience based on individual predispositions or context" (ibid.). This explains why the different forms of denial are observed in some climate cultures and not in others. When new information collides with people's worldviews, their original beliefs can become even more entrenched through this type of backfire effect. By now, a growing body of research has established a strong link between (explicit) denial of climate change and the support of conspiracy theories (Lewandowsky, 2021; Hornsey et al., 2018). What is also distinct about this type of denial is the central role emotional messages play in these discourses:

> The ferocity and grandiloquence of climate denial rhetoric suggests more than a rational, measured disagreement of a scientific nature, but an emotional reaction

---

8 Here I rely on Karl Popper (1980) who conceives of conspiracies as follows: "The explanation of a social phenomenon consists in the discovery that individuals or groups have a vested interest in the unfolding of an event and that they conspired to bring it about. (Their interests are sometimes hidden and must still be detected.) This (...) of course stems from the wrong theory that whatever happens in a society is the result of plans made by powerful individuals or groups. (...) In its modern forms this theory is the typical result of the secularisation of a religious superstition" (cited in Eco, 2021, p. 11f.). Such powerful individuals or groups are generally often referred to as 'the elite' by those endorsing such conspiracy theories. This rhetoric also has an antisemitic element to it and must be thoroughly distinguished from what is meant by 'elite climate cultures' in this study (i.e., those endowed with considerable cultural capital in Bourdieu's terms).

> grounded in threat, and the fear, anxiety and unease that such a threat might engender.
>
> Ford and Norgaard, 2019, p. 226

Norgaard however mainly deals with the other type, implicit denial: "What I observed in Bygdaby [the small Norwegian community studied] was not a rejection of information per se but the failure to integrate this knowledge into everyday life or transform it into social action" (2006, p. 352). Norgaard's conception is very nuanced. The remainder of this chapter thus elaborates on three aspects in her work and how they serve as point of departure for this study's own conceptual framework (defining climate cultures): the collective denial of responsibility for climate action; the denial of self-efficacy; and the denial of knowing in the form of this distancing from emotion. Now, the next section is concerned with what she has to say on the denial of responsibility.

Norgaard on denial of responsibility

The connection between denial and responsibility in relation to climate change (that lies at the heart of this study) has recently been granted increasing attention. Processes of moral disengagement such as the diffusion and displacement of responsibility are central to the denial of responsibility this study analyses. For example, Stoll-Kleemann und O'Riordan observe a shift from the outright denial of climate change towards the denial of *responsibility* for climate change: although in their study, all respondents claimed to find climate action important, a sort of *moral decoupling* was discernible: "There is still denial by favoring displacing responsibility or even assigning guilt to others (e.g., government, business and industry, lobbies, 'the rich', the 'egoistic people'), refusing to be a first mover and to engage in more than just low-cost behavior" (2020, p. 11). In her study of the people of Bygdaby, Norgaard similarly observes how people use a host of different strategies to practice this denial of responsibility. Here, she (2011, p. 68) refers to Frantz and Mayer who note that "climate change [...] is marked by a diffusion of responsibility" (2009, p. 214).

According to Norgaard, "the crisis of climate change makes clear how badly we need a mode of social organization that promotes organized responsibility rather than organized irresponsibility and denial" (2011, p. 226). However, since "current political economic structure is (still) intimately embedded in our petroleum-based economy" (ibid., 2018, p. 4), she observes a society-wide distancing from responsibility as "individualism and globalisation work together to create a disjunction between our morals and our practices" (Maniates, 2002, p. 51, cited in Norgaard, 2011, p. 226). Only by denying climate change, it is possible for Norwegian society to remain on this economic path. People from this community employed a variety of social narratives, some produced by the national government, to deflect responsibility for and legitimate Norwegian petroleum policy" (Norgaard, 2011, p. 140). Crushing ambivalences, like those caused by conflicting information, leave people feeling stalled and thus frustrated: "... climate change poses a new challenge for individuals to live morally coherent and responsible lives" (ibid., p. 226).

Norgaard then describes how people neutralise these negative feelings of inconsistency in various ways: "This dissonance is an unpleasant condition that people seek to resolve, often by changing one of their cognitions" (ibid., p. 68). Internalising the threat posed by climate change, the urgency there is to act on it and the totality with which behaviour would have to be adapted would be so disturbing and in conflict with so much that is taken for granted in modern everyday life that it is simply avoided. Norgaard here points to cultural "tools of innocence" that provide a *repertoire* or *toolkit* of solutions to everyday problems (see also Swidler, 1986; Rau, 2008). She sees these as "ideas, images and activities that are used to create distance from responsibility and to assert rightness or goodness" (Norgaard, 2011, p. 146). Here, she describes all sorts of strategies that the people in the community employ to justify their denying of responsibility. In this, she builds on Zerubavel's theory on the sociology of denial (2010) and social psychologist Morris Rosenberg's emphasis of "selective attention in the construction of reality" (Norgaard, 2011, p. 173): as Rosenberg writes, "people may shift their thoughts intentionally from one topic to another or selectively perceive, remember, attend to, and interpret events in ways that produce the intended emotional outcomes" (1990, p. 11).

Another mechanism to neutralise cognitive dissonance is seeking reassurance with those people one identifies with the most that one still acts condonably. "When we stray from social norms and our prescribed roles, emotions signal to us through feelings of discomfort that we are out of cultural bounds" (Ford and Norgaard, 2019, p. 221). We often seek absolution in the relational. "[...] cognitive dissonance is generated by threats to identity and individuals' desire to preserve a positive sense of self-esteem" (Norgaard, 2011, p. 217). Admitting to oneself all the ways in which one falls short in protecting the climate would however not benefit one's sense of self-esteem, which helps to explain this widespread phenomenon of denying responsibility.

Further strategies applied by the people Norgaard interviewed were, for example, that they often stressed they only needed to live a *simple* life as "images of simplicity connote innocence" (Norgaard, 2011, p. 161). Similarly, she reports that through emphasising the globality of the climate challenge, the Norwegian state managed to paint the Norwegian natural gas project in a climate-friendly light (ibid., p. 172). She also writes that leading politicians have emphasised that Norwegian industry is not the most harmful to the climate when compared globally, insinuating that Norwegian fossil fuel industries are "good climate policy internationally" (ibid., p. 173). Such cultural strategies employed to deny one's own climate responsibility and whether and how they may also feature in the German context thus forms one key interest of this study.

Norgaard finds there to be interpretative and cultural strategies of denial and classes the former narratives into the rubrics of 'selective interpretation', 'perspectival selectivity', and 'claims to virtue', and the latter category into 'norms of attention' and 'emotion/conversation norms'. One example of how the latter produce denial is that information about climate change may be perceived as too uncomfortable and thus people tend to choose to not concern themselves with it, which Norgaard calls "a new psychological predicament for privileged people" (2006, p. 366). Here, she observes how her respondents feel a "profound sense of entrapment" (2011, p. 195). People in western societies experience being "caught between the […] desire to do the right thing and to be informed (which they felt is a necessary first step toward responsibility and change)" (ibid.), whilst being stuck in a system that in so many ways depends on emitting carbon on a daily basis.

One further strategy used to push responsibility away was for example the application of so-called 'stock stories' in what falls in Norgaard's category of *interpretative denial*. This refers to the employment of a repertoire of ways to speak positively about Norway and thus neutralise potentially negative messages when confronted with evidence about its increasing climate impact.

Norgaard explains that this category of *interpretive denial* also involves the use of Rosenberg's notion of *perspectival selectivity* that refers to the way one approaches a particular situation: "People tend to assign those meanings to events that will produce the desired emotions" (Rosenberg, 1991, p. 135). Such perspectival selectivity was also applied to "deny self-involvement" (Opotow and Weiss, 2000, cited in Norgaard, 2006, p. 359). Here, responsibility is diffused as people "deny personal responsibility for an environmental harm by seeing it as the result of collective rather than individual decisions and actions" (Norgaard, 2011, p. 123). For the purpose of neutralising negative feelings about impending climate change, the members of the community also used humour as a means to "maintain […] conversational control over topics that were troubling (ibid., p. 125)". Here, Norgaard cites Nina Eliasoph who noted that "teasing let members keep the wider world at arm's length" (1998, p. 107, cited in Norgaard, 2011, p. 125), which is precisely what Norgaard observed was happening in this small Norwegian community. Norwegian people also deflected responsibility away from themselves by pointing to the US as another larger climate culprit and stressing Norway's comparatively small land area and population (ibid., p. 171). Norgaard goes on to say that ex-environmental minister Børge Brende had stated that "Norway is one of the countries in the world that has benefited most from fossil fuels. This gives us a special responsibility in the politics of climate change, especially with respect to poor countries" (Hovden and Lindseth, 2002, p. 143, cited in Norgaard, 2011, p. 71). Yet even in light of this acknowledgement, Norway had still substantially expanded its oil and gas production in recent years.

Norgaard argues that this diffusion of responsibility was also made possible by the strategy of habitually coming back to, focusing on and emphasising the positive sides of Norway. As Benedict Anderson (1991) has pointed out, "part of imagining communities is agreeing upon what people will collectively pay attention to […] and what they will collectively ignore […]" (Norgaard, 2011, p. 173). Accordingly, in conversations the members of the community focused on all things typically Norway: "By portraying Norwegians as close to nature, egalitarian, simple, and humble, these narratives of national identity served to counter the criticism and doubt Norwegians face with regards to climate and petroleum policies" (ibid., 2011, p. 142). These processes of national identity formation and protection were vital in maintaining a positive picture of one's country in the light of climate change and Norway's specific involvement in it. Since constant dripping wears away the stone, focusing on the positive and repeating it over and over will eventually make people believe in it, even when the evidence tells a different story. This strategy of *over-communication* (Goffman, 1959, cited in Norgaard, 2011, p. 142) serves to steer attention away from the fact that "Norwegian wealth, political economy, and way of life are intimately connected to the problem of global warming – not only through individual actions of automobile usage but also through the political economic structure that has created Norwegian wealth through the production and marketing of North Sea oil" (Norgaard, 2006, p. 353).

In a much more recent paper, Norgaard, together with her colleague Allison Ford, further develops these ideas about the links between climate change, culture, emotions and everyday life into their concept of *environmental subjectivities* (2020, p. 59) that "situates individual environmental practices in relationship to interlocking power structures" (ibid.). Here, responsibility again plays a central role: "For the Karuk people [US indigenous tribe studied], environmental subjectivity is shaped by a sense of responsibility to the natural world that spurred many creative, politically engaged responses to climate change and related environmental problems" (ibid.).

Efficacy and denial

To shed more light on such interlocking power structures within and between groups, the following section considers how in society there are different levels of both, actual and perceived efficacy, with respect to climate action. Norgaard also points to the links between responsibility and efficacy: "People with low self-efficacy will be likely to deny responsibility and concern because unless they feel able to do something about the problem, an awareness of concern or sense of responsibility would be a conflicting cognition" (2011, p. 68). She further refers to Jan Krosnick et al. who find that people only take on issues where they feel they can do something about them: "People stop paying attention to global climate change when they realize that there is no easy solution for it" (2006, p. 34).

With respect to the impact that different societal agents can exert on the outcome of the climate crisis, Norgaard stresses: "An individual can take shorter hot showers but the US military remains the biggest consumer of oil in the world" (Norgaard, 2018, p. 4). Elsewhere she points out that almost any effort from official sides to communicate climate change displays the 'severe limitation' of being addressed to the individual consumer. Here we again see the discrepancy between responsibility attributions and efficacy expectations at its finest.

Norgaard further elaborates on the relationship between privilege and climate change: "Privileged people reproduce existing power relations as they enact denial in everyday life" (2011, p. 218). To make visible such differences in actual power, one must become aware of the choices people have with regard to climate action: a business manager will have different financial means to forego certain mobility options than a single mother who lives in the countryside. Importantly, on top, both will have respectively different social pressures. "[I]t is important [...] to question the power structures that support and benefit from the invisibility of material realities. Both culture and emotions can be co-opted into supporting the status quo; or, channelled into challenging it" (Ford and Norgaard, 2019, p. 238). In many studies it has now been shown that it is precisely those who would theoretically be able to afford more climate action who deny most categorically: "Privileged people are protected from full knowledge of environmental (and many other social) problems by [...] their own fine-tuned yet unconscious practices of not noticing, looking the other way, and normalizing the disturbing information they constantly come across" (Norgaard, 2011, p. 219). All these considerations by Norgaard and others confirm the added value of conceiving of responsibility for climate action in direct connection with the impact an agent can actually have.

In her referring to efficacy, Norgaard widens these originally solely individually and psychologically conceptualised ideas about denial tendencies and self-efficacy (in Bandura's sense) by approaching it social-scientifically and also considering the role of emotions. Here, Ford and Norgaard refer to Kemper who "theorises that power and status are universally linked to the elicitation of emotions; when power and status are threatened, negative emotions motivate attempts to restore them" (1990, cited in Ford and Norgaard, 2019, p. 226). Norgaard also points to the fact that privileged people in industrialised Western societies profit from their denial of climate change in two ways – financially and also by "avoiding the emotional and psychological entanglement and identity conflicts that may arise from knowing that one is doing 'the wrong thing'" (2011, p. 72).

Underscoring the role of emotions, Norgaard also fiercely refutes information deficit thinking by calling for the recognition that "information alone is not enough to produce action" (ibid.). More so, expanding people's information about climate change can even prove counterproductive, as she and various other scholars (e.g., Kellstedt et al., 2008, see Norgaard, 2011, p. 2) have found that "respondents who are better informed about climate change feel less rather than more responsible for it" (Norgaard, 2011, p. 2). This is because being further inundated with details about the looming catastrophe is not a particularly motivating scenario. People then tend to look the other way or bury their head in the sand like the ostrich. This indicates that the relationship between increasing information and efficacy is anything but straight-forward. Thus, what is taken for granted and what counts as obvious and self-evident or what is seen as valid and legitimate in one section of society simply melts with reality. That this is in fact contingent only becomes visible from the outside of the social group: "[...] information on climate change may be accepted, resisted, navigated and interpreted differently depending on the sense of efficacy, self-esteem, and social support of the individual receiving it" (ibid., p. 72). This brings us to the link between efficacy and knowledge in Norgaard's work. As Goldblatt reminds us: "All knowledge is widely enmeshed in the operations of power" (2004, p. 124f.). Thus, the following third point of this subsection now considers such denying of knowledge that is simultaneously interlinked with denial of both efficacy and responsibility. Here, Norgaard writes: "The notion that people are not acting against global warming because they do not know about it reinforces a sense of their innocence in the face of these activities, thereby maintaining the indivisibility of the power relations that are upheld by so-called apathy regarding global warming" (2011, p. 71). This reiterates the pressing need to uncover these power relations if one is to make any significant progress in protecting the climate.

Norgaard and knowing

Norgaard then goes on to say: "'Information', like caring, cannot be thought of in generic and isolated blocs of facts with universal meaning and significance across all communities. Instead information is socially structured, is given social meanings and must be understood in social context" (2011, p. 72). This is because knowing is ambiguous and also serves political purposes: "Attention to the specifics of how people turn a blind eye [...] shines a light into more theoretical questions concerning the cultural reproduction of power" (Sutton and Norgaard, 2013, p. 498). In this, Norgaard shows that the social organisation of denial occurs first on the political, secondly on the emotional and thirdly on the social level: "[...] whether people notice information about climate change is related to socially shaped systems of perception and attention, whether they remember what they hear is a function of social systems of memory, whether it is considered morally offensive or not is a function of whether it is inside or outside socially defined limits of concern; [...] how we think is part of culture and marks our participation in community" (Norgaard, 2011, p. 5f.).

An examination of individual points of view that drift in a vacuum decoupled from social connections must therefore remain inadequate. As Stanley Cohen finds:

> The psychology of 'turning a blind eye' or 'looking the other way' is a tricky matter. These phrases imply that we have access to reality, but choose to ignore it because it is convenient to do so. This might be a simple fraud: the information is available and registered, but leads to a conclusion which is knowingly evaded. 'Knowing' though can be far more ambiguous. We are vaguely aware of choosing not to look at the facts, but not quite conscious of what it is we are evading. We know, but at the same time we don't know.
>
> Cohen, 2001, p. 5, cited in Norgaard, 2011, p. 72

People thus collectively "distance themselves from information because of norms of emotion, conversation, and attention, [*...using...*] an existing cultural repertoire of strategies in the process" (Norgaard, 2011, p. 9). Whilst it shall be emphasised that knowledge and information are certainly vital in sparking engagement, this relationship is far from linear and straightforward.

In this way, Norgaard's account of *socially organised denial* finally helps to explain the infamous *value-action gap*. All these examples point to the fact that emotions play a far greater role in climate action than has hitherto been recognised, maybe even more so than information provision:

> We contend that emotions – the affective interpretations attached to sensations – are central to the interpretation of cultural cues, signalling which frames are compatible with deeply held, often embodied beliefs and habits, and which ones would require the undertaking of what Swidler calls 'a drastic and costly cultural retooling' (1986, p. 277).
>
> Ford and Norgaard, 2019, p. 222

People refusing to contribute to climate action do not generally do this out of spite. In most cases, this flows from a (subconscious) fear of having to go through such uncomfortable cultural retooling.

There is, however, a certain reluctance in politics, society and most notably in science to give more attention to emotions in general, which is precisely why such insights remain masked from our understanding. Emphasising emotions is unpopular, probably for fear of sounding weak, unprofessional, unscientific or even polemical. This is also underlined by the fact that accusing women of behaving or negotiating 'too emotionally' has a history of being used to delegitimise their messages: "Emotion has typically been associated with femininity and irrational, disorganized behavior" (MacArthur & Shields, 2015, p. 40). However, if the role of emotions in the diffusion of responsibility continues being brushed under the carpet, climate action will remain inadequate.

In this context, Norgaard speaks of an observed "public apathy" (2011, p. 348) that stems from overwhelming feelings of helplessness in relation to climate change. As she points out, this collective apathy is increasingly puzzling scholars from different disciplines in the form of the apparent paradox that in Western industrialised countries there exists what Robert Lifton (1982, cited in Norgaard, 2006, p. 357) calls a double reality in relation to climate change: highly educated people simultaneously are well aware of the threats posed by rising temperatures, yet lead their lives as if they had never heard of it. Here, she follows Jennifer Kent: "Because climate change requires so much more than individual action, discourses of individual responsibility, rather than enhancing agency, merely 'alert individuals to their essential ineffectiveness in tackling complex global environmental issues'" (2009, p. 145, cited in Norgaard, 2011, p. 192).

Due to intensified liberalisation of global markets since Reagan and Thatcher, politics has successively shed more and more of its responsibility so that today "we have no politics of climate change" (Giddens, 2009, p. 4, cited in Norgaard, 2011, p. 224). Norgaard thus further criticises existing studies for overlooking the significance of political economy because it provides the background against which cultural norms emerge, thereby also influencing them. Choosing to (not) act upon one's knowledge should instead be deemed a political act, which illustrates once more the inadequacy of such conventional economic approaches like nudging theory. "The barriers to action on climate change are based in the distribution of social power in the economic, political, and cultural spheres. Introducing new messages or information into an otherwise unchanged socio-economic system will accomplish little" (Luke, 2005, cited in Brulle et al., 2012, p. 185). Norgaard similarly concludes that "unless we can also refashion our political and economic systems, we are trapped" (2011, p. 224f.).

Building on these insights, it is vital to also examine 'official' discourses in society and analyse which power structures operate, even if this is often diffuse and difficult to grasp. Antonio Gramsci's (1971) hegemony concept also rests upon the recognition that power is inextricably linked to culture, as Sutton and Norgaard write (cited in Sutton and Norgaard, 2013, p. 498). Privileged social groups in society uphold and secure their dominant status quo by means of subtly generating compliance instead of exerting outright control. They then refer to Eliasoph (1998, p. 233) who defines hegemony as an "ongoing cultural process that gerrymanders the boundary of perception; [...] the way people make sense of everyday experience usually discourages them from thinking thoughts that might challenge the status quo" (ibid., p. 232). Ford and Norgaard also make the following point in relation to this:

> Research that preselects environmental practices takes for granted that all environmentally concerned individuals share the political goals of elite-envisioned sustainability, such as green development that serves the continuation of modern nation-states. But some groups and individuals that are committed to addressing climate change are not uniformly aligned to support the continuity and extension of the current political economic system.
>
> Ford and Norgaard, 2020, p. 47

Recognising these variations and shedding the assumption that citizens can unequivocally be nudged into climate-friendly behaviour (cf. Nerlich et al., 2010; Suldovsky, 2017) would significantly advance climate action efforts: "One missing puzzle piece is the acknowledgment that the way people know about climate change is not uniform but filtered through cultural systems accessed from lived experience within hierarchical social institutions that sort people by status" (Ford and Norgaard, 2020, p. 44). This is so important because if these differences in the cultural operation of knowing remain unrecognised, progress remains unlikely: "Power is contentious and disputed, but has to be included in ways in which knowledge is produced within the social sciences" (Goldblatt, 2004, p. 125). It must urgently be acknowledged that "changes in knowledge systems and social changes are inextricably linked" (Foucault, 1977, cited in Goldblatt, 2004, p. 25).

Norgaard goes on to say that in situations where there is no trust in political structures, the individual's refusal to take responsibility is understandable: "Individual apathy is a rational response if there is nowhere to turn" (2011, p. 225). Citing one of her interviewees, she writes: I feel helpless because I know "I can do these things on my own every day, like walking, making those choices, but the big environmental problems are coming from industry, and I feel like I can't do anything about that" (ibid., p. 194). Elsewhere she elaborates on the strategy the members of the Norwegian community employed to make themselves small: "Not every usage of the phrase 'Norway is a little land' is meant to exempt Norwegians from responsibility. [...] It implies as well a sense of vulnerability and powerlessness" (ibid., 2011, p. 171).

Consequently, this study integrates these ideas about socially organised denial of responsibility, efficacy and knowing related to climate change into its own cultural conception and then examines how this varies within German society along different climate cultures that each share how particular actions are carried out. According to Erhardt-Martinez et al. (2015, cited in Norgaard, 2018, p. 3), "social organization and culture produce variation in values among stakeholders and decision makers, variation in the perception of risks and uncertainties, differences in costs and benefits, and variation in the capacity of decision makers to implement mitigation policies" (see also Beck, 1992; Fisher, 2006; Roberts and Parks, 2006). A principal recognition of the true diversity that characterises climate-related thinking and practice in different social spheres allows, it is argued, the development of more nuanced exchange and more effective (and, certainly and importantly, dual) communication between decision-makers and civil society. In relation to climate change, there often seems to exist some form of 'unwritten law' that functions as absolution not to put one's knowledge into practice. Therefore, Norgaard suggests: "Even talking about climate change with family and friends is an important way to break cultural norms of silence" (2018, p. 4). How this 'unwritten law' is sometimes ratified in one group whilst action is taken in another embodies the central focus of this analysis. Accordingly, knowledge about climate change is in fact processed in the majority of the cultural segments of society, yet consequential actions are often not taken.

Acknowledging the denial that is implicit in such looking the other way allows for the following consideration: perhaps, factual knowledge is rather secondary, and it may prove more conducive to focus on what is being valued as *legitimate knowledge* in certain circles and what does not gain such recognition, by contrast.

According to Nerlich et al., risks to humanity presented by climate change are still being interpreted as 'virtual' by some segments of society which "turns climate change from a purely scientific phenomenon into a cultural one" (2010, p. 2). This helps explain why climate action still remains inadequate even though it has been such a topical issue in recent years:

> Culture shapes how individuals see the world, and how they feel about what they see. And culture is anything but rational! Emotional relationships to culture can help us understand why some people outright deny climate change, while others live in fear of it, but do nothing to change its trajectory, and still others challenge the social systems that cause climate change, fighting passionately against injustices to overturn inequality.
>
> Ford and Norgaard, 2019, p. 220f.

The idea that there are different types of culturally contingent denial also reiterates what Bieling has found: "In contrast to the relatively coherent world view of the conceptual and opinion forming intellectuals, the everyday awareness of the general population presents itself in many ways as incoherent and fragmented as it consists both of conservative-conformist and resistant-rebellious, innovative aspects and those that push beyond the status quo" (2014, p. 195f.). Ultimately, a certain way to behave remains acceptable as long the social circles that carry the most importance in the eyes of the practitioner do not openly sanction it. Therefore, it must be recognised that "climate impacts are varied not only along dimensions of inequality and vulnerability, but are also a function of interaction between material impacts and their cultural interpretations" (Norgaard, 2018, p. 3).

Therefore, this type of socially organised denial manifests differently in different societal circles. Using the concept of *climate cultures*, this study thus captures varying constellations of how responsibility, efficacy and knowing are handled, which is outlined next.

2.6 Divergent cultures of climate action and denial

Although fundamental to public opinion and political (in)action regarding climate change, culture remains a marginal concept in climate change research. Each climate culture will transport its own idiosyncratic norms regarding attributed or experienced responsibility, its individual or collective expressions, its efficacy expectations and its actual contribution to climate action. This occurs in the carrying-out of particular practices.

This overall ignorance of cultural phenomena partly relates to their ubiquity, as well as the relative resistance of culture to conventional scientific definition and measurement. As Mike Hulme (2016) puts it, "culture, just like climate, is hard to see and harder to measure" (p. 6). Thus, most media coverage and public debates concerning climate change tend to be 'culturally blind', too, in addition to ignoring pressing social problems arising from a changing climate such as resource scarcity, poverty and forced migration. Culture is thus conceptualised as an inherently social phenomenon that shapes and reflects social interaction within groups and communities: "Rather than being idiosyncratic, cultures of emotion are structured by social norms and expectations" (Ford and Norgaard, 2019, p. 221).

Given this inherent difficulty in investigating culture, continued cultural blindness in research on climate action coincides with profound neglect of people's everyday experiences and daily practices that characterises debates on environmental challenges more generally, and climate change in particular. This reluctance to 'mind the mundane' (Rau, 2018) means that much climate change communication actually serves to disengage citizens (Fox and Rau, 2017). This includes fear-inducing catastrophic and apocalyptic messages that incorporate a rather limited view of human agency and that may thus prevent public climate action (cf. Kundzewicz et al., 2020 for a recent discussion of this particular issue). Importantly for the present argument, such a perspective completely ignores lived experiences of climate responsibility and of individual and collective efficacy.

In the tradition of Bourdieu and leaning heavily on Norgaard, conventional linear concepts of knowing are replaced with a conception that explicitly recognises the multi-directionality of knowledge creation and –transfer that manifests through culture. "Cultural frames, selective interpretative schema that simplify and condense information, filter out information that is incompatible with familiar ways of seeing the world" (Ford and Norgaard, 2019, p. 220). This, in turn, highlights the necessity of responsibility discourses and practices amongst the whole of society and of paying attention to the actual potential of different societal actors to make a difference in relation to climate action. "With sociological analyses the question becomes [...] under what circumstances are people able to move beyond a sense of helplessness, guilt or fear of the future and take actions that are in their collective, long term survival interest?" (Norgaard, 2018, p. 4). Therefore, such an analysis is uniquely suited to shed light on diverging cultural tendencies that prompt agents to look at climate change or turn their head, to not be discouraged by one's own individual insignificance and take responsibility for one's own marginal contribution or instead to resign and blend it all out. "The power of culture to shape the way we act arises from the way it makes us feel" (Ford and Norgaard, 2019, p. 224). In this study's conception of climate cultures, therefore, the three central concepts – responsibility, efficacy and knowing – and whether or not they cumulate in collective denial embody the demarcation lines between the different climate cultures that were identified when undertaking the research.

This said, an emerging body of literature deals explicitly with linkages between culture and climate change. Thorsten Heimann, a leading contributor to this research, links the origin of the idea of climate cultures in German-speaking research to Claus Leggewie's work on climate change-related questions of "social responsibility, cultural memory and intercultural differences" (2009, p. 176, cited in Heimann, 2016). Similarly, Welzer et al. (2010) argue that social-scientific inquiries into climate change need to concern themselves with:

> ... the cultural practices and contexts of meaning that have caused climate change, thereby challenging human interpreting and sense-making and the philosophical consideration of aspects of justice and responsibility [...] as well as the knowledge-sociological analysis of collective interpretative patterns.
>
> Welzer et al., 2010, p. 13

A culturally-sensitive analytical framework is urgently needed because "actors try to achieve different things, such as raise awareness, persuade people to vote for a political party, support government policies, *save the planet*, *greenwash* a business, expand a business into new and more profitable arenas, and many more" (Nerlich et al., 2010, p. 6, orig. emph.). Building on these considerations, this study advances a comprehensive analysis of people's reactions to climate change that explicitly acknowledges their inherently social nature and that closes some of the gaps left behind by conventional behavioural explanations that dominate current climate debates.

Embodied information practices

Responding to the limits of information deficit thinking in explaining climate inaction, there is an additional body of literature that explicitly underscores the importance of culture in the creation of (climate) knowledge. In their seminal work on climate cultures, Heimann and Mallick criticise that "factors to explain differences in perceiving and handling climate change *besides shared knowledge* remain blind spots" (Heimann and Mallick, 2016, p. 1, orig. emph.). Importantly, these authors challenge conventional understandings of knowledge as inherently cognitive, arguing that it instead needs to be understood as comprising "shared cognitive and normative framings (e.g., shared problem framings for climate change, general values, beliefs, and identities) as well as shared practices at the level of action" (ibid.). Incorporating this broadened concept of knowledge, Heimann and Mallick develop their model of *climate adaptation cultures*.

Building on this existing work on climate cultures, this study highlights the inherently collective and frequently tacit nature of knowing that is practiced within each climate culture. Yet, current literature (even on climate culture) "tends to privilege cognitive processes. Even variables like values and concern, which are infused with affect, may be reduced to their role in producing deliberative, rational responses to climate change" (Ford and Norgaard, 2019, p. 222). Therefore, moving beyond a purely cognitivist view of knowledge, it is built on Olsson and Lloyd's notion of knowledge as "embodied information practices" (2017) that recognises the centrality of non-linguistic, experiential types of knowledge:

> Knowledge is not what resides in a person's head or in books or in data banks. To know is to be capable of participating with the requisite knowledge competence in the complex web of relationships among people, material artefacts and activities.
>
> Gherardi, 2008, p. 517, cited in ibid, p. 3

Focusing on embodied knowledge in situ also emphasises the centrality of the body for knowing, whereby "information landscapes are not only shaped and represented socially and dialogically but also reflected corporeally" (Olsson and Lloyd, 2017, p. 8). Olsson and Lloyd's concept upgrades this study's understanding of knowing in that it allows to make visible knowledges that fail to be acquired by the Enlightenment's understanding of employing certain instructions for use from a *manual*. There are in fact forms of knowledge that "cannot be effectively expressed in written form" (ibid., p. 3) such as learning how to be a good parent, for example. These "rich sites of knowledge [...] are local/nuanced, drawing from expertise in situ and may be contingent and only available at the 'moment of practice'" (ibid.).

Therefore, in this analysis the conception of knowledge is substantially broadened to crucially include the everyday embodied information practices of societal actors, which are neither conceptualised as external to the system nor simply as an add-on, but instead seen "as dynamic entities in their own right" (Reckwitz, 2002, cited in Shove, 2010, p. 1279). Considering social practices elucidates to the dynamic "meanings of normal and the patterns of consumption associated with them [that] require constant reproduction" (Shove, 2010, p. 1279). Regarding affective and emotional aspects of knowing and their manifestations in practice, this study explicitly recognises shared forms of 'not knowing' that serve to protect people from unpleasant facts that may threaten their livelihoods and ways of life.

The centrality of everyday life

Adopting the concept of embodied information practices does not merely mean the extension of existing definitions of knowledge. Instead, it also implies an explicit recognition of relative resistance to efforts to transform everyday behaviour (Rau, 2018; Rau et al., 2020; Sahakian and Wilhite, 2014; Spurling et al., 2013). For example, eating habits and mobility practices have been shown to be particularly difficult to change (Godin and Sahakian, 2018; Heisserer and Rau, 2017). This, in turn, is key to understanding the public's (lack of) engagement in climate action. Cultural norms and prescriptions play a central role in this resistance to change in that they contribute to keeping alive a practice across multiple generations of 'practitioners' (Shove and Walker, 2010):

> [...] the stubbornness of habits depends on how deeply anchored the habits are in relation to three pillars of practices: the body – including cognitive processes and physical dispositions; the material world – including technology and infrastructure; and the social world – including settings, norms, values and institutions.
>
> Sahakian and Wilhite, 2014, p. 28

Arguably, the 'stickiness' of many routine practices does not always lead to inertia and stagnation. "Cultural meaning structures are malleable, but they are also durable" (Ford and Norgaard, 2019, p. 237). Instead, people's insistence on doing things in a certain way can also be essential to dealing with the complexity and unpredictability of everyday life. By acknowledging people's capacities to creatively solve problems in everyday life, for example by combining established routine practices to form new ones, a practice-centred perspective is uniquely suited to advance a view of human agency as socio-materially embedded (Rau, 2018, p. 219)[9]. Adopting a practice-centred perspective more generally, and especially a focus on embodied information, thus opens up new ways of understanding people's reactions to climate change and opportunities for engaging people more effectively in climate action measures.

The concept of climate cultures with its inclusion of collectively undertaken everyday discursive and material practices such as the coming into being of all kinds of different artefacts (waste disposal, releasing of CO_2) allows deeper consideration of how to achieve more successful climate action. Moreso, the requirement to consider different societal entities has recently been acknowledged in social scientific climate research. Therefore, I propose a perspective that analyses how cultural conditions influence everyday practices and vice versa. This study's newly developed concept of climate cultures is uniquely equipped to meet this challenge.

In this way, a culturally sensitive view of climate-relevant profane everyday practices can actively challenge simplistic conceptions of a linear, unidirectional transfer of knowledge between science and society that have beset much thinking on climate science and action to date. In particular, it questions the capacity of such *knowledge transfer models* to mobilise people to accept responsibility, recognise their own capacity to act, and engage in effective climate action. Therefore, it is argued for an explicit linking of this ever so broad, multi-directional, dialogic knowledge concept with notions of responsibility and efficacy to make sense of the lack of public engagement in climate action to date.

Understanding variations in responsibility, efficacy and knowing: The concept of climate cultures

Besides embodied information, climate cultures shall be distinguished by the similarities and differences in statements made with regard to who in society (individuals, politicians, the media, private sector, scientists) holds responsibility for climate action and who is thought to be able to make a substantial difference. Thus, this study is further built on the conviction that appealing to people's sense of responsibility and demonstrating their capacity to act are central to effective climate action (Buschmann and Sulmowski, 2011, p. 283). At the same time, a focus on *variations* in how responsibility and efficacy are viewed and practiced can contribute to the identification of different climate cultures, including those that are commonly attributed to elites that dominate many public climate debates due to their large stocks of cultural capital. Charles Wright Mills "finds it to lie in the remit of social scientists and

9 See e.g., Norgaard, 2018, p. 4: "Other scholarship on cultural inertia, culturally patterned receptivity (Fox, 2014; Fox and Rau, 2017) sheds much light on the profound potential for normalization of the climate threat across society".

other intellectuals, to investigate the consequences of the actions of power elites and to publicly confront them with their respective responsibility" (2016, cited in Wendt and Görgen, 2018, p. 60). This is the challenge that I have accepted. For this study's conception of climate cultures, the following interpretation of responsibility is particularly apt:

> Responsibility does not appear as an overarching, universal and cross-temporally valid concept, instead, time and again, it is produced afresh and in different forms as a concrete and both historically and culturally situated, practice-specific phenomenon.
>
> Buschmann and Sulmowski, 2011, p. 287

Although it may be true that considering responsibility is somewhat *en vogue* (cf. Heidbrink, 2003), it has hitherto only been linked to efficacy to a certain degree, and quite crudely so. Therefore, a more nuanced consideration and subsequently, a more wholesome integration of the two concepts is needed. Importantly, this goes beyond the analysis of the individual and information deficits in order to really help explain the lack of public involvement with climate action to date.

This is based on the conviction that climate action unfolds on the interface of emotion and culture. Climate cultures thus constitute shared repertoires of cognitive, emotional and behavioural responses to the threat of climate change that characterise particular segments of society and that are reflected in public climate debates. As Ford and Norgaard contend, "culture and emotion are simultaneous and co-constitutive. [...] however in practice emotional responses to cultural attachments may be fleeting, unregistered or contradictory" (2019, p. 237), which renders them so much harder to grasp that the continued reluctance to investigate them is unsurprising.

Attention is therefore paid to the unfolding of practice patterns in social circles as this indicates how people perceive their everyday lives differently. Just like in Ford and Norgaard's concept of environmental subjectivities, this study rests on the application of practice theories that would do well (c.f. Ford, 2019; Hargreaves, 2011; Shove and Walker, 2014, cited in Ford and Norgaard, 2020, p. 47) in taking the place of approaches that look out "for researcher-defined pro-environmental behaviour" (Ford and Norgaard, 2020, p.47). Accordingly, their concept of environmental subjectivities "calls attention to situated knowledges of climate change that emerge in relation to differences of indigeneity, race, and class" (Ford and Norgaard, 2020, p. 59). This is the point where the present study parts ways with (Ford and) Norgaard's framework and instead presents its own analytical conception of climate cultures that reconnects this work with the three key concepts of responsibility, efficacy and knowing:

Building on the conceptual considerations discussed in this chapter, **climate cultures are therefore defined as dynamic variants of social organisation that provide a framework for recognizing culturally relevant information regarding climate change and that are (re-)produced through climate-relevant everyday practices that reveal diverse forms of 'lived' responsibility and 'everyday' efficacy. The latter includes responses to more abstract attributions of responsibility and efficacy in 'official' climate change discourses that may or may not clash with people's lived experiences.**

Thus, the analysis of different climate cultures grants an insight into certain telling conventions, values and mind-sets that can differ substantially between the climate cultures that are present within one society. For example, more fatalistic cultures (that can be based on religion) may believe in some 'higher power' and therefore attribute very limited efficacy and influence to the individual (while a pastor himself may actually display large influence as multiplicatory figure). Alternatively, a climate culture may define itself by who is included in it and who is not, perceiving of its members as 'the chosen few' which again has certain implications for efficacy attributions (and respective actual power).

The approach pursued in this study responds directly to the lack of recognition of the centrality of everyday practices and their links with more abstract attributions of responsibility and efficacy vis-à-vis actual practical manifestations of responsibility and efficacy. This is particularly pertinent because divergences between abstract attributions and 'lived' experiences of responsibility and efficacy appear to be central to variations in climate culture.

2.7 Conclusion

The differing weight and priority given to each of the three concepts of embodied information, responsibility attribution and efficacy expectation in relation to specific social actors marks the distinction between the different climate cultures discussed in this study. The question of what role climate action plays in people's lives (if any) and whether official approaches to climate action fit their everyday practices serves as an apt starting point. An appropriate culture concept first includes an investigation of how responsibility for climate action is collectively attributed within a certain climate culture. Second it investigates whether the group perceives itself as being in the position to make a difference when it comes to climate action (vis-a-vis how large their actual impact is). This interpretation of efficacy as an inherently social phenomenon is central to this study. Making a clear distinction between individual and collective forms of responsibility and efficacy, and focusing on the collective level, can yield important clues as to why people do (not) act when confronted with the challenges of climate change. As Ford and Norgaard emphasise: "People who occupy different strata within a hierarchical structure hold different cultural schema and have access to different resources. This becomes apparent when we compare specific social groups and their knowledge about, and response to, climate change" (2020, p. 44). This approach is also uniquely suited to acknowledge differences in the everyday realities of groups within the German population that are endowed with different stocks of economic and cultural capital, which is urgently necessary for achieving social fairness and maintaining social stability:

> By remaining inattentive to how differences in social location and culture shape people's knowledge of and response to climate change, public and professional conversations about climate change over-represent elite sensibilities, marginalizing those who fall outside of what Audre Lorde calls 'the mythical norm' of whiteness, heterosexual masculinity, and economic privilege
>
> Lorde, 1987, cited in Ford and Norgaard, 2020, p. 44

Lastly, this study also investigates whether there emerge differences in the conception, understanding or definition of the three key terms responsibility, efficacy and knowing.

3 Methods

3.1 Introduction

> We seldom realize, for example that our most private thoughts and emotions are not actually our own. For we think in terms of languages and images which we did not invent, but which were given to us by our society.
>
> Alan W. Watts, cited in Marr, 2008, p. 97

In accordance with this pertinent realisation, the present analysis' research design has at its heart *relational* methodological elements (comment threads on social media, focus group interviews) in order to investigate socio-cultural phenomena that lie beyond the purely conscious and cognitivist attitudes and opinions the individual has access to. This rests on the conviction that explanations for the lack of (individual) assumption of responsibility paint at best an incomplete picture. These include for example information deficit hypotheses, theories of the diffusion of responsibility and de-politicisation, the power of materialism or the thesis of "disintegration of collective orientations and obligations" (Beck, 1986, cited in. Bremer, 2004, p. 13) that allegedly comes with liberalisation and increasing individualisation. Therefore, the research design consisted of a mixed-methods approach that fused the following three qualitative empirical steps together:

- Semi-structured expert interviews
  individual
- Innovative media analysis (flow model)
  relational
- Focus group discussions with already existing professional groups/work teams
  relational

Climate cultures reveal themselves through variations in discursive practices in the public realm concerning climate change and -action. This study is thus concerned with publicly expressed views about climate change and climate action across, firstly, a range of media and secondly, across different occupational fields. It conceptualises the latter as providers of culture: one's professional field brings with it a certain culture with respect to climate change and –action and thus impinges upon the worker. At the same time the employee brings his or her idiosyncratic cultural composition to the workplace and in turn shapes and restructures the occupational cultural environment.

This study's methodological triad was uniquely suited to examine its central questions, as the main interest lay not in what individual people thought and said, but instead in how the topic of climate action was dealt with collectively. Collective handling of climate matters is precisely what climate cultures are about. Therefore, what was being said in conversation between people and, importantly, also what was not necessarily being consciously communicated presented the focus of this investigation. The question was therefore how such deeply relational, multidimensional concepts like responsibility- and power attributions can empirically be captured and analysed in their social context.

Such relational knowledge, and above all what unconsciously and tacitly swings along with messages, is extremely difficult to investigate, especially because the participants were not actually being observed in how they actually behaved in their everyday lives (with the exception of the statements made on social media). The nature of interviews remains that questions are being verbally answered and thus tracing back how people actually live their lives is a difficult endeavour. Yet some insight into practices and ways of thinking the participants habitually engaged in could still be gained through the application of the two relational empirical steps. For instance, when focus group members of the craftsmen and the industrial enterprise each stated outright that they did not care about the carbon emissions of their respective vacation flights, this indicates that in these two groups, at least, such behaviour was not commonly being socially sanctioned (as then they would not have dared to state this so boldly). The presence of the rest of the group rendered it likely that participants did not deviate too far from how they would normally talk. These insights would have been lost if only single interviews were undertaken: here, a little white lie for fear of being judged by the interviewer would not have been noticed. Similarly, the conversations on social media that were analysed unfolded 'in real life' so to speak – there was no interview situation in this case. Since such unobtrusive data on social media is readily accessible, it provides particularly rich access to how people actually handle certain topics and express their feelings and opinions about them. These two elements (and in particular in combination with the expert interviews where the narrative was in fact quite different) allowed new (and often enough quite surprising) insights into societal perceptions of climate change.

Accordingly, Corner and Randall stress that studies (Haythornthwaite, 1996; Valente and Pumpuang, 2007; Fell et al., 2009) show that "pro-environmental behaviour change will be enhanced by targeting social networks rather than individuals" (2011, p. 1011). According to Bremer, research also shows that social spaces with common life patterns do still exist, the principal difference to former times lies however in the fact that the categories cannot readily be classified according to past existing social classes (2004, p. 14). Instead, today, social spaces include all group constellations of everyday life such as family contexts, friendship groups, communities that form for leisure activities like music groups and sports teams, groups that form because of life events (birthing classes, bachelorette parties, house building cooperatives) and work teams in the professional occupational sphere. In this study, two social spaces were chosen for analysis, namely particular camps appearing and interacting on (social) media platforms (media analysis) and professional work teams (focus group analysis).

3.2 Background

The wider context within which much of this study's empirical material was collected is also highly relevant: at the time of the 2019 European elections the *Fridays for Future* movement in Germany was growing significantly and gaining influence. There was a public call for stronger action on climate change and a push from numerous directions that politics should prioritise the issue. It was ceasing to be the exclusive topic of the Green Party and making its way more towards the political mainstream. A so-called climate cabinet was established two months prior to the election, with the aim of synthesising legislation for mitigating climate change. Therefore, the question of how climate change should be approached politically featured prominently in public discourse. This general call for political action may thus also reflect the wider social and political context at the time of gathering the empirical materials. It was however also repeatedly mentioned in the interviews that politicians were publicly perceived as acting solely according to the rationale of upcoming elections to please voters rather than with authenticity.

3.3 Research design

The data for the present analysis was collected over a time period of twelve months (March 2019 – February 2020) in and around Munich. The multi-method approach was chosen to enable a more detailed, multi-layered capture of the research topic. The insights gained in each research step informed subsequent analytical components, which aided the synthesis of a more nuanced picture as in this way the different steps informed and legitimised each other.

Figure 2: Methodological proceeding (own presentation)

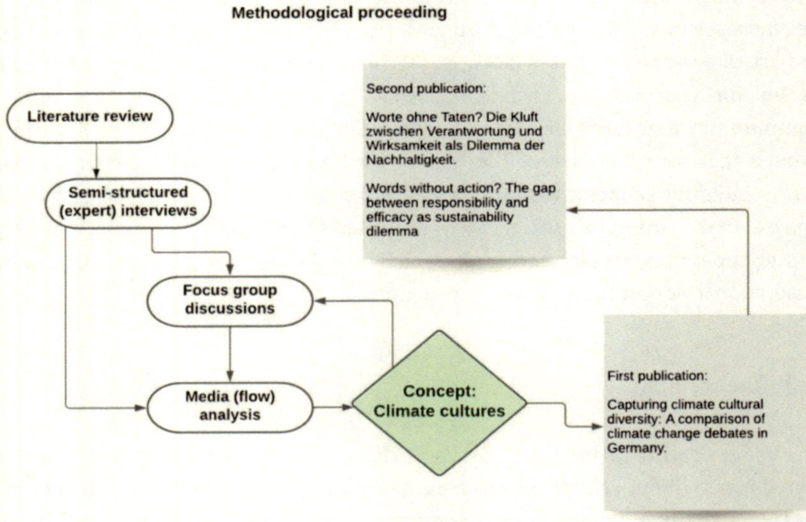

As a preliminary step, an extensive literature review was carried out from September 2018 until May 2019. Key terms were searched in different combinations in German and English in relevant literature data banks and online libraries like *Google Scholar*, the *International Bibliography of the Social Sciences (IBSS)*, the *International Bibliography of Periodical Literature* as well as the internal OPAC of the *Ludwig-Maximilians-Universität (LMU)* and the online catalogue of the *Bavarian State Library*.

The following terms were searched:

climate change, climate action, climate policy, sustainable development, green consumption, green growth, de-growth, sufficiency, education for sustainable development, responsibility, climate responsibility, responsibility diffusion, self-efficacy, efficacy, power, power relations, societal power relations, climate justice, culture and climate, climate cultures, practice theory, individualism, cognitivism, embodied information, social space, habitus, rationality, denial, climate change denial, collective denial

Core concepts and key ideas were subsequently collected, organised, excerpted and edited further. Based on the overview gained through this literature review, the guideline for the semi-structured expert interviews was developed.

3.4 Expert interview analysis

In this first empirical step, interviews were exclusively held with experts (mainly scholars, government officials, politicians, representatives of NGOs), i.e., individuals who had specialised knowledge on the topic of the societal reception and treatment of climate change and climate action.

The following table shows the interview partners' professional roles:

Table 1: Interview partners/experts (own presentation)

Date	Interview partners (IPs)
19/03/2019	Academic (sustainable consumption)
26/03/2019	Division head (climate change) at private foundation
12/04/2019	Head of environmental NGO
16/04/2019	Chairperson socio-ecological think tank
25/04/2019	Academic (sustainability innovation)
26/04/2019	Expert 1 federal environmental agency
02/05/2019	Expert 2 federal environmental agency
08/05/2019	Academic (sociology and sustainability)
21/05/2019	Teacher (secondary education)
27/05/2019	Member of Bundestag (CDU)
16/07/2019	Member of Bavarian parliament (Freie Wähler)

Here, the aim was to gain a comprehensive overview over the current state of 'official' knowledge in connection to climate related responsibility attributions, efficacy expectations and the role of scientific information for practical behaviour in society. These official discourses presented an apt starting point for gaining access to the stances that exist in German society: however, here I was acutely aware that they represented only a fraction of the population, namely certain privileged segments of society (that hold high levels of what Bourdieu considers to be *cultural* capital). Therefore, they can be classified as *elite discourses*.

Guided semi-structured interviews with experts were chosen as a qualitative method, because the interview partners can be considered 'part of the practice field' (Meuser and Nagel, 1991, cited in Schirmer et al., 2009, p. 194). Therefore, they are 'intimate insiders' (Liebold and Trinczek, 2002, cited in ibid.) of a particular societally relevant topic, in this case climate change and -action. Because of his or her presence in the field, the expert is an experienced specialist with regard to the practices and ways of thinking that are commonplace in German society in connection with the topic of climate change and -action.

As Schirmer et al. write: "In general, this method is part of a comprehensive examination of a research subject. By itself, expert interviews and their analysis do not make much sense" (Schirmer, 2009, p. 193). This is because it is imperative that further perspectives beyond the view of the expert are considered, so that more inclusiveness can be attained. Precisely for this reason, this method only embodies the first out of three steps for data collection within this study.

The method of the semi-structured interview, hence an interview that uses a rough guideline, was chosen because according to Meuser and Nagel this does justice to both, "the thematically bounded interest of the researcher", as well as the expert in his or her function (1991, p. 448). The preparation necessary for the conception of the guideline (here, the extensive literature review) ensured that the researcher was already familiar with the foundations of the research subject necessary for the conversation. Besides, "even though this might sound paradoxical, it is indeed precisely [...] the guideline itself, that guarantees the openness of the interview" (ibid., 1991, p. 449). When it is seen not as a recipe, but instead as a backup tool, the interview will be kept alive and not be impeded by it.

Of course, the choice of the interview partners does also hold significance – i.e., experts who are qualified to grant their insight into the stances of the public as well as to give their own personal perspective. Here, the selection criterion was that the expert needed to have significant professional contact with the topic of climate change. Additionally, the aim was to paint as broad a picture of expert assessment as possible, hence professionals from the fields of science, politics, NGOs and private businesses (albeit them still all belonging to the exclusive category of *elite* discourses) were included. Generally, initial contact was established via phone and email. The interview partners were partially recruited via the researcher's own network and partially, in order to prevent the interviews from becoming too biased by this one specific societal position, via internet research and subsequent cold call. Hence recruiting was not carried out according to a random methodological scientific strategy, which did however bring the advantage of alleviating initial reservations through the superficial connection that did already exist (in some of the cases). This helped in the research moment, making it resemble a more relaxed private and therefore authentic conversation.

Furthermore, in two cases the method of *snowball sampling* was used, i.e., people were contacted on the recommendation of individuals already interviewed who knew someone who could further contribute meaningfully to the research subject. Already in 1958, James Coleman believed this strategy to be particularly helpful for social-scientific research, as it enables the creation of a setting along existing and naturally interacting entities. There is however a certain apprehension that in this interview situation, there is an increased risk for *social desirability* to occur, namely a distortion of response behaviour that is attributable to the need for social validation. This then manifests itself through expected answers and a fear of rejection or judgement by the interview partner if an authentic response were to be given (cf. Bundesamt für Naturschutz, 2014, p. 21). Udo Kuckartz gets to the heart of this issue by saying: "Of course it is not difficult to respond to the questions, similar to those one is asked by border authorities when entering into the US, in the right way and immediately you find yourself in the delicate presence of committed protectors of the environment" (2010, p. 145). This obstacle was dealt with by completely anonymising the interviews, which was clearly communicated to the interview partners beforehand and guaranteed via a data privacy form.

Of course, in this way the researcher's classification of who is seen as an expert played a fundamental role: "Already at this point it becomes apparent that at the end of the day what enters into the thesis as expert knowledge lies in the discretion of the researcher" (Schirmer, 2009, p. 195). Moreover, it is necessary to reflect on what role the person speaks in in the research moment. Since the expert status in most cases resulted from the experts' occupational roles, they potentially saw themselves as representatives of their particular field which may have had consequences for the openness with which it was spoken. Therefore, it must be recognised that the experts did not provide *facts*. Instead they presented matters that they judged out of their special professional perspective, which in turn was being supplemented by personal motivation as well as aspects stemming from several social contexts. "Hence it is about open, secluded, secret, reflected, un-reflected, formal or informal, conscious or subconscious knowledge" (ibid.). Since all these knowledge types are important in their own right, the challenge consisted in bringing to the table a certain sensitivity for reading *between the lines* in order to adapt the interview strategy to each conversation respectively as well as for the subsequent analysis.

In one of the expert interviews it became apparent that the questions in the two sections *responsibility* and *efficacy* were not perceived as distinct (enough). Consequently, the interview guide was adapted slightly. Overall, the guideline succeeded in repeatedly prompting the conversations, yielding a series of relevant and comparable answers in each interview. Furthermore, a few high-ranking politicians could be recruited, which allowed a valuable insight into the connection of information and power that presents one key focus of the present study.

It proved unproblematic to find interview partners as they all, by the nature of their occupation, had a pronounced interest in the topic. However, disappointingly, an AfD-member of the Bundestag cancelled his (long planned) interview on very late notice. It would have been particularly interesting to see how a politician who does not speak out for climate action would have answered these same questions.

3.5 Media analysis

This study's main aim was to establish "the connection to the social fields of practice and the specific expectations for concrete [relational] offers and etiquette" (Bremer, 2004, p. 16). As one-on-one interviews alone are not equipped to deliver this, "figuratively speaking, the bigger picture [...] needed to be refined through a close-up" (ibid.). In doing so, this study went beyond the individual and gained access to social dynamics unfolding in the collective, as such group dynamics and –effects have hitherto remained substantially under-researched.

Responsibility as relational concept

How responsibility for climate action and related expectations of (perceived or actual) efficacy were being handled collectively was therefore, in a first instance, investigated through an analysis of media discourses.

This comprehensive media analysis was carried out to fulfil the following two goals:

1. Investigating the *collective* societal treatment of climate action (by using material that referred to one another as well as analysing comment threads and discussions on social media)
2. In order to paint a more inclusive and complete picture, gaining an insight into the *public's* thought patterns and motives for action, so that they could be compared with the individual elite discourses already recorded through the expert interviews.

In doing so, insight was also gained into the stances of those social groups who occupy social spaces between the two poles of climate scepticism and strong support for climate action, i.e., the large share of the population who is not particularly opinionated in either direction when it comes to climate action.

In addition to conventional media types, this empirical step was also concerned with the new forms of social media, "which indicate new vehicles for the transmission of knowledge [and] may transform power relations and ultimately what counts as knowledge" (Goldblatt, 2004, p. 122). Here, those who are the loudest and most opinionated are generally also the most visible, which one must be aware of when undertaking research. Leading communication scientist Mike Steffen Schäfer (2012) identifies a certain discrepancy between the influence and efficacy commonly ascribed to social media and the attention that they have hitherto been granted by research. Research has so far also "mainly focused on individual-level effects on peoples' problem awareness, their level of information, and their willingness to act" (ibid., p. 9). By contrast, in this study, the focus lies with the diverse cultural influences that can be identified on social media platforms. This part of the study concentrates mainly on 'embodied knowledge' as these non-linguistic, experience based embodied types of knowledge are paramount as forms of socially shared information. As Peter Dahlgren argues, particularly in online environments it is necessary to:

> … examine how the hegemonic and contested currents find expression in the Web 2.0 milieu, and we can assume that these currents are driven by both rational and affective elements, with the latter seemingly on the ascent. Media culture generally overall seems to be moving ever further away from the ideals of the traditional public sphere and its rational character.
>
> Dahlgren, 2012, p. 9

This study's engagement with social media content and its insights into cultural standpoints towards climate policy is therefore uniquely equipped to do justice to these alternative but by no means inferior emotional aspects of 'knowing'. Promisingly, these are increasingly being recognised as bringing some of the answers that considerations of information deficits have not.

Whether in its conventional or new social vesture, media coverage of climate change provides particularly rich evidence of climate-cultural variations, a fact that remains seriously under-appreciated in much social-scientific work on culture and climate change. This study responds directly to this research gap by examining diverse media reports on climate change in Germany around the 2019 European elections, with a view to demonstrating which climate cultures (do not) feature in public debates on this important topic. A qualitative approach to data collection and analysis was chosen, with material deriving from four interrelated sources across TV, print and social media:

A. Debates on climate change in three German prime-time political talk shows: *Hart aber fair* (hard but fair) presented by Frank Plasberg (25/03/2019), *Anne Will* (05/05/2019) and *Markus Lanz* (27/06/2019)[1]. The format of these three talk shows is very similar, with prominent politicians and public figures discussing current affairs in a more or less confrontational way. This said, *Markus Lanz* deviates somewhat from the other two in that this show appears a little less elitist due to the less formal demeanour of the talk show host and the wider selection of guests which often includes both prominent political figures as well as members of the public 'with a story to tell'.
B. Comments and discussions posted on two social media platforms (Facebook[2] and Twitter[3]) following social media postings by the producers/administrators (when possible) of the three talk shows. Examples of dialogue and exchange

1 These talk shows typically reach an audience of approximately 3.5 million viewers.

2 *Anne Will*: No Facebook: https://www.daserste.de/specials/service/community-index-spalten100.html (accessed 02/06/2019).

3 *Hart aber fair*: https://twitter.com/hartaberfair/status/1109100001685319682 (accessed 02/06/2019). *Anne Will*: https://twitter.com/AnneWillTalk/status/1125302263906480128 (accessed 02/06/2019). https://twitter.com/AnneWillTalk/status/1125289706000912386

received particular attention. For example, responses divergent to the previous participant that suggest differences in climate culture are listed **in bold** in the second table under 'direct opposition' (see chapter 5). In connection to *Hart aber fair*, the analysis covered two threads on Facebook and Twitter that emerged in response to the administrator's introductions of the talk show guests Ulf Poschardt, editor-in-chief of the conservative Welt news group, and then German Minister for the Environment Svenja Schulze. The editorial team of *Anne Will* did not maintain a Facebook account (at the time of analysis) but two Twitter threads were analysed. Regarding *Markus Lanz*, it was more difficult to find social media content, so the material was limited to one Twitter thread.

C. Online news articles from influential German news producers and leading weekly political magazines that covered and commented on the three talk shows.
D. YouTube videos by the two well-known influencers Rezo (channel: *Rezo ja lol ey*) and Mai Thi Nguyen-Kim (channel: *maiLab*) on the topic of climate change, which appeared around the same time as the talk shows.

The choice of sources reflects the intention to capture as broad a range of views and statements as possible (without being representative in the statistical sense of the term). Data collection took place from October to December 2019 and was carried out almost exclusively online, with the exception of a printed version of an article in Der Spiegel (23/2019) covering the posting of the famous Rezo video (the destruction of the CDU) and its aftermath. The talk show material was transcribed and subsequently translated from German into English, complementing printed text and social media comments.

Using Kuckartz's (2012) typifying approach to qualitative content analysis, the collected material was examined to identify and subsequently compare statements regarding climate action and related issues of responsibility, efficacy and knowing. Given that there is no societal consensus regarding who should take the lead in promoting climate action in Germany, the responsibility attributed to, and efficacy expected of different societal actors (individuals, politicians, the media, private sector, scientists) received particular attention. The iterative analytical process combined deductive and inductive elements. An a priori interest in the role of different societal actors in climate change debates, the use of apocalyptic/catastrophic vocabulary and the topic of individual responsibility informed the initial choice of methodology and material. The subsequent identification of different climate cultures happened inductively through a very close and repeated (re-)reading of the data.

(accessed 02/06/2019). *Markus Lanz:* (difficult to find) https://twitter.com/Markus__Lanz/status/1144308596257230849 (accessed 02/06/2019).

3.6 Focus group interviews with professional groups

As the concept of climate cultures synthesised by this comprehensive media analysis attracted wide interest and proved particularly fruitful, I chose to continue to work with it. Here, the occupational context presents a promising further analytical frame as most adults invest a large portion of their lifetime into gainful employment. Furthermore, work environments often remain stable over longer time periods and the group of staff or work team embodies one of the social subuniversa this study is particularly interested in. This way, societal regularities and power relations related to climate change and –action could be filtered out and made visible.

Therefore, as a second *relational* method, focus groups were chosen. By means of "decoding certain patterns of social practice" (Bremer, 2004, p. 12), this shifts further attention onto the importance of social space. Each social group's respective social space and the naturalised social practices that habitually and conventionally occur within it have a substantially underappreciated influence on public reception and collective practice in the context of climate change and –action: "The relationship between an individual and her social context is complex and is shaped and constituted by social, cultural, economic, political, legal, historical, and structural forces [...] [and] this relationship is multidirectional, co-constitutive and constantly in formation and the multi-layered influences in which the individual is embedded are often beyond the level of individual consciousness" (Burke et al., 2009, p. 66S). Over time, people develop certain types of *habitus* according to the different social groups they are surrounded by in their daily lives. In contrast to individual interviews, focus groups thus allow the analysis of social interaction and thus enable insights in relation to "the joint construction of meaning" (Bryman, 2008, p. 501) in the form of, for example, social norms. In this way, "the more latent, less cognitively controlled schemata can better be discovered. In this sense the method is actually more suited to the exploration of habitus as [individual] interview techniques" (Bremer, 2004, p. 105).

From this perspective, travelling long distances by plane (especially for pleasure) is no longer perceived as a 'lifestyle choice' but instead as a socially and culturally specific practice (Shove, 2010, p. 1280) that carries with it a whole battalion of further motives (perceiving oneself as cosmopolitan and widely travelled as in some circles this brings high social valuation) besides the initial one merely related to mobility. These socially initiated and internalised, 'embodied' (Olsson and Lloyd, 2017) and often subconscious meanings constitute, it is argued, some of the missing pieces in the hitherto incompletely remaining explanation of why nudges and individual calls to action related to climate action still remain far behind what is needed.

Professional environments as social space

As one of the social networks mentioned above, the work team or group of staff embodies and apt starting point for the investigation of social space. Here, the focus group as a method is uniquely suited, since it enables the witnessing of a more natural discursive flow (than individual interviews) similar to everyday conversations. As Elke Pirgmaier states in relation to this:

> As social beings, people continuously communicate with each other. (...) Language is a powerful medium of communication but as soon as we choose words, we provide a one-sided description of reality. As soon as we pin something down, we leave other aspects of reality out. Theories – stories we tell each other about the world – are therefore always biased. This matters, because word as a medium of communication and work as acting on the world are united in praxis – both in the old-to-be-transformed and the new-to-come-into-being. The choice of language and framings is therefore key for reproducing and reshaping reality.
>
> 2019, p. 281

Therefore, as a third empirical step, seven focus group discussions were carried out between July 2019 and February 2020. Each conversation lasted between 60 and 90 minutes and was held with already existing social groups, namely work teams, in and around Munich. The focus of the investigation lay in the participants' collective stances, again, vis-à-vis representations of climate change and –action, particularly to whom in society they ascribed responsibility for climate action and whom they perceived as influential in this regard. Moreover, it was examined where the groups stood collectively with respect to the creation of knowledge and information about climate change and –action and whether (and if so which) denial tendencies could be identified as a consequence of what was being said.

The focus groups, like the experts for the individual interviews, were partially recruited via the researcher's own network and partially via internet research and subsequent cold call. Generally, one person was contacted initially and then asked to recruit his or her own social group. Therefore, recruiting was undertaken via snowball sampling (making use of existing social ties and networks) and not according to a random methodological scientific strategy. Working with already existing social groups instead of using a random sample increased the probability that conversations could be experienced that actually resembled the commonly practiced discourses in each social group (Fox, 2014, p. 85). The stances and convictions that are taken for granted and passed on over time in certain circles (and that embody the aspects the present study set out to capture) only come to the surface when working with such natural groups (cf. Fox, 2014). Therefore, access to these aspects that lie at the core of this study cannot be gained when samples are randomised. From this follows that investigating participants' social milieus is simply incompatible with randomising samples.

Arguably, this type of sample facilitates the uncovering of how group members that are familiar with each other collectively approach climate matters with the help of routine (discursive) practices, classifications and dispositions that characterise their respective social space (cf. Fox, 2014). Consequently, the present study is concerned with how climate action measures resonate differently in the public, by investigating of how these appeals (*calls to order* in Bourdieu's terms) in relation to climate action are received in each focus group (cf. ibid., p. 11), whether they are even noticed initially, whether they are then taken up and internalised and lastly and most importantly, whether people report to actually act upon them.

For example, the use of 'collective expression' (Callaghan, 2005, cited in ibid., p. 85) and 'embodied information practices' (Olsson and Lloyd, 2017) both hint towards how it is normally spoken in each setting. Although the conventional group-specific discourses will be influenced by the contribution of each participant (and to an extent the researcher and will in turn influence the rest of the group), they resort back to references that connect the group to the wider community or field (Callaghan, 2005, cited in Fox, 2014, p. 85): "Under such circumstances the focus group may act as a *portal* to the social space within which much of the participants' life is unfolding" (Fox, 2014, p. 85, my emph.).

Additionally, in order to present as broad a picture as possible, participants were included whose work did not directly relate to the topic in of climate change (teachers, craftsmen). Particular interest was paid to how such groups who may be further removed from climate discourses handled the topic. Besides, "the focus group method's interactive component offered a means of studying the micro dimensions of societal power relations and regularities in the development of climate change receptivity" (Fox, 2014, p. 86). Moreover:

> ... the research moment is not an exchange of *rational* positions and perspectives. The goal of the research was never to merely record and input the claims of participants into the thesis. To do so would be an acceptance of the rational choice position on human beings.
>
> ibid.

Table 2: Overview of focus group discussions

Focus group	Craftsmen	Green startup	Local environ-mental NGO	Farmers	Industrial enterprise	Mobility provider	Teachers
Time of inter-view	08/2019	09/2019	11/2019	07/2019	10/2019	02/2020	07/2019
No. of par-ticipants	5	9	6	6	4	4	9
Sex	Male: 5	Female: 7 Male: 2	Female: 5 Male: 1	Female: 4 Male: 2	Female: 3 Male: 1	Female: 3 Male: 1	Female: 5 Male: 4
Age	heterogeneous	homo-geneous	heterogeneous	heterogeneous	homogeneous working students	heterogeneous mid 20s to late 40s	heterogeneous

The pitfall that focus group discussions are treated merely as a series of individual interviews was carefully avoided as this would once again yield only the attitudes and opinions of the individual. Instead, the aim was to gain access to the societal dynamics that unfold in the everyday lives of the focus group members through the interactions of the participants. Thus, attention was paid to what was collectively synthesised as a group and whether and how statements were perceived (i.e., sanctioned or welcomed).

Using vignettes

As an 'unobtrusive issue' (Schäfer and Bonfadelli, 2017, p. 2), climate change cannot directly be perceived with the human senses. Visualisations thus present a helpful means to make this abstract issue more tangible. For these reasons so-called 'vignettes' were applied to stimulate a conversation among group members. These were prompting *snippets* in the form of "short stories about hypothetical characters in specified circumstances, to whose situation the interviewee is invited to respond" (Finch, 1987, p. 105). This had the clear advantage that instead of being asked about their own contribution to climate action and how this potentially deviated from what they (morally) thought it should be, respondents were invited to judge how others (represented by the vignettes) behaved with regard to climate change and how their gap between conviction and actual daily practice could be apprehended. This helped to somewhat avoid the trap that is presented by *social desirability*.

This study used six of these vignettes: firstly, an open introductory question (what are your first thoughts when it comes to societal responsibility for climate action?), then four vignettes each corresponding to different societal actors (politics, corporate sector, single consumers, civil society) and their respective responsibility and efficacy and lastly one vignette related to the creation of climate related knowledge in society. These were presented to the respondents as pictures (as well as one short and one slightly longer video clip) within a PowerPoint presentation. "It is important that the stimulus is able to reach the core of the issue, for example by means of a provocative or challenging hypothesis" (Bremer, 2004, p. 104). The rationale behind the use of these vignettes lay in being able to assess, in this way, "whether there is agreement about 'the proper thing to do' in a given set of circumstances" (Finch and Mason, 2003, p. 12) within each of the different social spaces analysed. Ultimately, the goal was to draw some conclusions about how these different societal groups actually habitually behaved in relation to climate change.

As opposed to single interviews, here, the role of the researcher merely lay in the moderation of the discussion. Care was taken to contribute as little as possible as regards content. In certain situations, it proved however useful to play the role of 'devil's advocate', hence "to give the discussion new impulses through purposefully interspersing standardised teaser arguments" (Bremer, 2004, p. 104) that challenged what was being said. This was done in order to gain even deeper access into the thought patterns that existed in each group.

The method of the group interview allowed the identification of "some of the ontological hierarchies (what is valued within inner circles) that manifested within the focus groups" (Fox, 2014, p. 148). Climate change was habitually processed by means of these connections (ibid.). Apart from the industrial enterprise, recruitment of the groups proved unproblematic. This may again be attributed to the time of the research which was carried out in the year that the *Fridays for Future* protests were gaining considerable momentum in Germany and therefore climate change became the public issue that was by far most discussed. As with the expert interviews, it again appeared that where there was thematic overlap with the topic, people were eager to contribute to the research, whilst otherwise there was noticeable hesitation. The corporate entities approached for an interview on *responsibility for climate action* may therefore have feared that they would have to justify themselves. Two of the focus group discussions (teachers and craftsmen) unfolded in a somewhat unstructured way, since participants joint or left the interview at different stages, which could not however have been prevented by the researcher. Overall, each of the focus group discussions yielded an intensive and fruitful debate.

A commonly raised critique of the use of focus groups as empirical method lies in the fear that "the results obtained in a focus group may be biased by a very dominant or opinionated member. More reserved group members may be hesitant to talk" (Stewart and Shamdasani, 1998, p. 509, cited in Fox, 2004, p. 87). As Fox discusses, "these criticisms overlook the social basis of human existence and how conversations in daily life often feature dominant voices. Such voices can be indicative of the levels of interest in the issues under discussion and/or the differences in embodied capital which reflect power relations in a group setting, and in wider society" (2014, p. 87). Considering whether there were particularly dominant voices and if and how they were reacted to by the rest of the group thus served as an important way of gaining insight to the operating power relations in these social spheres.

3.7 Conclusion

The present pragmatic multi-method approach was chosen to gain as broad a picture of (collective) societal positions on climate change and –action as possible. Since the three separate empirical steps built upon each other, the findings could be integrated particularly well and therefore yielded coherent insights into the constitution of societal hierarchies. The application of two different relational methods ensured that collective stances were captured. The concept of climate cultures developed through the media analysis was subsequently tested by being applied in the context of the focus groups, which to a very large extent confirmed the findings gained up to that point. From this follows that the methodological triad chosen for this study was uniquely equipped to answer the key research questions asked in this study. Thus, this innovative research design delivered new and particularly telling insights into the collective stances on climate action and responsibility, efficacy and knowing that the different social spheres endorsed respectively.

Part III – Empirical findings

The following three chapters describe the findings of the three empirical steps.

4 Expert interviews

4.1 Introduction

In this first research step, experts were interviewed to attain access to the current constitution of societal knowledge about climate change and -action. Questions asked related to this study's key concepts of responsibility, efficacy and knowing and either concerned the experts' own opinion or their take on what the public believed.

The aim was thus also to gain an insight regarding *to what extent*

- these experts conceived of responsibility in relation to or even in terms of efficacy,
- they valued the provision of (cognitive) information,
- they classified climate action as an inclusive project involving the whole of society – and –
- they observed diffusion of responsibility in society.

4.2 Statements concerning responsibility

This excerpt from one of the interviews immediately exemplifies the complexity the concept of responsibility conveys in connection with climate action:

> I think, one takes responsibility for things one has not caused. And one causes things for which one does not take responsibility. I think, for a long time, this had been more or less congruent. And that's also how the term responsibility was meant [originally]. But, in the modern knowledge society, if you will, so at least since the sixties, these connections have become so complex that you can say: you are buying a piece of butter at a discounter. You are now responsible that nitrate levels[1] in the water are rising because this is why so many cows are on the

1 Nitrate contributes to climate change, see for instance: https://www1.wdr.de/wissen/natur/nitrat-stickstoff-100.html (accessed 16/09/2022).

> pasture. Or rather, they are not on the pasture but in stables and produce masses of manure that then lands on the fields. In some way this can be said. Of course it can also be said: that's complete nonsense!

Academic (sociology and sustainability)

Amongst the experts, there was a general recognition for the many layers and facets as well as the cumulative nature of the responsibility question. Responsibility was termed *an object of negotiation* by one of the experts (academic sustainable consumption), indicating that its attribution in general and with respect to climate action in particular is far from straightforward and oftentimes fiercely contested.

Here, in some of the interviews, the moral component of the responsibility question was referred to:

> … in any type of green consumption, my conscience always plays some role.

Expert 2 at federal environmental agency

One interviewee (head of environmental NGO) cited Immanuel Kant in voicing that individual freedom is limited by it infringing upon someone else's freedom. One of the experts (academic sustainable consumption) also stressed that individual responsibility was bounded. Determining what was right beyond what lay in one's own responsibility for oneself was paternalistic in her eyes. By contrast, one other participant (expert 2 at federal environmental agency) deemed the application of such moral demands to be quite unhelpful at times. With respect to voluntary carbon offsetting, he emphasised that despite its reputation of being no more than 'indulgence trade"[2], this was indeed efficacious, whilst the environmental movement failed to recognise it as such because it was imprisoned in its 'moral high ground type of thinking'. At another point in the interview he did however point to his observation that people tended to flee into individual behaviour, thereby losing the political dimension. He often heard that people were allegedly contributing as much as they could whilst they forgot that climate action also had a *normative* dimension.

When asked who in society held responsibility for climate action, in most cases in these interviews the answer came quickly and staunchly along the lines of "everyone". So, in a first instance, responsibility was overall attributed to the whole of society. Delving deeper into the conversations, several nuances could however be filtered out with regard to this aspect:

in some cases, this reply, "everyone", referred to the single consumer. Repeatedly, it was recommended, also by two scientists (academic sustainable innovation,

2 *Ablasshandel* in German original statement.

expert 2 at federal environmental agency) that for decades had worked extensively on this question, that *strategic* distinctions should be prioritised when thinking about one's own carbon emissions. Moreover, some of the experts (particularly the teacher and the conservative politicians interviewed) had quite an individualised concept of responsibility for climate action, presenting it as a personal choice that should not be interfered with:

> I think that we fare well here in Bavaria by living by the maxim 'live and let live'. So in terms of diet, I do not want to dictate... It is however important to raise awareness...
>
> Member Bavarian State Ministry (Freie Wähler)

Therefore, in wondering how to mobilise the consumer, the other politician emphasised that her party wanted to frame the topic of climate action in a positive way:

> With incentives, with technology, with innovation and not from the start with prohibitions and regulatory law. [...] so that we achieve acceptance. And that is perhaps also the focus that sets us apart from the Green Party. If we, for example, raise the fuel tax, we won't score any great hit and this will only cause contempt...
>
> Member of Bundestag (CDU)

This clearly illustrates how the responsibility is shifted from the political to the individual sphere. Interestingly, when employing this individualised concept, it was often insinuated that there was a moral demand for the individual to contribute to climate action whilst at the same time the consistency and dedication with which this was practiced was being judged (e.g., how consistent the *Fridays for Future* protestors were in their own consumption decisions) *even though* it was deemed to be a personal choice:

> ... when I'm for example hearing that the average age for cheap or short-distance flying is sinking, then I wonder whether they [the young protestors] are contributing themselves [to high emissions]...
>
> Member of Bundestag (CDU)

In line with these individualistic conceptions, it was repeatedly pointed to carbon footprint calculators and individual purchasing decisions when it came to climate action:

> Principally, it begins at your own door. So from the moment that I actively participate as a part of society [...] [I have] an individual footprint [...] and therefore I have to begin with myself and think about how I move about, what trips I take, what my consumer behaviour is like, how I live, whether I heat to 19 degrees, 21, 23 for my own well-being or whether I just wear another sweatshirt. So principally it is a bit the attitude of the individual, at first. [...] So [climate action] begins with oneself and then it is of course rolled out institutionally...
>
> Member of Bavarian state ministry (Freie Wähler)

In relation to this, another interview partner stated:

> So I don't think that the responsibility can be pushed off towards politics. Because they are in their own sphere of tension. Say the Green Party won the next election, even then they could not simply turn everything upside down, because at some point you would anger so many people that [...] the far right would gain from this and then climate action plays no role at all any more. [...] So if everybody took responsibility, then there would be no need to pass the buck [in the first place].
>
> Teacher (secondary education)

In one interview it was noted that the responsibility question tended to polarise within the climate debate. Here, three "extreme" positions were identified: this aforementioned focus on the individual, then a deep trust in innovation that salvaged the individual from foregoing consumption and lastly, voices that were asking for more regulation, which in this case were deemed to be underrepresented. It was then problematised that focusing on one of these groups immediately deflected from the bigger picture as each of them were connected and interdependent:

> So if you say, the individual has to change their consumption behaviour, then you overlook that there are framework conditions that determine these consumption practices. It is easy to say: don't drive. But when you live in the countryside and there is no infrastructure, then you don't have the choice. I believe many of the protests in France can be attributed to this dilemma.
>
> Academic (sociology and sustainability)

These yellow vests protests (*Mouvement des Gilets jaunes*) that happened in France around the time of the interviews were often mentioned when speaking of the need for public acceptance of political actions. Here, the interview partner recommended to consider the different actors concomitantly and ask in what kinds of practices each of their behaviour was embedded respectively. Decision-makers should examine from what type of demands behaviour emerged from and who must be activated in what manner so that behaviour could unfold differently. So the question also needed to be, who is not acting and what kind of interests were at play in the current situation. This was also emphasised by a different expert:

> ... the incentives in everyday life are such that often one once again opts for another [non climate-friendly] alternative...
>
> Expert 1 at federal environmental agency

Following from this, we see a particular area of tension emerge between responsibility attributions to the individual versus to the political sphere. One expert said the following in relation to individual responsibility:

> I think, you should not make life too hard for the consumer. When I go to the supermarket and I only want to buy, for example, a tooth brush or some tooth paste, do I have to trace the supply stream all the way back to the country of origin? Do I have to investigate whether there is child labour in the bristles of the tooth brush? Sorry, no-one has that kind of time. [...] You can think about it a bit, as a consumer you can at least avoid the worst excesses, but ...
>
> Chairperson socio-ecological think-tank

This idea of *avoiding the worst excesses* resembles the recommendation made above in terms of making *strategic* consumption decisions. Overall, there was some agreement amongst the experts that this was as much as what could be asked of the consumer when it came to individual responsibility for climate action.

However, in general, choosing the option with the least climate impact on a voluntary basis was not deemed sufficient by most experts:

> ... simply pleading for a change of behaviour doesn't work. This we know. Already in 2008 there was a voluntary self-commitment for the automotive industry to reduce carbon emissions, of which nothing was implemented in the end.
>
> Division head climate change private foundation

It was further problematised that climate action could become a divisive force for society, as only more affluent segments would be able to afford the moral absolution granted by 'consuming climate-friendly', rendering the issue somewhat an elite project. In this respect one academic (sociology and sustainability) referred to literature that had found climate action to have become a means of *distinction* through which the middle class was valorising itself vis-à-vis lower and upper classes. She deemed this to be responsible nevertheless, even when the key motive was distinction and not climate action per se.

The following was also stated by another expert:

> So there are people who do perceive this (need for climate action) and who do suddenly switch their behaviour and that on all levels I think. But of course it is the case that those who are socially deprived, who receive social assistance, who are underprivileged or who feel disadvantaged, always point the finger up to those at the top.

Head of environmental NGO

One expert nevertheless found voluntary climate action to be underrated within the climate movement, not least because of the potentially positive relational effect setting a good example could have in his opinion. In relation to the aspect of voluntariness, the two conservative politicians were in favour of incentives in the form of nudges so that prices would steer consumers into a climate-friendly direction:

> [...] and in fact, this (emission trading scheme) would be the most supreme instrument, the scientists who are currently writing the report for the chancellor all agree on this, to extend this market-based instrument to other sectors, and ideally also to the European context right away. And right now would actually be a historic opportunity with the results of the European election[3].

Member of Bundestag (CDU)

Accordingly, these two politicians were against prohibiting by law certain climate-harmful forms of consumption:

> We can also try to interfere with the use of taxes. We can introduce incentives. This is still much more congenial than steering things with the use of regulations. I find incentives to do certain things still much nicer [than regulations].

Member of Bavarian state ministry (Freie Wähler)

3 Where there had been much demand for more climate action and the Green Party had significantly gained votes.

> If we prohibit the combustion engine by, say, 2020 or 2025, but then we don't have an alternative for the old lady in the Rhön Mountains [...], then the AfD is going to become stronger and stronger...
>
> Member of Bundestag (CDU)

Here, one participant (teacher secondary education) elucidated to people, in this case politicians, potentially harbouring a different concept or definition of responsibility. In referring to an imaginary FDP-politician, he stated that what would be irresponsible from their perspective would be acting according to lobby-interests for his or her own personal advantage. If it was instead the politician's conviction that the market should operate freely and this was best for the climate, then this conformed to this person's understanding of what it meant to act responsibly. Opinions over the right course of action with respect to climate change varied and although the participant himself had a different political orientation and therefore a different concept of climate responsibility, he still classified this as responsible behaviour.

Overall it can be said that there was a trend in these elite discourses to go beyond calling the single consumer to action and beginning to emphasise the need for political action, as this statement exemplifies:

> I actually find it problematic when responsibility for climate action is so vehemently unloaded onto the consumer. And also that ultimately the political courage or the political will for implementation of stricter regulatory measures is somewhat missing.
>
> Expert 1 at federal environmental agency

The politicians interviewed did also (at least in principal) acknowledge their own responsibility:

> Indeed, we politically responsible do, we belong (-)– we cannot further delegate this responsibility.
>
> Member of Bavarian state ministry (Freie Wähler)

Acting responsibly as an individual with respect to climate change was therefore increasingly described in political terms. For example, voting for a kerosene tax even though one enjoyed vacationing by plane was seen as displaying individual responsibility for climate action. One expert said in relation to this:

> ... to me it really seems that in Germany seventy percent of people are pro environmental protection [...], but of course they don't transfer this into their voting behaviour because there they care more about their own comfort but at least a general willingness [exists] and more people know that something has to happen. We don't have a critical mass yet...
>
> Chairperson socio-ecological think-tank

Hence, individual responsibility was repeatedly referred to in terms of one's role as political agent or voter. This also echoes the evolution that has taken place in more progressive elite discourses from purely individualistic responsibility attributions that revolve around the power of the consumer and go along the lines of "your grocery receipt is a ballot"[4]:

> So I consider it to be the job of politics. And thus indeed also to lie with the citizenry. But as citizens, who take responsibility for political processes, yes, as voters. As citizens, yes, ...
>
> Academic (sociology and sustainability)

Whilst agreeing that climate change needed to be prioritised more, the politicians however also described the difficulties they faced when trying to move into this direction. Those politicians who were currently part of the government voiced that they in some ways felt treated unfairly as in their own view, they were already doing a lot to advance climate action:

> I always hear, "Yes, politics finally has to do something. Do something! You haven't been doing anything for 30 years" [this refers to the recent accusations made by Rezo in his infamous Destruction of the CDU-video], and that is completely without any foundation.
>
> Member of Bundestag (CDU)

This politician further admitted that she felt treated unfairly by the message of the video because she personally had done a lot for climate action in the course of her career. She then added that if Rezo had looked into her as a person, the video would have had to have been different. Generally, even though political actors were under increasing pressure to prioritise climate action, there was discontent with how serious politicians were about this:

4 https://www.derstandard.at/story/1385169710727/der-einkaufszettel-als-stimmzettel.

> We simply have to be aware that politics is just not objective or interested in solutions, it works exclusively according to power dynamics.
>
> Division head CC at private foundation

Occasionally it was however also said that politicians were acting increasingly responsibly, for example by allocating funds for more climate research. Yet it was for example also repeatedly criticised that political sanctions over the automotive industry had been much too lax in the aftermath of the *Dieselgate* scandal.

> There is a large discrepancy between how current politics are perceived and what people want politics to be like in the future.
>
> Expert 1 at federal environmental agency

Corporate interests were repeatedly deemed too influential over political decisions and public opinion was said to mirror this perception. Frequently it was stated that corporate decision-makers were too profit-driven and self-interested to act responsibly in the light of impending climate change. It was however also recognised that corporate actors were themselves embedded in certain structures:

> The automotive industry is asked to come up with solutions that it is not equipped to deliver. The automotive industry is stuck in its own system logic.
>
> Expert 2 at federal environmental agency

Especially within large corporations, change was deemed to be slow and shareholders' short-term interests were also recognised as a hurdle. Here, it was again the single consumer in the role of the investor who was thought to hold the responsibility to invest in climate-friendly sectors (chairperson socio-ecological think-tank).

There was overall a strong call for the reduction of lobbying by the companies themselves. Moreover, it was found necessary that corporations acted socially and environmentally responsibly...

> ... under their own roof instead of doing a little pseudo-CSR. At the same time, companies are also responsible to shape framework conditions in a way that economic aspects are compatible with ecological and social ones, since as long as we have these preconditions like global competition and so on, the sticks are just not all the same length...
>
> Academic (sustainability innovation)

One of the experts answered the corporate responsibility question as follows:

> There is some room for manoeuvre. You do not need to jump over each stick and take part in every competition. Within the framework and structure that does exist, you can take responsibility, first and foremost for your employees. You can close contracts that let your people work properly. You can move away a little from exclusive profit optimisation. As much as is possible, yes. And this can mean that you are not competitive in some sectors, yes.
>
> Academic (sociology and sustainability)

Some responsibility was further attributed to NGOs and environmental associations. Their main role was perceived to lie in holding other societal actors responsible for climate action. Holding others responsible or calling them out on supposedly behaving hypocritically was in some instances however strongly rejected:

> I cannot stand this reasoning anymore! The Greens, they drive to the organic supermarket with their SUVs... I don't think that is the client base of the Green Party. I think there is this statistic that green voters earn almost as much as FDP-voters, which I find remarkable, but when I'm at the organic supermarket I don't see an SUV and in front of a discounter I see a whole series of SUVs. I think this comparison is unwarranted. Responsibility, yes, I think a lot of people sit comfortably, they lean back and say, politics has to fix it. ... but please no interdictions!
>
> Head of environmental NGO

Repeatedly, responsibility for climate action was also ascribed to the scientific community in pointing society towards the right direction. One expert said:

> Even if, say, everybody starts living super 'de-growth-like', then this would also have consequences that cannot be foreseen. Yes. [...] I think it is important that this is critically accompanied. There I see a responsibility for the scientific community.
>
> Academic (sociology and sustainability)

One participant (division head CC private foundation) said in relation to this point that he actually found those funding research to be even more responsible than the researchers themselves, and this he found to be particularly true for public funding bodies, as the sums that were given out there were so substantial. Consequently, this placed a large portion of the responsibility once again into the direction of political agents.

Different opinions surfaced however with respect to who held the responsibility to communicate scientific findings. The previous participant said he was against training researchers to become science communicators as this task required a completely different skill-set as the one a scientist typically had. Another participant (expert 2 at federal environmental agency) emphasised that it lay in the responsibility of the scientific community to present knowledge in more practically relevant forms. Repeatedly, it was demanded by the experts that the messages sent out in relation to climate action should be unequivocal and clear in order to stimulate action.

When asked who was responsible for scientific knowledge actually reaching the public, one expert said:

> I see this as a two-way-street [between science and the public].

Head of environmental NGO

Lastly, at times it was pointed elsewhere when confronted with the question of responsibility, for example when the Bavarian politician referred to *the lack of creativity on the part of Berlin* (in the context of energy efficiency of private homes) whilst in Bavaria one was supposedly *trying with 100 different measures to get somewhere.*

Hence, as unequivocally as it was stated that responsibility for climate action lay with the whole of society, there was also an explicit mentioning of such 'diffusion of responsibility'. Oftentimes this phenomenon was deemed to lie at the heart of the problem:

> People push the responsibility away. Why should I act when 80 million other people don't?

Head of environmental NGO

Here it was noted that often there was preoccupation with ascribing responsibility which deflected away from actually acting responsibly. It was perceived that societal actors often pointed to each other and shifted the blame, which could easily be done due to the many interdependencies that surfaced with respect to the question of responsibility.

4.3 Statements related to efficacy

That to a certain extent responsibility attributions depended on the power and influence societal actors held was prominently mentioned in the interviews:

> ... and then there is this kind of implicit approaching of responsibility in terms of agency or opportunity or true power [over societal outcomes]...
>
> Academic (sustainable consumption)

Initially, this connection was mostly portrayed as being quite straightforward:

> ... to say it bold and simple: it's like with spiderman. With a lot of power comes a lot of responsibility.
>
> Academic (sustainability innovation)

Accordingly, it was stated that more could be asked of privileged people who had the means for more climate action, they were however often the ones that allegedly contributed the least.

It was also reported that this relation between responsibility- and efficacy considerations had previously extensively featured in some of the experts' work. This surfaced for example in terms of the concept of 'competencies' and in this case was framed as follows:

> I used to have a little pre-text, 'searching for the next step', [...], where it was asked: what can the consumer do next? What can the politician do next? What can corporate actors do next? A corporation can indeed somewhat shift the structures that it is influenced by. [But] it cannot jump out of them. [...] This is precisely my perspective [...], so to say: how can the single consumption decision be transformed or initiated in a socially relevant way?
>
> Expert 2 at federal environmental agency

Relatedly, another one of the experts painted a picture of an 'architecture of responsibility':

> ... where everyone makes use of his or her opportunities that exist in their field and makes sure that when they are in that position [...], they extend other areas of opportunity; because industry as well as politics have the ability to also increase the scope for action, including that of consumers. And consumers have the ability to increase politics' scope for action, when they accept certain laws more or vote for a

> party that pushes certain things through. Thus, you have this kind of dependency, because you can increase or lessen the agency scope of other actors.

Academic (sustainable consumption)

In most of the interviews it was soon acknowledged that this relationship between responsibility and efficacy was one of the key aspects that rendered the attribution of responsibility for climate action so fundamentally complex and difficult:

> So, it can be seen particularly clearly in the agricultural sector: so you have farmers. And then you could say: you are overusing fertilizers on your fields. And you produce too much manure. You need to produce less manure. But the fact that the farmers themselves are embedded in this quasi-industrial complex, where there is also a chemical agribusiness industry and one that produces utility vehicles and so on... So that the farmers are also embedded and that they are actually only the last... the interface or the border agent towards nature and that so much plays into this situation that hardly leaves them much room to act differently...

Academic (sociology and sustainability)

One interview partner did however reject the idea that a lot of influence brought more responsibility:

> If this was the case [...], then you would get to push responsibility away. Because if I have less influence, then I also have less responsibility. And right now, I definitely have much less efficacy than Merkel... (Interviewer: yes, but as a teacher, you also have a lot of efficacy...) Yes, you are right...

Teacher secondary education

Thus, while this deep complexity was acknowledged and with it the recognition that finding the most effective measures brought considerable uncertainty, one academic went on to argue that taking responsibility for certain things as a consumer, this imposing matters upon oneself through consumption practices resulted in others (with more actual influence) being let off the hook:

> .... so of course there is an agricultural sector and an agricultural lobby and industries that serve agriculture, that at the end of the day all work towards this butter ending up on the shelf.

Academic (sociology and sustainability)

Additionally, in the eyes of another expert, holding the single individual accountable was not ever going to be sufficient since consumers were not willing to display the dedication needed to achieve meaningful climate action:

> Exceedingly few or nobody actually is willing to go that far. And this we see in all markets, no matter whether it is fashion, even vegan and vegetarian diets that are having an enormous boom in the last ten years [...], that's still only a fraction, a couple of percentage points, we see a lot of flexitarians and so on but this corresponds to this escaping a guilty conscience...

Academic (sustainability innovation)

As a result, one of the experts emphasised that besides these intricate interdependencies and all this complexity, there were still areas where there was much agreement over the necessity of implementing measures for climate action and for her it was fairly obvious that political agents were the ones needing to take action, for example in the meat industry. She believed that whilst politicians held significant influence over such matters and did have the means to initiate changes, they instead opted to even more effectively responsibilise the single consumer:

> ... whenever I visit conferences [by the government] for sustainable consumption, every time they present this app, 'too good for the trash', for them, that's climate action, that people have an app with which they can determine whether the best before date is even relevant for them, well, great! [...] [but] this is going to make zero difference!

Academic (sustainable consumption)

It was further granted that effective political environmental action consisted in actually restricting consumption and the challenge therefore lay in gaining the necessary societal acceptance.

Consequently, for one of the experts, acting responsibly as an individual began with considering the areas that one actually had an influence over:

> I believe that where my actions actually make a difference, where I can do this or this, that is where one should take responsibility and consider: do I really have to get the maximum out of something? Do I have to act strategically here? Or can I maybe actually just act out of solidarity in this case? [...] And take responsibility for the mutual relationship and not for the maximisation of my utility. [...] but these areas are quite small and maybe they are getting even smaller...

Academic (sociology and sustainability)

She went on to say that in her eyes it was central to involve oneself and contribute to one's community. Here she stressed that the means to do so differed, and somebody struggling to make ends meet may not have the capacities to do so. Thus, the initial inherent complexity of ascribing responsibility for climate action was exacerbated by people in modern life being exposed to multiple pressures, especially in young adulthood when trying to make a living, raise children and in some cases also care for their elders. Climate change communicators often failed to establish some form of connection to these everyday realities of people. Furthermore, individual consumption decisions for more climate action were welcome but at the end of the day, they were no more than *a drop in the ocean*.

For these reasons, there was a general consensus (except to an extent amongst the conservative politicians) that this focus on the single consumer was unhelpful if not counterproductive in everyday life:

> The consumer is told that they can do so much for climate action, thousands of little things, things that systematically overstrain them, if with each coffee they buy they have to consider whether from a climate perspective this makes sense or not....

Academic (sustainability innovation)

Or in another interview:

> I think that this is a kind of overstrain, because firstly you cannot really know exactly all that comes with this piece of butter that you are buying and at the same time, as I said, in many cases, one is embedded in certain necessities where you don't really have a choice...

Academic (sociology and sustainability)

In conclusion, with respect to the role for climate action of the single consumer, the predicament was described as follows:

> ... climate change will only work if every single one contributes. On the other hand, there are a lot of people who are right in saying: it's completely irrelevant whether I go by car or not. And at first, this is a completely rational statement because it is true. [...] But on the other hand, if we want to achieve a climate neutral society, this of course has to be reflected in the actions of the individual...

Expert 2 at federal environmental agency

However, there was also an argument with respect to the efficacy of the individual that went into the opposite direction. In this respect, Greta Thunberg was for example referred to as an 'ignition spark' that then mobilised the *Fridays for Future* protests (chairperson socio-ecological think-tank). Yet arguably this once again has to be put into (social-scientific) perspective as Greta Thunberg did not achieve this momentum for the climate movement truly on her own. Instead, the issue had already been simmering in society for quite a while and when she started her school strikes, the time was right for collective action to mobilise and have an impact.

Therefore, in the eyes of one expert, the influence that could actually be exerted by the individual over societal outcomes consisted in the following:

> ... exerting pressure from within society... through the formation of coalitions... yes, and being present, being uncomfortable, being loud, being seen. With demands that are articulated clearly...
>
> Head of environmental NGO

Overall, many interviewees reasoned that political actors held particular responsibility as they actually had the most influence over societal outcomes. One expert was hesitant at first with regard to this point, arriving however at the following conclusion:

> ... it is often marginal groups [that initiate change]... as long as you are in this stage, you cannot really criticise state actors for not reacting fast enough, as the state is hardly ever a first-mover and you also need a whole lot to have majorities, you need a majority in parliament to pass laws or to get funding approved, yes. But at a certain point, when a problem has been known for twenty years, then you can and you have to hold the state responsible. Yes, because the state is not acting and it is the only one who can. The state cannot give this obligation [...] back to civil society, even though this happens all the time: you people simply have to scream a bit louder and then we create some legislation. Of course, politicians need acceptance, you see this in the example of the yellow vests... that's very discouraging to politicians.
>
> Chairperson socio-ecological think-tank

Yet, there was considerable scepticism over whether state actors actually met this responsibility:

> Let me put it like this: they [the politicians] are effective in legitimising politics, so politicians legitimise their role, so they do do something, they carry responsibility in their political role, but they don't carry responsibility as climate protectors.
>
> Academic (sustainable consumption)

This participant went on to say that in her perception political actors often saw themselves as very limited in their own actual agency by the will of the voter and in her eyes this was true to some extent as polemics and elections did in fact limit their efficacy. Political actors themselves confirmed this perception:

> Our influence over outcomes, it does exist, but it is much more limited than you would sometimes think – also how we ourselves would want it to be.
>
> Member of Bavarian State Ministry (Freie Wähler)

Or in another interview:

> But if we, say, raise taxes at just one segment (-)... and then we don't even know whether people will only get mad but still continue to drive their cars. Then I have ruined more than I have gained.
>
> Member of the Bundestag (CDU)

While these politicians by and large accepted their special responsibility for intensifying climate action, they perceived their ability to make a difference, so their own efficacy, to be much more limited:

> At the moment, I see a certain discrepancy between: do you want politics to do more for climate action? 80 percent agree. Do you want carbon pricing? 70 percent reject this. And that is the great challenge we face...
>
> Member of Bundestag (CDU)

Elsewhere in the interview she did however express that she did feel self-efficacious:

> So I would certainly say that in the position that I am in I have a lot of power. Also because I am really close to the chancellor. And to her employees. Last week I spoke on the phone to the person who is drafting her foreign economic policy [...] but

> then again, I don't have the final say. I am not transport minister or energy minister. And therefore, my power is limited once again by what I can attain within my fraction. But if I manage to achieve things by going via the chancellor... I like that she is making this [climate action] a matter for the boss[5]...
>
> Member of Bundestag (CDU)

Wondering why conservative parties were however not recognizing the extent of the urgency and threat climate change presented and thus not trying harder to win people's acceptance, one expert said:

> ... at the end of the day climate action has a lot to do with where you come from, your place of origin... and with conserving these places... and thus it would make sense for the CSU to be the typical climate action party [...]. And they do try to some extent, but at the same time they want to keep economic liberalism because it secures our standard of living, at least allegedly, but to me it is obvious, we cannot keep this form of affluence that we generate at the moment, no way, in fact we must not! [...] but they simply keep clinging onto familiar patterns and it is hard to let them go [...]
>
> Head of environmental NGO

This clinging to what is familiar he also ascribed to the politicians' need for convenience and thus demanded that laws would be introduced that forced actors to leave their comfort zone. Relatedly, there was particular disagreement on the use of regulations. Whilst the conservative politicians interviewed were against 'telling people what to do', some of the other experts demanded their implementation:

> ... at the end of the day, issuing laws and actually also prohibitions, even when people will say this is socialism and [call them] the "prohibition parties" and so on, at the end of the day we have seatbelt regulations and non-smoking laws. They also used to be prohibitions and today nobody cares about that, they are commonplace... [...] only then will we see some development.
>
> Head of environmental NGO

This expert also voiced incomprehension regarding the legislature's failure to harvest even the 'low hanging fruits' as in a recent poll, one third of people had said they would give up their cars if there was sufficient public transport available close to where they lived. He further criticised the government's reported inconsistencies,

---

5 *Chefsache* in German original statement.

for example them wanting to protect 40.000 jobs in the coal industry whilst passing legislation in 2011 that "*killed the entire photovoltaic* sector" where considerably more people were employed. Thus, while he believed it was politicians who held the largest responsibility for climate action, he saw them as displaying only limited efficacy. On the other hand, he attested the growing movements from civil society (*Fridays for Future, Extinction Rebellion*) considerable supportive (vis-à-vis politics) efficacy even though in his view, these efforts could not readily be expected of civil society. Yet, another participant saw it like this:

> At the end of the day, civil society can also not be successful if it continues to only criticise state actors as an instrument of capital and of the lobbies and so on... often enough this is true but government is also the miracle tool of democracy... I'm not saying that government doesn't make mistakes and isn't structurally venous [at some stages]... [...] I think civil society and these young people can be criticised for this tendency to have very little faith in politics and then I wonder: who else is supposed to make the laws?
>
> Chairperson socio-ecological think-tank

On numerous occasions it was also noted that in Germany one was much too dependent on the automotive industry. One participant voiced deep disappointment in its executives as instead of being a role model, its representatives had been setting such a bad example:

> They truly would have been the ones who had the power, and I mean financial resources, intellectual resources, technical resources, to initiate and push change themselves and instead they sacrificed this for profit...
>
> Academic (sustainability innovation)

Another expert also observed a concentration of power with large companies, but she did however not attest them the corresponding amount of responsibility, as these actors were also embedded in power relations. She thought that framework conditions should be established that allowed or forced those who have this kind of power to act properly and that this was the task of politics, even if this resulted in less votes or donations:

> I think a certain amount of courage to become unpopular is part of being responsible.
>
> Academic (sociology and sustainability)

On the other hand, it was recognised that within a corporation one could have a much larger impact as a single person than as a consumer:

> ... if I campaign in my company that from now on, we only use recycling paper, this is not peanuts anymore, because suddenly we are talking about an organisation with one hundred employees, with a paper demand of potentially tons, several tons. That adds up and can really make a difference.
>
> Expert 2 at federal environmental agency

It was further pointed out that, in line with consumers, corporate actors also had the strategic option to operate in climate neutral ways and whilst there was already some movement into this direction, this remained below what could be expected, given that consumer demand is already shifting to more climate-friendly products.

The scientific community was deemed very efficacious, especially through the international institutionalisation of the subject of climate change within the IPCC:

> The IPCC has caused a societal level of knowledge for a specific environmental challenge that is unique in my opinion...
>
> Expert 2 at federal environmental agency

At times, one could notice in the interviews a deep trust in the efficacy of technological innovation, mainly in the case of the more conservative participants:

> The topic of climate action and sustainability will be advanced with the help of technological solutions...
>
> Member of Bavarian State Ministry (Freie Wähler)

One expert said in relation to the efficacy of the scientific community:

> Science does indeed play a role, I think. But more indirectly. In what the media then brings to the public. But not, I think, nobody really notices these things... [...] since the eighties it cannot actually be said any more that scientific knowledge is superior [to practical knowledge]. But of course, there is some knowledge in any kind of practice. I think it is right that science as an entity that generates secured or legitimised or neutral knowledge is centralised. And I think it is important to integrate local knowledge into this.
>
> Academic (sociology and sustainability)

On the other hand, one other academic (who also worked in more inclusive, transdisciplinary research projects) reported that this was much more complicated than often assumed, and this was very difficult to convey. She said that in relation to this, she faced a lot of scepticism towards science with people saying that what she was doing was completely irrelevant.

It was also criticised that currently, ministers were ignoring even their own expert panels (expert 2 at federal environmental agency), pointing towards science also sometimes lacking efficacy and assertiveness. Furthermore, on numerous occasions it was pointed out that messages were heard most where there already was established concern for climate action.

In line with all these presented incongruences between responsibility attributions and efficacy estimations, one of the academics came to the following testament:

> So, there is actually this cut between the action and its effect that I can take responsibility for. […] And I believe this holds true for both directions, so on the one hand I take responsibility for things that others could indeed for once also see themselves responsible for. And also, I am being made responsible for things that I cannot even fathom what they are about. […] So I think it is really difficult to establish this nexus between action and responsibility [for action].

Academic (sociology and sustainability)

Furthermore, it was emphasised that climate action remained a topic exceptionally difficult to communicate as it was firstly so abstract and secondly there was this problematic uncoupling of cause and effect with respect to climate change. This was exacerbated by the fact that carbon emissions could not be experienced directly by people's senses:

> … the further away or the more abstract or the more invisible a danger is, say poison for example, fertilizer, in small amounts CO_2 is harmless anyways, is part of nature, all this makes us less and less able to react to this danger…

Chairperson socio-ecological think-tank

4.4 Statements about knowing

This relates to the dominant view that the public needs to be provided with more detailed information about the threat of climate change in order to act responsibly (information deficit thinking). This perception also featured prominently in some of these interviews. For example, one of the conservative politicians (member of the Bundestag, CDU) affirmed that if the public were only informed better, there would generally be more effort to protect the climate.

Turning back to the topic of responsibility attribution, one interviewee responded as follows:

> Of course it lies with politics, as politicians are the ones who hold the most leverage and who by definition of their occupation are supposed to have the most information density at their disposal as they are sufficiently advised by scientists, there are enough committees to all sorts of topics [...] and thus it is on the politicians if they do not listen to this advice or are turning a deaf ear to it or prioritise other matters...
>
> Head of environmental NGO

This excerpt thus epitomises that just as responsibility cannot be contemplated without concomitantly considering the agency or efficacy an actor holds, both concepts are at the same time also deeply intertwined with the notion of knowing. More precisely, it must also be asked if and under what circumstances people are motivated to act on the information they have at their disposal.

As one of the experts (academic sociology and sustainability) remarked, consumers are often, and in her eyes unfoundedly, ascribed responsibility with the argument that they would have had every opportunity to inform themselves about their actions' consequences for the climate. One other academic (sustainable consumption) stressed that carrying responsibility entailed that the actor *actually knew* what the right course of action was – a prerequisite that can be difficult to meet given the complexity of climate change. These statements indicate that responsibility cannot be considered without asking about power. Since we have known since Bacon and Hobbes that *knowledge is power*, responsibility and efficacy both cannot be considered without asking to what extent it is knowledge and information that causes people to behave in certain ways:

> ... I think responsibility lies with everyone who knows [about the threat of climate change].
>
> Head of environmental NGO

The link between responsibility and knowledge also surfaced in the following statement:

> ... so I think, I am deeply convinced that the responsibility is greatest where there also is the most opportunity; that means someone well-educated has more responsibility than who is uneducated, someone rich has more responsibility than someone poor because everybody who is well-off and educated has the means to inform themselves...
>
> Chairperson socio-ecological think-tank

Nevertheless, this same participant did not ascribe to a call for more information about climate change:

> Honestly, I think what we lack the least is more knowledge!

Like this expert, several of the interviewees believed that people were currently well aware, for example about the impact of flying on the climate and that this awareness had increased in recent years. However, expert 1 at the federal environmental agency found that while attitudes towards climate action were overall very positive, yet when compared with actual market data, there appeared a relatively large gap between both aspects (i.e., between value and true action).

Another point related to knowledge and information was repeatedly mentioned, namely the problem of people being confronted with contradictory messages. One expert (academic sociology and sustainability) remarked that people often felt demoralised when the information they faced was too heterogeneous. Another participant put it like this:

> ... but it is also extremely difficult to be completely informed. If today I decide from now on I will only buy organic, then tomorrow I read in the paper that organic meat has much greater emissions than conventionally produced meat, at least with beef this is the case. And I immediately feel hard done by because I actually want to be doing the right thing...
>
> Head of environmental NGO

4.5 Statements pointing towards denial

From this it follows, firstly, that even though knowledge and information are essential for combatting climate change, they are not sufficient. Secondly, this indicates that more information can even be counterproductive, as it often overwhelms and demoralises people:

> I mean, that's the thing with knowing[6]. The more detailed my knowledge is, the more I know what I don't know. […] to the same extent that you know more, your resistance increases. And I think this can indeed be observed that the more complex it gets and the less people understand [therefore], the more tendency there is for them to withdraw themselves into these different reverberation chambers[7] in order to search for simpler explanations that allow them to remain capable of acting…
>
> Academic (sociology and sustainability)

Or as another participant put it:

> … I think everybody knows that they have to work on themselves […]. But many also go by this motto of the ostrich and say, Oh well, I still want to go on holiday [by plane], never mind…
>
> Head of environmental NGO

This type of ignorant behaviour, people putting their head in the sand or looking the other way, was often mentioned in the interviews. Overall, when it came to the responsibility for climate action and people acting on what they know, from the interviews it emerged that there was widespread **denial** present in German society. Mentioning of this phenomenon of denial occurred in different contexts:

> I think as an adult, it is your responsibility to inform yourself. Ignorance does not protect you from being held accountable, I think. You cannot just put your head in the sand and say: as long as I don't know about this, I can take planes and eat meat as much as I please. Of course, it is inconvenient once you know. […] the (nineteen-)twenties and thirties must have been awesome, when smoking wasn't unhealthy yet. Of course, you make life difficult for yourself… But you also want to escape your own sense of powerlessness[8] somehow and you want to understand the bigger picture…
>
> Teacher secondary education

---

6 Jamison, 2001, p. 23: "Paradoxically, the more expert knowledge we have, and the more use we make of it, the more calamitous the ensuing problems seem to be".

7 YouTube universa, echo chambers, cultural cocoons; cf. Lütjen, 2016 here.

8 *Unmündigkeit* in German original statement.

Another participant said the following in relation to this:

> … it is not only that we say we want to do more, but we don't manage to, it is also that we don't actually want to do more, because we believe that we have already done a lot […] people are simply no experts in ecological balancing…
>
> Expert 2 at federal environmental agency

In order to escape uncomfortable feelings of fear and hopelessness, people tended to flee themselves into resignation as one expert described:

> … also in the face of the sheer magnitude […] that says we all have to act immediately, otherwise the world ends, and so on… I mean, this is not a discourse that is particularly motivating anyways, it is more one that maybe causes you to adopt an attitude along the lines of, I cannot do anything anyways, so I'm going to enjoy what I can […], so an attitude of I just don't care…
>
> Division head CC private foundation

It was further stressed that in order for people to contribute meaningfully to climate action and be efficacious, it was necessary that people felt like something could still be done to mitigate climate change. However, statements like this one painted a somewhat hopeless picture:

> I think that from our capacities […], I think we are not even able to adequately face a problem of this magnitude. This will only happen when the level of suffering is large enough but then it will be too late….
>
> Academic (sustainability innovation)

One of the experts said that he also often observed a rejection of responsibility with centre right politicians and high-income corporate actors who still took planes for work and leisure without thinking about it. Secondly, he attributed this to comfort and habit and said that it was hard to leave patterns of practice behind that one had followed for long times. Here, laws were needed to force more uncomfortable practices. Thirdly, he gave the following explanation:

> … also because it [jet-setting] is what is chic at the end of the day. It is chic to show off, it is chic on Instagram […]. It is part of [modern] lifestyle. So what, then I fly from time to time. But that this is the biggest climate killer and that this messes up your complete balance of emissions of the whole year, I don't think people know

> this. And they don't take responsibility... [...] they also want to show their children the world.
>
> Head of environmental NGO

Or as it was said in another interview:

> ... societal framework conditions render travelling by plane extremely attractive... and not only financially but plane travel takes me to destinations that are deeply fascinating... nothing against campaigns that promote the beauty of regional destinations, but a Grand Canyon is just something else when compared to the Wutachschlucht in the Black Forest. That's simply how it is.
>
> Expert 2 at federal environmental agency

Several of the experts, like these two, elucidated to people truly acting according to what held the most social value instead of what factual information would impel them to do.

> So you would think that somebody who grew up as part of the 68 generation would, on some level be, sensitised [for environmental matters]. But when you are in a certain professional environment, where it [flying] is commonplace, then you can ask whether someone is the type of person to go into this occupational field... But I think, the professional field is something that needs to be looked at more closely. So, the context of practices in which certain types of behaviour are formative [...]. So how to approach this? Only few will change this behaviour when kerosene becomes more expensive... How can a shift in consciousness or a change in the framework conditions of this practice be achieved? Only really through stigmatisation. But how do you stigmatise flights?
>
> Academic (sociology and sustainability)

One expert (academic sustainable consumption) also emphasised these often non-cognitive aspects that emerged out of the way people habitually behave and interact. In this respect, the influence of the social surroundings was repeatedly (academic sociology and sustainability, expert 1 at federal environmental agency) deemed to matter more than the provision of more detailed information. One participant (academic sociology and sustainability) said that she thought that people who acted with no concern for the climate did so because that was their way of acting without thinking about it that much. When these people were then confronted with the topic of climate change, they often defensively argued that their individual behaviour did not make an actual difference. Furthermore, there were several pressures in everyday life for most people like being time poor, which made prioritising climate action even harder.

In relation to this lingering collective denial there was also some marginal mentioning of outright climate change rejection in the interviews:

> Apart from maybe the AfD, they say: climate change is not caused by humans. They are not saying that it is not happening. But it is not caused by humans. They are walking around quite destructively...
>
> Member of Bundestag (CDU)

Or in another interview:

> What I see is more some kind of regression. Regression in the sense that climate change is seriously doubted. And there one has to say that the lobbyists and, well, how do I call them? PR-people, they were very successful.
>
> Academic (sustainability innovation)

However, denial was mostly spoken of in its more unintentional, subconscious, ostrich-type form described above.

Therefore, one academic concluded that if climate action was not part of one's particular culture, then it was even less likely that one would act accordingly:

> ... so I think, it is more a matter of your direct surroundings that influences you. So, your work environment, your living environment, your friendship circle...
>
> Academic (sociology and sustainability)

This also links to the following statement:

> Here in Munich, you very much see this other picture, where it is all about your lifestyle and you enjoying yourself and people revel in this. [...] and then you post this on Instagram and everyone likes it and wants to relieve it. But you also have the other picture, like in my personal environment, where people do act responsibly. And of course, these are the people that you choose to be with because you always look for like-minded people...
>
> Teacher secondary education

One of the experts noted that from an outside perspective, in each case, there was actually more room for manoeuvre than what it seemed from the inside, including for the consumer, as it were also entirely possible to just not go on holiday. According to her, for different reasons, some room for agency was always closed off. These reasons included matters of perception, of competence and, most importantly, of socialisation:

> ... otherwise, it is very much due to socialisation. With the repair movement, it is nearly always people [...] that have had some sort of positive social experience. So Dad, Mom, someone had [always] repaired...
>
> Academic (sustainable consumption)

This was indirectly also indicated by one of the conservative politicians:

> It is also a matter of how you grew up...
>
> Member of Bavarian State Ministry (Freie Wähler)

Another point raised was related to the diversity of motives actors held, as there simply did not exist *one* citizenry that would react to a universal call to action with respect to the climate:

> ... interests are just too heterogeneous. On the one hand one wants the cobbles because it's sustainable and rain can drain easily, on the other hand it's pretty loud and one would rather have tarmac. [...] I think it is these contradictions that make it [regulations] take so long and lead to compromises...
>
> Academic (sociology and sustainability)

In line with this, one politician (Freie Wähler) elaborated on this by asking what is seen as 'hip' in society. Progress would be achieved if an energy neutral house is seen as 'hip', as opposed to some fancy interior. Another expert (Head of NGO) pointed into the same direction in saying that today [caring for the] *climate was just not [perceived as] sexy*.

Experts asking these kinds of questions points to the hitherto underappreciated relevance social valuation exerts in decision-making. Taking this into consideration was however somewhat incompatible with a perception that worked exclusively according to numbers and measurements as one academic (sociology and sustainability) pointed out. Those experts living according to such a more quantitative worldview also displayed a deep trust in technology and innovation, particularly with respect to alternative technologies in the automotive sector (Head of NGO, chairperson of socio-ecological think-tank):

> We count on innovation, on economic advantages, on incentives.
>
> Member of Bundestag (CDU)

Here, flying was described as *ground-breaking technological accomplishment* (head of environmental NGO). This might help explain why it is so difficult for privileged people to distance themselves from flying as they live in a world where technology and innovation are so all-encompassingly glorified. Again, this indicates just how mighty and influential social valuation is.

Perhaps somewhat unsurprisingly, the secondary education teacher also leant more on the side of factual information:

> Of course, you have to reach students emotionally somehow, but not only emotionally. That should not be paramount. The focus should definitely be on the facts and on the scientists. And through this scientific understanding of the facts, ideally the motivation for action should follow.

Overall, there was strong contestation on this question of knowledge provision (versus social valuation) with some other experts fiercely rejecting the focus on information and knowing. One expert who had worked extensively on environmental awareness stated:

> ... knowledge, for example from climate science, is actually only helpful to a very limited extent. I think it is actually the type of knowledge that emerges from concrete local spaces where there are real interactions between people [that must feature more] [...] and I think that knowledge must not be 'given' to the public, it must actually emerge from the public [...] because everybody is the expert for his or her own everyday life.
>
> Expert 1 at federal environmental agency

One expert (division head CC private foundation) was similarly convinced that the slow progress with climate action was not due to a lack of knowledge and information about climate change. He emphasised that in order to act, people had to *feel* some sort of personal concern. Convinced that much more could currently be achieved through the exploration of alternative angles, he demanded that within the climate community, there needed to be more examination of the true motives people held to become active:

> We see this everywhere in the world, where climate action is actually taking place, in the rarest of cases this is at the end of the day primarily due to reasons related to the climate. For example, health is a strong trigger, there are several other trig-

> gers that can be used to achieve the right things for climate action, without always employing only the climate narrative. [...] innovation is another one, nutrition and diet, foreign and security policy, [...] climate change is a cross-sectional issue [...] and therefore we need to look deeper into this and think about which milieus, which societal groups can potentially be reached through which type of rationale.
>
> Division head CC private foundation

For these reasons, most of the experts were generally not in favour of introducing further public information campaigns about climate action:

> It is simply not enough to try, to say somewhat naively, we now want to make sufficiency policy popular, that is just not going to work. Or the Deutsche Umwelthilfe's current campaign *Don't buy nothing (Kauf Nix!)* – I don't know what they were thinking. They are just shooting in the dark...
>
> Expert 2 at federal environmental agency

One expert came to the following conclusion:

> I do indeed believe that more knowledge is needed. And inevitably so. But this only leads to more dedicated climate action in an indirect way.
>
> Academic (sociology and sustainability)

Overall, in the interviews there was a growing consensus that for people to act climate responsibly, one needed to go beyond factual information. Another expert voiced the following:

> ... how you can act also has a lot to do with having made experiences and I am not a fan of providing recipes [for people to act in certain ways]...
>
> Academic (sustainable consumption)

There was growing recognition that experience-based knowledge and emotional messages needed to be given more attention. At the same time, some experts were frustrated with people still not acting in light of increasing extreme weather events and manifestations of climate change even in front of their own doors:

> ... currently we are in a phase, we have always complained in relation to environmental protection that people are not experiencing environmental change [...],

> but at the moment people experience this the whole time. There is no lack of understanding in this regard...
>
> Expert 2 at federal environmental agency

Here, another participant stated:

> ... science has been generating data for 110 years [for this location] that we can use and that is robust. There is no way that one can say, I don't see it, it doesn't exist. People who go through life like this are in fact preventing any chance for a future worth living[9]. Of course, we are all feeling this already in the form of heavy rain, melting glaciers, increasing snowfall...
>
> Member of Bavarian State Ministry (Freie Wähler)

4.6 Conclusion

This chapter has shown that initially, most experts interviewed voiced that climate action needed to be an inclusive project involving the whole of society. Yet political figures were particularly responsible since they actually held the most influence over societal outcomes. There was thus already an implicit assumption that responsibility had to be contemplated in accordance with efficacy in many of these discourses. Acting responsibly as an individual with respect to climate change was therefore repeatedly described in political terms. The experts were generally weary of corporations, probably due to the recent *Dieselgate* scandal in Germany's automotive industry. Further, it emerged from the interviews that there is widespread denial present in German society. Knowledge concepts varied, with some interviewees basing their judgements on others' alleged information deficits whilst others conceived of people acting according to what held the most social value. Non-cognitive aspects that regularly emerged out of the way people habitually behaved and interacted were also mentioned here.

Although different (financial) circumstances, the profound influence of respective socialisation and, in one case, people employing diverging conceptions of, for example, responsibility were mentioned, overall the fundamental societal differences in the reception of climate messages were not recognised by these experts. In general, the public was here treated as a quite unified entity.

9 ... *vergehen sich an der Zukunft* in German original statement.

5 Media analysis: Public debates about climate change
Divergent views and variable voices

5.1 Introduction

This section presents the results of the media analysis, combining descriptive statements and direct quotes with interpretative efforts to ensure maximum readability, accessibility and analytical transparency. The data was initially sorted into two main groups of climate cultures. On the one hand, a comparatively homogeneous set of rather visible climate cultures was detected. These were associated with political elites, prominent public figures and well known influencers. These elite climate cultures reflect ways of knowing, sense-making and speaking associated with educated elites in German society, including choice of language and how scientific information is handled. What makes these climate cultures (including the subculture of young activists and influencers) 'elite' is their exclusionary nature (mainly with reference to cultural capital), given that only highly educated and media-savvy members of the public can follow and actively participate in these discourses.

This contrasts with a less visible, heterogeneous group of climate cultures 'from below' that encompasses diverse views held by members of the public. Here, various ways of understanding, arguing and reasoning can be detected, many of which relate to everyday experiences of lived efficacy and responsibility. Some of these public views explicitly contradict or challenge elite practices and dominant ways of knowing while others accept their supremacy while offering potential alternatives.

A subsequent fine-grained analysis of the data revealed four separate climate cultures – two linked to elite actors' public statements, and another two from the general public. Additionally, some displayed certain variations or *shades* that were found to comprise a *subculture*. In this study, a subculture represents a variant or shade of the cultural leanings associated with the parent culture. Whilst internally the subculture strives to achieve some distinction from the parent culture, upon closer examination these deviations remain subtle enough to place them within the same general cultural category.

The first group (the elite climate cultures) finds expression in the three TV talk shows, online news portals, prestige print and influential political magazines and, perhaps more surprisingly, climate-related YouTube clips by young influencers that received significant attention[1].

In contrast, the second group of climate cultures 'from below' features very prominently across different social media, including comments sections linked to the aforementioned talk shows. In addition, some of these 'non-elite' climate (sub-)cultures appear in 'alternative' media outlets such as print magazines focusing on green lifestyles and climate action and political magazines that endorse anti-establishment views. However, these were not included in this study, due to their extensive range and diversity. Admittedly, some degree of overlap exists between some of the climate (sub-)cultures, for example regarding trust in expert opinions. However, I nevertheless decided to distinguish between these four climate cultures and their respective subcultures because of fundamental differences in key areas such as attributions of responsibility and expectations of efficacy vis-à-vis actual experiences of 'lived' responsibility and efficacy.

5.2 Elite climate cultures

Two separate elite climate cultures – individualist and collectivist – emerged from the analysis, with the second displaying a distinct subculture of young activists and influencers. Amongst these elite climate cultures, similarities included a shared language associated with 'official' positions on climate change and action as well as more or less explicit acknowledgements that anthropogenic climate change existed and presented a serious challenge to humanity. At times, participants from this elite category saw themselves as well-informed and sufficiently competent to educate the public. For example, the arguments and terminology used by prominent influencers and YouTubers revealed their high educational status (Rezo holding a masters- and Mai Thi Nguyen-Kim a doctoral degree) and their commitment to informing the public about climate change. Rezo's video clearly demonstrated his ability to 'speak the language of science' (e.g., citing relevant studies, summarising and synthesising studies). This was also evident when analysing the 'open letter' video 'signed' by 90+ YouTubers. Here, the authors of the letter spoke of 'risk hierarchy', 'scientific consensus' and being 'discredited'. All three elite climate (sub-)cultures featured some or all of the following arguments, many of which related directly to the aspects of responsibility and efficacy discussed in chapter 2:

1 Clicks to date (04/06/2020): Rezo: Die Zerstörung der CDU: 17.347.533. maiLab: Klimawandel: Das ist jetzt zu tun!: 866.947. maiLab: Die Klimawandel-Therapie: 88.652. Ein Statement von 90+ YouTubern: 4.395.518.

- Responsibility of political sphere versus individual responsibility
- Efficacy of individual purchasing decisions
- Social fairness of political decisions
- References to the role of the private sector (responsibility and efficacy)
- Efficacy of scientific knowledge/technological innovations (perceived vs. lived efficacy)
- Use of apocalyptic and catastrophic vocabulary (perceived vs. lived efficacy)
- The questioning of the growth-dependent capitalist free-market system (perceived vs. lived efficacy)

Table 3: Excerpts from elite climate debates

	Individualist culture	**Collectivist culture**	**Activist/influencer subculture**
Exemplary statements	Ulrich Reitz (journalist, FOCUS-online): *In the past, actually just a couple of weeks ago, it was all about your own very personal (carbon) footprint that you leave our offspring with every light-pink T-Bone-Steak […]. This has now been literally chewed out, however, now it is about way more…*	Robert Habeck (co-leader of the Green Party): *… the point is that we live in serious political times and that our party is expected to carry an amount of responsibility like never before and we work extremely hard to do justice to this expectation. […] and now we have the situation that almost every day another stone is being added to our backpack and then someone says, 'come on, run faster'!*	Mai Thi Nguyen-Kim (YouTube science channel maiLab): *[…] there are two very important things, every single one of us can or even must do. Firstly, stop using bogus arguments. The climate debate is befouled by bogus arguments, that not only keep politicians from acting responsibly but also often come in the disguise of something like this (Twitter posting): "Double standard á la Luisa Neubauer, attacks government for its alleged lack of political will for climate action but has visited more countries at age 23 than most people. […]".*
Exemplary statements	Ulf Poschardt (editor-in-chief of the conservative Welt-group): *A car is way more than an object that lets you travel from A to B. […]. We have to ask ourselves what else people do with their cars. They communicate, they enjoy themselves […]. I think*	Annalena Baerbock (co-leader of the Green Party): *… and then there was this major fraud* (Dieselgate scandal) *that affects us all and that is why politics has to assume responsibility and compensate for this loss of trust.*	Rezo: *Well maybe (one could say) our efforts are being thwarted by other countries? Maybe we want to do a lot… What? Okay, other countries are starting initiatives and want to fight the crisis way more and we are thwarting that and are not joining in? Huh. Right, ok, CDU maybe is thwarting the fight against global warming, but hey, maybe*

	Individualist culture	**Collectivist culture**	**Activist/ influencer subculture**
Exemplary statements	*the question must be how electro-mobility can also be emotionalised. And here I remain unconvinced because the electro-cars I've driven have been interesting in terms of acceleration – but they have no soul.*	*[...] and the current problem lies in the fact that those who want to sustainably drive electro-cars have to pay way more because of the fossil subsidies [...] and this is what we want to end...*	*they have a good reason. So economically, this is unbearable. Coal is huge in Germany... What? Only 20.000 jobs in the whole of the coal sector? [...]*
Exemplary statements	Michael Kretschmer (CDU politician): *... what we need again is rationality, calm and sober acting. [...] but the whole thing has to happen with rationality and sound judgement... [...] There have to be ideas and ways to do this rationally... [...] we want to do everything we can to make this work. Supply security, reasonable prices, independent of other countries.*	Jan Grossarth (Journalist, SZ): *Differentiating and balancing, out of responsibility, whilst being aware of the complexity, that'd actually be the more bourgeois-conservative approach. [...] What would a family business be without a lively environment? [...] in the long-term, climate action in fact supports the conservation of the market-based system.*	Luisa Neubauer: *At this point, I would recommend re-reading the IPCC-report.* And later: *[...] and it's a shame that there is no climate scientist here...* Mai Thi Nguyen-Kim: *But do not be fooled, when people claim that research and innovation (alone) will save us all – no!*
Exemplary statements	Ulf Poschardt: *... I believe the challenge concerns us all, my criticism [...] concerning the school and university protests has been, that with spreading panic and with this kind of apocalyptic rhetoric...*	Dietrich Brockhagen (Atmosfair-CEO, SZ-Interview): *... But I am responsible for what I have control over. I cannot impact airports in China. But for their Mallorca-flight everybody is responsible themself.* Kevin Kühnert: *[...] I believe that capitalism and market mechanisms have perforated our society too deeply.*	Mai Thi Nguyen-Kim: *(Title: Climate change therapy; therapist:) Nobody finds climate change easy. Knowledge and rationality are a good basis, but generally they don't provide a personal motivation. What you need is a strong emotional trigger. (Patient:) But I am a very rational person. (Therapist:) Every person is susceptible to emotional triggers; the key is finding the right one.*

5.2.1 Elite with individualist tendencies

Current debates on climate action in Germany frequently attribute responsibility for climate action to the *individual* citizen-consumer, asking them to reduce unnecessary consumption to arrest climate change. Such views characterise this first elite type of climate cultures, coinciding with a more or less direct rejection of any legislative restrictions. The sarcasm in FOCUS-author Reitz's choice of discourse indicated his rejection of lifestyle questions being made anything but his own business. Ulf Poschardt also vehemently stressed individual responsibility. Politicians who fell into this climate culture also tended to call for minimal political intervention to avert climate change. For example, they argued against a carbon tax, citing low public acceptance for such measures.

Interestingly, representatives of this climate culture ascribed considerable responsibility to private companies but, at the same time, emphasised that these already took sufficient responsibility given their exposure to other economic pressures such as profitability and competitiveness. In this context, the power and influence of individual consumers (*Verbrauchermacht*) was emphasised once again.

In contrast, experiences of 'lived efficacy' by members of this particular climate culture did not correspond to this official discourse. Instead, representatives expressed little or no confidence in individual behaviour change and self-restriction as effective means of climate action. Thus, the moral imperative to act for the greater good of the climate was not recognised here. Support for laissez-faire politics and an (over)emphasis on individual decision-making featured prominently in this first elite climate culture.

Although social fairness was seen as essential for stability in society, many members of this climate culture rejected political efforts to redistribute wealth. Instead, trust was placed in the market to steer companies in the right direction, for example to develop technology to advance climate action.

Table 4: Excerpts from climate debates among members of the general public

Exemplary statements	**Inaction climate culture(s)**		
Pro-climate action culture	***Inaction subculture 1: Sense of inefficacy***	***Inaction subculture 2: Scepticism***	***Inaction subculture 3: Denial***
Christian Wirth: *What nonsense! It has never been easier for the individual to avoid CO_2: heaps of cheap meat, cheap flights, cruises, skiing holidays. All are ways to practice what you preach and fast CO_2. But this can only be done by practicing restraint.* Lila: *yes, Ulf, one is supposed to feel bad if one drives the planet against the wall and with it the life of younger people. Let's finally take responsibility, particularly people like Poschardt. He wants to discredit the youngsters, so he can keep on denying what people like him have neglected and not having to leave their comfort zone.*	Ed Dy: *As long as container ships on water pollute the air, major industry and pretty much each larger country only cares for greed for profit, no-one talk to me. The truly easy stuff is not being considered, instead every single time the small man is turned to for money or taken the piss out of.* Lisias Apolopulus: *In 10 years the CO_2 saved costs us 500 Billion Euros. China is having the same amount for breakfast within three months.* Klaus-Dieter Walter @starwarrior1958 @AnneWillTalk @MPKretschmer: *Who wants to pay for climate action? The individual? I am not stupid Industry? Help, competitive disadvantage The state? Who is*	XY: *We don't need climate hysteria, but WORLDWIDE [...] purification plants, recycling [...].* -> link posted: environmental management instead of CO_2-ripoff Bernd Lehmann: *About 2.8 billion people in India and China hang on German environmental minister Schulze's every word as they know, humanity's rescue will come from Germany. At least in the left-green grandeur delusion [...].* Christoph Drescher: *Why not still do better? I don't understand this pub-argument »but the others are much much worse«. [...]* Joanna Li @Christoph Drescher: *I think, pushing the responsibility onto »the others« in the distance is easier than changing oneself, doing without and limiting one's consumption.* Alfred Wechsler @Joanna Li: *We don't push anything on others. It just remains patchwork if we do it alone. And as long as new coal plants are being connected to the grid in our neighbourhood, we don't have to switch off ours!* Dirk Evers: *All in all 100.000 flights per day in the world!! And those who drive are being blamed!! Just so you know, these flights fly with water and are 100 % clean [...], but once*	Ferdi Krüger: *I no longer drink sparkling water, beer and other carbonised beverages. This way I surely significantly support the reduction of the human contribution of overall 0,04 % of the CO_2 monsters that are in the atmosphere. Germany go! And if it's the last thing we do!* Maba man: *Why should I intend to save CO_2? It is vital for plants and at the end all living beings! With more CO_2 the earth becomes greener.* SarbazeSardar_Soleymani @AnneWillTalk and @KuehniKev: *This guy [Kevin Kühnert] is a liar. The only thing he wants is the disownment of the people and the curtailing of freedom.* Thomas Gollinger: *All these TV-debates are always the same sorry it is not against you the same guys always sit there, and that the the earth is sweating is just far-fetched.*

Statements in ***bold = statements in direct opposition***

Exemplary statements	**Inaction climate culture(s)**		
Pro-climate action culture	***Inaction subculture 1: Sense of inefficacy***	***Inaction subculture 2: Scepticism***	***Inaction subculture 3: Denial***
refllex. *#fridaysforfuture: [...] he does not want it to become uncomfortable to live irresponsibly* Sonja Straate: *[...] it is the fundamental obligation of each citizen to contribute to the protection of the natural environment and [...] to prevent all forms of ecological destruction through the introduction and support of environmentally-friendly practices and rules.* **Jonathan Gruner: *Freedom of the press means [...] [to not always agree] Main thing is that eventually EVERYONE in the circle sees eye to eye, isn't it?***	*he going to pay? EU? It only works world-wide UN? With China and the US having veto rights? ERGO-climate protectors-why don't you do this on your own !* Christian Beetz: *As long as I HAVE TO cover each palette at work with X meters of clingfilm for load securing but am expected to pay for a plastic bag because of the environment, I'm gonna kill myself laughing ...* Petra Maier: *[...] Why am I as individual consumer supposed to mind that the products offered to me increase business profits and, at the same time, ruin the environment? Why do you ask me to take responsibility for the damage they do?*	*again he who drives is responsible for all of it!! I wonder who is taking the piss out of whom!!! And why people go on believing this!!!* Andre Vogler: *All this is nonsense. Do they really believe what they ask? Where is all the electricity going to come from if there are only e-cars? Wind turbines? Of course! Wants everybody in their front yard. The electricity also has to be transported. [...] What about recycling the batteries? Nobody talks about that. All nicely blended out. All of this is a farce.* Ludwig: *I couldn't find the facts mentioned by Greta. Which are they? I increasingly understand the climate sceptics! The changing climate cannot be related to the increase in CO_2-concentration. I'm technically trained (btw).* Sammy Man: *Every cow farts methane and is as harmful for the climate as an SUV. therefore one should become vegetarian and NOT invade burgerking or mcdonals after the Friday demo.* ***Arthur Schuessler: these are just dumb insinuations, rg. Mc Donalds etc. But unfortunately some people are this narrow-minded.*** **Steve Müller: *Rise against Leftgreen incitement!***	fAKt 111: *I am curious who will be held responsible for the ice age 115.000 years ago ;).* Martin Hoffmann: *Our young environmentalists should maybe for once critically question whom they actually protest for and who is really behind Friday-for-Future [...] (then follows whole conspiracy theory that the originator of the greenhouse-theory was the cousin of Greta Thunberg's great-grandmother).* Voeegele@akivoeg: *Command economy is what is being asked for.Living in socialism, Venezuela etc. All possible with the #climate lie.People wake up and vote out this mob.Flee out of Germany if you can, go to the USA, Switzerland etc.This reminds me of the mine and Gulag state GDR. #fleefromGermany* ***Arthur Schuessler: I recommend reading a good book about the topic some time.***

*Statements in **bold = statements in direct opposition***

Expert advice and scientific insights were seen as central to effective climate action. In addition, rational decision-making was highly valued, translating into high levels of scepticism concerning the role of emotions in climate discourse and action. An exception to this lay in Ulf Poschardt's explicit recognition of the centrality of emotions in consumption (in this case, car ownership and use). He believed that people responded very strongly to emotional messages (as opposed to 'cold' factual knowledge), for example when considering their mobility options[2]. Nevertheless, the overall privileging of ('cold') factual knowledge also put responsibility on individuals to inform themselves to make the right decisions. This, in turn, deflected attention away from the responsibilities of more influential societal players.

Besides, catastrophic and apocalyptic statements were largely absent from this climate culture and only featured insofar as they were being criticised. Lastly and unsurprisingly, in this climate culture there occured no questioning of the free-market system.

5.2.2 Elite with collectivist orientations

The most prominent difference between the first and this second elite climate culture lay in their divergent attributions of responsibility. The second climate culture acknowledged the gravity of the climate crisis and the resulting need to act. Accordingly, and importantly, it ascribed much responsibility to political agents across the party-political spectrum. Criticism of current government inaction featured prominently, an argument that was largely absent from the individualist climate culture described above.

Members of this much more progressive climate culture also cautioned against a narrow focus on lifestyle, albeit for entirely different reasons than their individualist counterpart. While representatives of the previous elite climate culture did not want to be told what to do, members of this second elite culture instead questioned the impact of lifestyle changes. Thus, statements suggested that individual responsibility was overemphasised in public climate debates, not least because it stood in direct contrast to the limited influence individual consumption could actually have (lived efficacy). Consequently, they focused on the political sphere as a main lever of change (lived efficacy). Some members of this climate culture nevertheless argued for a shift in individual consumption habits, recognising the shared moral imperative to do so (hence the label 'collectivist').

---

2 This points to the different attributions of meaning certain practices carry with them besides the obvious primary one. According to Andreas Ernst, often a coupling of initially separate functions can be uncovered: "A car is not only used for mobility but also serves for social prestige, image cultivation and probably satisfies deep-rooting imaginations of freedom and independence" (2010, p. 138).

Another possible reason for redirecting attention away from the subject of lifestyles may have been to pre-empt and refute accusations of hypocrisy that were regularly levelled at elite advocates of climate action, most notably members of the Green Party and *Fridays for Future* activists.

Again, the impact of the private sector was considered to be high (lived efficacy), mirroring some of the statements made by members of the more individualist climate culture. However, existing efforts by private actors were deemed to be insufficient, and responsibility was instead attributed to political actors.

Concerning social fairness, this climate culture argued for sharing the burden of climate action much more equally than is currently the case. Politics was deemed to be largely responsible for organising this burden sharing, including through financial redistribution. This emphasis on the (interventionist) role of politics stood in stark contrast to the market-focused, laissez-faire perspective endorsed by many members of the individualist climate culture.

With respect to knowledge and technological innovation, some parallels existed between the two elite cultures: information deficit discourses, a prioritisation of science and faith in expert-knowledge loomed large. This said, here catastrophic and apocalyptic storylines featured to some degree, reflecting the idea that strong negative emotions (e.g., fear) would mobilise people.

Lastly, many members of this collectivist climate culture blamed current systems of production and consumption, politics and governance for accelerating climate change. However, not everybody expected solutions to emerge from a radical systems change. For example, journalist Jan Grossrath believed in the compatibility of the market economy and successful climate action.

Collectivist subculture: Emerging elite discourses of activists and influencers

The discourses of young German activists and influencers represented a subculture of the collectivist elite climate culture, as the discursive practices of its members closely resembled those of the parent culture. They equally stressed the importance of information provision, coupled with a firm belief in the effectiveness of scientific reasoning. Representatives also frequently deployed scientific arguments, techniques and terminology to promote climate action. For example, YouTubers Rezo and maiLab regularly referred to scientific studies and prominent climate scientists and campaigners. They also cited particular scientific findings to rebut skewed and misleading arguments used by climate sceptics to deflect responsibility (e.g., accusation of eco-hypocrisy aimed at politicians, ad-hominem arguments[3]).

---

3 Definition of *ad hominem* argumentation: https://www.merriam-webster.com/dictionary/ad%20hominem (accessed 05/05/2022) 1: appealing to feelings or prejudices rather than intellect; an ad hominem argument 2: marked by or being an attack on an opponent's character rather than by an answer to the contentions made.

Communicative mechanisms for promoting immediate climate action were a key interest of members of this subculture. Here, the explicit use of colloquial language served the purpose of motivating its primary target audience (young people) to accept their responsibility and act accordingly. Examples included Rezo's use of the term 'mate' (*Diggi*) to address his viewers or Luisa Neubauer's use of 'most-massively' (*massivst*) to accentuate the scale and urgency of the climate change problem. maiLab also used youth language but to a lesser extent as she directed her videos at young people interested in science. Moreover, members of this subculture highlighted the central role of emotional triggers in mobilising different societal actors to accept their responsibility for climate action and to act accordingly, which is what set them apart from the other two elite climate cultures discussed previously. It was for example regularly resorted to catastrophic language to mobilise audiences to take immediate climate action.

While having internalised individuals' moral obligation and responsibility to contribute to climate action, members of this subculture also questioned the efficacy of the individual, ascribing responsibility and efficacy to the political sphere instead. At the same time, they doubted the ability of current political leaders to legislate for effective climate action. The willingness of private-sector actors to engage in serious climate action and to do so voluntarily was questioned too, revealing a discrepancy between attested responsibility and efficacy. For example, some YouTubers viewed private businesses as very powerful actors that would always put their own interests first, unless laws and regulations forced them to act in the interest of the climate.

The 'system question' was hardly ever raised within this elite subculture. Overall, the participants of these elite climate cultures were unified by their implicit and explicit acceptance of 'official' narratives regarding the societal imperative to 'do something about climate change', albeit with varying degrees of urgency.

5.3 Climate cultures 'from below'

Only by analysing reactions on Twitter and Facebook to ideas presented by members of these elite climate cultures in the TV talk shows, the diversity of climate cultures in Germany became fully apparent. In fact, climate cultures 'from below' presented themselves as much more diverse and eclectic than those in the elite group, which has not yet adequately been recognised in climate-related research and policy. This invisibility of the climate-related views and practices of members of the public can be partly attributed to the fact that they rarely have access to the same kinds of elite platforms (e.g., political talk shows, prestige print media).

Two distinct climate cultures (action and inaction) were identified, with the latter displaying three subcultures (I: inefficacy, II: scepticism and III: denial/anti-

(youth)activism), each of which displayed its own discursive patterns and logics. Whilst none of the elite climate cultures questioned the authority of the IPCC-consensus, here the complaint repeatedly surfaced that the media was practicing a bias by not covering precisely that:

> **Frühlingsklima Heimatlooserx**[4,5]: Many "media professionals" (e.g., I refer to the lack of variety in talk show invitations) view themselves as advocates of certain interests, as activists even. However, freedom of press is about NOT always joining into the choir of majority opinion.
> Or elsewhere:
> **NicoHB**: When the smallest party of the opposition secretes its bullshit, frenetically cheered on by the hand-picked audience, then you know: you are watching the forced fee financed public television.

These sceptical and even denialist voices were also **the loudest**, which manifested in the data with an abundance and wide variety of expressions belonging to these three subcultures. This was surprising because German society is not usually considered to be particularly climate-sceptical in the literature (cf. Grundmann, 2007; Tranter and Booth, 2015; Walter et al., 2018). What also stood out is the polarisation of the public debate between radically 'green' pro-climate discourses on the one hand, and especially these sceptical and denialist discourses on the other.

5.3.1 Pro-climate action culture

This first bottom-up climate culture was characterised by its ample cultural reference to 'green' values that were ultimately also mirrored in political affiliation. There was some overlap with the collectivist elite culture presented above. Opinions among its members tended to revolve around the following points:

- Debates about the individual holding responsibility and 'quiet' acceptance of some form of individual responsibility
- Rejection of conspicuous consumption
- References to the 'climate consensus'
- Strong support for, and celebration of, the electoral success of the Green Party in the 2019 elections.

---

4 Twitter statement, political talk show *Anne Will*.

5 In these social media statements, style, grammar, and punctuation were kept to convey a picture as close as possible to the original statements (albeit them originally having been in German).

Importantly, representatives of this climate culture embraced the idea that people should 'practice what they preach', signalling efforts to rebut eco-hypocrisy arguments. This coincided with moralist appeals to be consistent and authentic and to set a good example. Furthermore, some expressions were quite alarmist. At the same time (and in contrast to the collectivist elite culture), there was little evidence of members of this climate culture recognising the many real practical obstacles that prevented citizens from leading their everyday lives in a climate-friendly way (lived efficacy), which left individual responsibility unquestioned. Responding to Kevin Kühnert (SPD politician) addressing this issue in the *Anne Will* talk show, some members of this climate culture raised the 'system question' and related aspects of climate justice:

> **G.D.S.**: A politics relying on annual growth of 2 % is going to miss any climate targets in this world. A politics that enters into economic contracts with countries that will obviously be exploited through them does not deserve the name politics!
> **JohannE.Dressel**: Kevin is right. Placing capital above animal or human lives is Satanical
> **Unbequeme Wahrheit (gern geschehen)**: If we don't change radically, through our actions we will be the murderers of our children. this is a fact. no matter what any capital marionettes say, then this will be fact!

They nevertheless denounced the apparent inefficacy of the current government with regard to climate action.

Scientific experts were also well respected by members of this climate culture, and there was some significant overlap with the collectivist elite climate (sub-)cultures concerning responsibility attributions to different societal actors, including the media (even though opinions differed regarding the responsibility of the individual, as mentioned above).

5.3.2 Inaction climate culture(s)

By contrast, this second climate culture 'from below' was characterised by its (at times fierce) rejection of current public calls for more climate action. As reasons for this rejection ranged from experiences of inefficacy to outright climate change denial, statements have been assorted into three subcultures:

Subculture I: Sense of inefficacy

This first subculture rejected current calls for climate action due to a lack of trust in the effectiveness and consistency of 'official' climate action measures. So even though its members may to some extent have admitted that protecting the climate should be attempted, they either saw it as overrated or did not deem it realistic. Here, there was an abundance of arguments explaining why climate action was either utopic or not worth it.

Members of this subculture also remained largely unconvinced that society and individuals could afford wide-ranging climate action, pointing to the high cost of measures such as the promotion of electric vehicles or the purchasing of organic food.

Statements thus also exemplified the clear difference between 'official' attributions of responsibility and efficacy to the public and the way people actually experienced their role and options for decision-making.

> **Markus Quetsch @hartaberfair @SvenjaSchulze68**: "Even if citizens feel a duty for the environment, they often have no alternative to environmentally harmful behaviour in their everyday. They do not succeed in leaving their car for the distances they need to travel... or not flying for work" – ! (quotes SPIEGEL ONLINE article[6]: ecological assessment: "When it comes to environmental policy, Germany is a developing country")
> **Robert Schuchmann**: Lack of realism when it comes to alternatives: BMW towards disappointed test driver: we very much regret that in your case the reach (of the e-car) does not correspond to what has been tested by us. As you have noticed already, in this weather driving without heating is intolerable.

Debates also unfolded within this climate subculture concerning who in society should be held responsible for acting on climate change. Similar to representatives of the previous pro-action subculture, members of this subculture were angry that politicians did not remain true to their particular responsibility. This contrasts the sceptical and denialist subcultures, where the political responsibility itself was not recognised (as the existence of climate change itself was refuted, at least in part). Further issues discussed in this subculture included the limited efficacy of the individual in their private sphere and the inherently profound climate impact within the realm of work-life and industry that seemed of much higher significance. These thus caused further doubt vis-à-vis individual responsibility and the overall feasibility of meaningful climate action.

> **Kjell Leinte**: [...] Mothers in Stuttgart receive fines for driving a three-year-old Diesel but luckily there exists an [...] Audi e-Tron with gluten-free or vegan batteries. As long as locally we have ecologically daft double standards with self-

6 Ecological footprint: "Germany is a developing country when it comes to climate policy": Ökobilanz: "Bei der Umweltpolitik ist Deutschland Entwicklungsland" – SPIEGEL ONLINE – Wissenschaft: spiegel.de https://www.spiegel.de/wissenschaft/natur/umweltpolitik-was-deutschland-von-anderen-laendern-lernen-kann-a-1259518.html (accessed 16/09/2022).

> righteous delusion, there is no need to debate melting pole caps.
> **hart aber fair**: Dear Kjell Leinte! You are right with regards to double standards. Still, the approach to create awareness and wanting to change something in small and local contexts is not generally wrong
> **Kjell Leinte**: Of course. How much do we do in small contexts? I try to not buy anything wrapped in plastic. Do you know how hard that is? [...] I am just angry that humankind is just not earnest. [...] (today) we only consider ecologically secondary battlefields, to calm our conscience. Thus my comparison plastic bag – monster cars.

In addition to questioning the effectiveness of proposed climate action measures, members of this climate subculture also did not seem to believe that these measures can be reconciled with social fairness:

> **Stefan Krüger@Krüger**: This demand (that flying becomes more expensive) I find outrageous. There are enough people who can already hardly afford to look at something else than their workplace and/or their own four walls.
> If one was at least to say that frequent flying should become more expensive, that I would support!

This could also be seen through statements like *are rising incomes not the starting-signal for increasing consumption?* The efficacy of national-level climate action measures taken in Germany was also doubted, with climate change having been seen as a fundamentally global challenge (which stood in direct opposition to the above-mentioned statement by the YouTuber Rezo). Instead, they voiced that any successful domestic attempt would inevitably be cancelled out more or less immediately by the demands of rapidly industrialising economies (e.g., China, India) and global population growth.

Finally, many of those belonging to this group did not see how climate action could feasibly and practically be integrated into their everyday realities (= lived efficacy), even when they acknowledged that they had at least some responsibility to act.

Subculture II: Scepticism

There was, however, ample evidence of more radical objections to current calls for climate action across the data studied, yielding a second inaction subculture: its members tended to view climate change and related calls for action as no more than *scaremongering*, *hysteria* or a *ridiculous hype*.

Here, increased climate action was seen as unnecessary and excessive and the extent of the threat posed by climate change was not recognised and therefore played down. Thus, discourses regarding individuals' responsibility did not feature. However, there were regular references to morality and efficacy, for example when members talked about 'double standards'. There was also elaborate complaining as direct backlash against the currently growing climate movement in general and a critique of costly measures that to them occurred in areas of everyday life that they did not consider to be very important.

Politicians were generally deemed untrustworthy, most of all the Greens. In fact, statements revealed a deep-seated lack of trust in establishment institutions and their ability to act decisively on the alleged climate challenge (where it was recognised), as well as many other issues.

> **Martin Rücken**: We witness a new era of fascism – through environmental fascists.
> **Ma Drosch**: You're not serious?!!
> **Martin Rücken**: Yes, indeed. [...] and it has nothing to do with the warranted demand towards the population for responsible treatment of creation and nature. Environmental fascism is an ideology, that derives itself from a self-defined elitist expectation in the conviction to possess the only moral truth, that rests upon the opinion to be saving the world.

Politicians were also criticised for placing the burden of crisis management largely on the shoulders of the public.

Subculture III: Denial

Even more radical yet, in several social media threads the truth content of current climate science was questioned, complemented by more or less overt discourses of climate change denial:

> **Michael Rühl**: Without climate change, we would not exist. Whoever stands for something else must be not quite right in their head.
> **Jens Thölking @Michael Rühl**: Plants cannot live without water. Too much water and they die.
> **Michael Rühl @Jens Thölking**: And are we living in drought?

For example, in some cases, climate change was treated as a conspiracy, led by the rapidly growing climate movement.

> **Alfred Wechsler**: The population doesn't even realise how their freedom is being messed with. Don't give me this CO2 immisions stuff. The real beneficiaries sit in the IPCC. they make the whole world crazy with computer programmes that are scientifically supported by wrong data.

Like in the two previous inaction subcultures, establishment politicians and institutions (for example the IPCC) were largely deemed untrustworthy, albeit more harshly this time.

> **Dr. Heiko Kallweit**: Please make sure to invite enough 16year old wise-ass kids who from their major life experience give a proper chewing out. Here, there still exists a serious gap, as gender and migration have been treated sufficiently.

One rhetoric strategy repeatedly resorted to here was the use of quasi-religious insinuations as shown by the following social media debate:

> **David Ziegele**: There is sensible environmental protection and there is quasi-religious eco-extremism. Right now the latter tends to dominate. The climate-dschihadists must be stopped.
> **??**: You should reflect your blue-brown choice of words a bit. To call environmentalists dschihadists seems a little strange.
> **Chris Ruröde**: Right, but you don't see that only radical measures will work? You ignore that 23000 scientists from faculties support these people?
> **Max Fritze Neumann**: Millions of flies cannot be wrong.
> **David Ziegele**: and what is meant by "blue-brown"? Göring-Eckardt (leading green politician) calls Greta a "prophet". And many are not open for other arguments. This is an extremist political movement with religious traces
> **Kerstin Ralf Nier**: A new religion " the climate protectors "

This exchange once again exemplified the hatred that was expressed vis-à-vis 'those at the top', i.e., the political and scientific establishment and people in power in general. Overall, the data showed that the opposing attitudes regarding the role climate change should play in people's everyday lives collided with each other in new and interesting ways on such social media platforms.

5.4 Conclusion

Discursive variations that became visible through this in-depth analysis of media coverage of climate change topics around the 2019 European elections highlight the centrality of notions of responsibility and self-efficacy for understanding clashes between climate cultures. Here, a decoupling of responsibility and efficacy was clearly discernible across a number of climate cultures. For example, individual consumers were routinely blamed for not doing enough to protect the climate, including by climate activists, which placed the burden of responsibility on the shoulders of those who were least able to act. In contrast, powerful societal actors like politicians and business leaders were portrayed as limited in scope for climate action, despite their actual capacity to do so. This (perceived) inefficacy and irresponsibility of established actors was utilised by other political and civil society actors to challenge dominant scientific and 'official' climate cultures and to advance counter-arguments ranging from a radically green, pro-climate agenda to variants of climate change denial.

Climate cultures that have formed both within and outside elite circles also incorporated a broad range of emotive aspects that related very closely to notions of responsibility, efficacy and knowing. Elite discourses frequently emphasised the centrality of rationality and scientific knowledge in climate action. At the same time, they revealed beliefs of an inherent 'information deficit' among members of the public that targeted climate education could help to overcome. This emphasis on the cognitive dimensions of knowledge contrasted with climate debates 'from below' that were interspersed with references to everyday practices, emotional messages and embodied knowing.

Climate-related debates that occurred across different media formats were far from consensual and revealed variable voices that harboured the potential for serious societal conflict. Importantly, a significant gap existed between climate-related arguments and debates that members of elite climate cultures engaged in, and those that could be assigned to climate cultures 'from below'. Here, it was possible to identify culturally distinct notions of responsibility and self-efficacy and divergent ideas around what counted as acceptable knowledge. This shows that the ways in which people talked about climate change links more or less directly to cultural norms and conventions that contribute to the social regulation of everyday life, and that guide and shape people's engagement in climate-relevant practices across domains such as food and mobility. In some cases, there appeared to be a complete disconnect between those who debate climate change and climate action on mainstream media and those who use social media channels to express their views. Moreover, the nature and content of many elite contributions to the debate seemed to be of limited relevance to members of the public who commented on climate issues through social media channels, including those attached to mainstream media such as TV talk shows. These observable climate-cultural divergences have likely contributed to the slow progress in relation to climate change mitigation and adaptation, at least partially, a fact that remains under-appreciated in scientific and public debates on climate action. An explicit recognition of climate cultures that emerge 'from below', including those described in this chapter can help to overcome the persistent disengagement of large parts of the public from elite climate debates and cultures and related political and practical projects.

6 The seven focus group discussions

6.1 Introduction

As the last section has demonstrated, the increasingly pressing imperative for climate action resonates in different ways with differing segments of society. These variations reflect and at times shape various climate cultures. Here, the occupational context is one of the factors that play a decisive role in people's engagement with climate change. Thus, this chapter turns to the professional context, where profound climate-cultural diversity was again observed. Practitioners from various professional fields were group-interviewed regarding their opinions on climate action between July 2019 and March 2020. The content analytical exploration of the interview material yielded both similarities and differences between the groups regarding climate-related discourses and practices and connected climate-cultural orientations. Once more, particular focus was placed on the attribution of responsibility to different societal actors, related efficacy expectations as well as the role of different forms of (not) knowing/refusing to know.

6.2 I really don't care what comes out of the plane in terms of CO_2 – Craftsmen

The men in this group were of different ages. The group agreed in saying that climate action did hardly play a role in their lives (even though they thought that the environment should be protected). The reasons for this were quite varied, however: one person (that was comparatively dominant) had extensively prepared for the discussion in order to convincingly present his conviction that climate change was not caused by human influence. Another person did not perceive climate change as an issue, whilst the rest of the group was generally aware of the issue, but had not internalised it to the point where it would have been deemed necessary to adapt one's everyday practices because of it. There was no objection towards the lengthy statements of the climate sceptic. The group concurred that wasting of resources definitely needed to be avoided. The participants were generally very connected to nature and the countryside, whilst it was spoken dismissively about urbanites. This was also reflected in regionality being the only climate-related factor that played a role when making purchasing decisions. Overall, one was wary of rich people and mistrustful towards any kind of elite.

Table 5: Overview: The focus group of craftsmen

Group: Dimension	**Craftsmen**
Responsibility	Diffusion of responsibility + pronounced externalisation of responsibility for climate action (to politics, corporate agents, the media and science)
Efficacy	Low individual efficacy expectation, little trust in decision makers, overall, very sceptical towards 'the elite' and 'official discourses'
Knowing	Patchy knowledge of climate change (exception: where there was work-related overlap; yet IPCC-consensus not accepted by majority of the group), low problem awareness, clear preference for factual information (= information deficit thinking; aversion towards manipulation/'framing'), well-informed in own perception
Denial tendencies	Pronounced outright denial (e.g., conspiracy theories), imperative to protect the climate not internalised, if at all treated like a trivial offence

Lived responsibility

As members of a small firm, the respondents did not perceive themselves as responsible for climate action. Instead, they thought it was larger companies that needed to act, but deemed this improbable as they were generally profit-driven and corrupt. Here, the *Dieselgate* scandal was again mentioned. Large firms were perceived to get away with a lot that would immediately have consequences for smaller firms, especially due to lobbying. Although it was stated that the individual was responsible for climate action, in sum the responses did not indicate that the participants applied this to themselves (ergo it may have been said due the interview situation, social desirability). For example, one group member said:

> I like flying! [...] I really don't care what comes out of the plane in terms of CO_2.

This statement shows that in this group, behaviour that is harmful to the climate is generally not socially sanctioned. Besides, it was not deemed realistic that enough members of the population would contribute to climate action, as people were 'too lazy'. Moreover, politics was attested responsibility to protect the climate, the group however believed that this was currently not being practiced. The global nature and temporal complexity of the climate crisis were cited as reasons for political inaction:

> Why is Germany supposed to invest 15 billion in climate projects when this has no benefit for it whatsoever in the present?

Such diffusion of responsibility was quite pronounced in this group.

Everyday efficacy

The members of the group voiced that the individual could hardly make a difference and that this inefficacy was being exacerbated by the inconclusive knowledge and information the population was being supplied with.

The following exchange illustrates how one group member (**B3**) objects to the previous participant by employing the strategy of pointing to his own everyday practice instead of disagreeing outright (to avoid the discomfort of direct confrontation):

> **B4:** But there, the cucumber wrapped in foil is just as good as the cucumber without any plastic. If you eat that cucumber, then there is not really any difference between the two. They taste the same.
> **B1:** Let me put it like this: why would anyone as a single human being try anything to make things better, when at the end of the day it turns out, like for example with the cucumber, that it does not make any difference anyways? In fact, the cucumber that causes less CO_2 until it ends up in the supermarket is the one that is wrapped in plastic. And then there is one without plastic, but that one causes more CO_2 due to its transportation. That's where the mistake is.
> **B3:** I buy organic cucumbers from Bavaria.

The group was further annoyed that politics did not direct its focus where it would really make a difference as measures were often employed on secondary battlefields. The group also talked very critically (almost spitefully) about the actions of corporate agents:

> The problem is, there is a jour fixe for everything, congresses, conferences...

Hence, political- and corporate decision-makers were deemed inefficacious and there was hardly any trust in politics. It was taken particular issue with people who were seen as role models (footballers, politicians) oftentimes not meeting this expectation. Interestingly, at the same time, one could also sense a certain amount of respect for business people (take planes, because they have such little time, a frequent flyer status is justified and aspirational).

Embodied information practices

Overall, climate knowledge in this group was patchy and the scientific consensus on climate change had not been internalised. Where there was thematic overlap due to the nature of the respondents' work, one was more confident:

> We have to know about emissions, we are energy consultants.

The members of this group generally thought that they were well informed about climate issues, which was based on their closeness to nature (as opposed to people living in the city) and one's work. The educational system was not credited here.

One was also suspicious towards the media and science. One member called the reporting of public media channels *one giant infomercial for the Green Party*. Being asked where society's knowledge about climate change originated from, one group member said:

> Yes, because the 'Mr. scientists' simply discover this at some point and then bring it to the public. Someone claims it, somebody else doesn't believe it.

How climate change was dealt with was also strongly determined by experiences of the weather. On the one hand, a shift was recognised:

> We now have a situation like in South Tyrol.
> We don't have a real winter anymore.

On the other hand, this was not taken as a reason to change one's behaviour. The concept of thresholds and tipping points was simply rejected:

> **I:** But I wanted an answer to what was just said, that it is cumulative and irreversible?
> **B3:** I can't say, I have no idea. There was an ice age, and then again no ice age.

The knowledge concept this group employed was quite narrow. Although one group member recognised the role of emotional messages, this was perceived exclusively negatively (one did not want to be manipulated through framing). Beyond this, the group followed information deficit thinking. The wording *Mr. scientists* insinuates the resentment that exists towards the influence of the knowledge elite.

Disagreement featured in questions about consumption, which was dependent on problem recognition. One group member (who had referred to his family as 'connected to the countryside') reported that quality of produce and regionality played a role when shopping groceries whilst a (price sensitive) young father, who did not perceive climate change to be a problem, said:

> **B4:** Ok, but nowadays you can actually buy anything. Because today, you have such strict rules. Like at Lidl, Rewe, they have to...
> **B3:** Yeah, but when half a kilo (of meat) costs two Euros, then?
> **B4:** Yeah, you might as well buy packaged meat at Rewe, Lidl, Penny, that is just as good.

Extent of denial

This group exhibited marked denial of climate change. The issue did hardly play any role in its members' lives and therefore it was not deemed necessary to attribute responsibility to oneself or think about one's own efficacy. Instead, the responsibility was seen to lie with decision-makers in politics, corporations, media or science who were however not seen as trustworthy or competent. Since knowledge about climate change was so fragmented and serious recognition of the problem more or less non-existent, these assumptions on the low efficacy of those societal agents did not particularly bother the members of this group. There was a whole series of strategies employed for practicing this denial:

Denial strategies

One member of the group extensively endorsed conspiracy theories in relation to climate change, which the other group members did not object to. The rest of the group treated climate action as if it were a rather trivial offence. Humour and sarcasm were used to deflect from not-knowing and to save face:

> Ok, so if we save the world only with a non-plastic straw, then I like it, then I won't use plastic straws anymore (laughs).

Climate activists were smirked at. Accusing decision-makers and influential figures of hypocrisy and the spread of conflicting knowledge also served to reinforce denial. Overall, the members of the group were very sceptical towards elites and 'official' discourses. Calls to climate action were also questioned on the grounds of social fairness:

> Save the bees? Yeah, but who signed this petition? Those who can afford it. Look at Grünwald [affluent Munich borough], how did they vote? (Laughs). We vote green, because we can afford it. That should make us think... Because somebody from Grünwald does not care whether the honey costs three or twenty euros. But those

who live in Aschaffenburg or back somewhere else, who have nothing to get by, do care in fact.

Lastly, it was collectively deflected away from the climate crisis due to its globality, the temporally distant effect of its consequences as well as the higher priority of other societal challenges.

6.3 We only worry about climate change because we are well off – Green startup

This group was particularly homogenous. All respondents had extensively thought about climate change, including its moral aspects. The fact that they worked for a carbon conscious company alone showed that climate action played an important role in their lives. The imperative to protect the climate had been internalised as a task for the whole of society. The members of this group were well informed and aware of the complexity of the debate. Disagreement featured only rarely and if so, in relation to details. Regarding the responsibility of the individual, the members of this group expressed to be in a kind of elite dilemma when climate action came into conflict with other (identity providing) motives. Accordingly, flying was ultimately deemed an (almost untouchable) personal decision by nearly all group members, in connection to which a series of justification strategies were employed (CO_2-compensation, short trips even worse etc.).

Table 6: Overview: The green startup focus group

Group: Dimension	**Green startup**
Responsibility	Strong emphasis of own individual responsibility, little externalisation
Efficacy	Focus on consumption; recognition of relational efficacy, individual efficacy unresolved High efficacy ascribed to corporations, yet overall little trust in conventional companies High efficacy ascribed to politics, yet attested inadequate implementation
Knowledge	Very well informed (due to occupational centrality of the topic), quite broad knowledge concept, climate change perceived as ›elite project‹; Ubiquitous justification of the knowledge-action gap, pronounced ›bubble thinking‹ (but this reflected by the group)
Denial tendencies	Partial denial as own climate impact quite large, e.g., due to continuation of flying

Lived Responsibility

The members of this group did see themselves responsible as employees of a green startup. Besides, this group believed that as an individual one was responsible for informing oneself sufficiently about the climate impact of one's own behaviour, since *ignorance did not protect one from stupidity*. There was however recognition of the differences in access to alternative behaviour, which was ultimately cited as a reason not to ascribe too much responsibility to the individual end consumer.

Politics was attested the responsibility to regulate the corporate sector, since corporations were exposed to profit pressures and global competition, which caused them to simply load off responsibility onto the consumer. Still, the group members believed that at the end of the day, companies were also responsible for climate action as it was them who determined the supply of (climate-friendly) options. Consequently, the behaviour of conventional companies was deeply condemned by the group:

> I find it completely perverse that H&M spits out a new collection on a weekly basis!

One further aspect that added complexity was seen in the diffusion of responsibility: the group stated that the threat posed by climate change was denied in ways that were reminiscent of denying the dangers of smoking. However, with smoking, the consequences only hit the originator themself, whilst the damage done by climate change accrued to responsible and irresponsible people alike:

> It is a bit like in a shared apartment (WG), you have to still feel responsible somehow for what is happening...

Accusations of hypocrisy caused intense annoyance. One person said that when speaking of her climate-friendly diet, she had repeatedly been confronted with the question of whether she still flew, which made her angry. Thus, she argued that it was not really reasonable to ascribe so much responsibility to the individual, especially since she and the other members of this group were already trying to adapt their behaviour because of climate change. From this emerged that for this group the question of individual responsibility in relation to air travel embodied a particularly emotionally charged aspect. For them it was exceptionally difficult to arrive at answers for themselves on how to handle the topic of flying in the future as they deeply disliked these feelings of cognitive dissonance. There was much talk of feeling guilty or bad when flying and the group members were definitely aware of the negative consequences for the climate. Still, the group managed to suppress these feelings and continue to fly (most group members admitted that they had already flown in the running year). It was also stated that in certain circles one did not dare to admit any more that one had taken a plane. Here it was stressed that rationally, one understood that it was bad for the climate, but one was still surprised that there was so much social sanctioning nowadays. Therefore, the group concluded that ultimately flying was everyone's own and very personal decision. Here, the members of the group went to great lengths to justify the continuation of flying:

> Of course, we can talk about climate change in relation to flying, but we can also talk about how it has brought us all closer together (collective agreement). And as you said, we know so much more about the world since we have had this level of connection. And it used to be a major hassle to be able to travel to the US and now you can easily go there for vacation and then you come back with amazing experiences.

A lot of responsibility was also ascribed to the media and the scientific community in terms of knowledge transmission. Here, there was explicit mentioning of the responsibility of science communication.

Everyday efficacy

In terms of individual efficacy, there were different opinions: one group member said that as an individual, you cannot save the world but in the collective, there was much that could be achieved.

Accordingly, the group mentioned a certain relational efficacy of the individual: through behaving responsibly, one could inspire others and be a role model. Then they wondered how other groups in society could be made aware of their climate impact. This was however deemed a tricky question since raising awareness was seen as important but at the same time, one did not want to talk down from a moral high ground. Navigating this was seen as deeply difficult.

One other group member disagreed with the statements made so far and stressed that flying as a practice had by far the largest impact on the climate and as an individual one should be aware of that (high individual responsibility). He however also pointed towards politics having to regulate through pricing.

Accordingly, at first, politicians were deemed efficacious as they had a lot of influence and room for manoeuvre, which in the eyes of the group was however not done justice to. This led to disillusion and anger.

The group disagreed on the role of corporations when it came to climate action. Although they were deemed efficacious (*companies' carbon footprints are much larger than those of individuals*), there was much mistrust regarding the authenticity of climate efforts of (other, conventional) companies, which were for example deemed to be no more than *greenwashing* as one group member voiced. Someone else said, however, that the messages of large companies did have a considerable impact. Then other factors were mentioned that further complicated the challenge of climate change, such as its global nature that caused climate harmful consequences to often simply be relocated to other countries.

The media and the scientific community were both deemed largely inefficacious by this group. Even though the role of the media was seen as important, there was not much trust in it (lack of independence), which resulted in the educational system being responsible for teaching media competency. This was exacerbated by the fact that media was consumed selectively according to one's own convictions, which further reduced true efficacy. The fact that scientific insights hardly ever reached the population was also deemed problematic. For example, the IPCC-consensus had not really been internalised by the population before it had reached public awareness through *Fridays for Future*:

> I think that there has been a lot of misinformation. In the sense of: well, it's not actually that bad. Whenever someone fears that the truth is becoming more established, then they simply send out an 'alternative truth'. Or a perceived truth. And if that is powerful enough, then it already suffices that the issue seems 'unclear' and 'not entirely certain' and then I can lean back on the basis that it is not totally certain.

Further, this group believed that prominent people could make a considerable difference for climate action. *Fridays for Future* and Greta Thunberg were also accredited with considerable influence, especially because they reached people on an emotional level and were *not as anonymous as politicians in suits*.

Embodied information practices

Initially, it was criticised that the current climate-related information landscape was too incomprehensible – there were, for example, too many different labels for organic food. The group believed that knowledge about climate change existed in society, in everyday life this was however often not put into practice. For example, people were aware of the climate impact of mass meat production, yet daily decisions were not being failed accordingly. It was further pointed to the role one's cultural surroundings played:

> In terms of flying, I find it really telling, because until I started my internship here, I was not very aware of the consequences. At university, I studied International Business, and in my course it was all about who travels the most. That was a completely different mind-set and here, it is entirely different, again.

The media was seen as *the number one source of information*. Although *Fridays for Future* was credited with being very efficacious, the group still questioned whether the students were actually informed sufficiently and whether they put this knowledge into practice consistently. Here, it was speculated that there actually were a lot of followers present in the movement. One group member concluded that then, at least, these would be *followers into the right direction*. At times, there surfaced a quite simplistic, linear, and somewhat naïve understanding of knowledge. The group for example took issue with there not being a climate scientist present in the newly established climate cabinet of the government, as then, *politics would just have to put such insights into practice*:

> Of course, we also need people who screen the whole issue in such a way that it becomes measurable, because at the end of the day, numbers are the only truth that we have.

The group repeatedly employed such information deficit logics, yet they were refuted by other group members in most instances. The respondents also voiced that scientific insights did not really reach their daily lives as scientists mainly communicated with their colleagues within their own discipline:

> Now everyone in the ivory tower please read this pamphlet!

The public was not being included in this communication. Here, emotional messages were deemed much more efficacious. Overall, this group had a quite broad knowledge concept that went far beyond the provision of only factual and cognitive knowing. Emotional messages were unequivocally deemed more relevant to people's everyday lives and thus certainly more efficacious:

> Human beings are emotional beings. People don't think about facts and it is facts that science brings, one degree, two degrees, but what does that mean?

Lastly, the group stressed the role of like-minded and relatable others in instigating climate action.

Extent of denial

For this group it was very important to take climate action seriously and take responsibility for it, be it in the professional or private sphere. There was much reflection and conversation about it. In many ways, behaviour was aligned with the motive of climate action. However, and maybe surprisingly, there was still considerable denial in this group. Although one was well aware of the consequences of different consumption decisions and accepted the moral obligation to protect the climate, in some ways these aspects were often overshadowed by other motives:

> Every day we have to think so much about what alternatives there may be as all things that are fun are bad for the environment...

Denial strategies

One denial strategy employed by this group was the portrayal of worrying about climate action as being a 'luxury'. This made it seem rather unnatural instead of urgent:

> **B4:** Simply because we are well off, we worry about this.
> **B6:** I also think that it is a luxury to a certain degree that we get to worry about it and that it is a trend [...]. I have just recently spoken to somebody from India who campaigns for climate action, and he said that there this doesn't reach people, since they have completely different issues they have to concern themselves with. [...]

The most prominently applied denial strategy by this group consisted in the emphasis of individual freedom and the aversion against 'pointing one's finger' and accusing another of behaving hypocritically. At the end of the day, the majority of the group concluded that consumption decisions were everyone's personal choice. Flying (in contrast to e.g., driving an SUV within the city) was classified as a necessity without alternatives. This shows that there is a deeply rooted concept of autonomy and freedom of choice of the individual present in this group, even though one deeply cared about the climate.

> I also travelled the world for a year and took thirty different flights. I am not proud of these flights, but I also do not want to miss having seen the world.

This exemplifies that here, the culture was one of well-educated young professionals that struggled to reconcile their past cultural experience that honoured individuality, progress, globalisation and freedom with a growing imperative to protect the climate as this collides with much that the group had been taking for granted in their lives so far.

6.4 There is no [basic human] right to travel by plane – NGO

Like the green startup, this group was also very connected to the topic of climate change, both privately and professionally. One was again deeply familiar with the complexity of the issue. The employment of several technical terms and concepts showed that there had been deep engagement with climate action, which was further intensified through the occupational centrality of the topic. It was treated very much as a moral issue (*CO_2-compensation is like indulgence trade*). The level of reflection displayed in this group was so pronounced that its members were even aware of the ubiquitous tendency to deny (which can be seen as the opposite of the denial practiced in the other groups), which shows that there was hardly any denial in this group. Only the continued emphasis of information deficits can be seen as some indication.

Table 7: Overview: The NGO focus group

Group: Dimension	**NGO**
Responsibility	Very nuanced notion of responsibility, own responsibility perceived considerable, political responsibility stressed (vis-a-vis individual responsibility that was thought to foster diffusion); thus group tended towards regulation
Efficacy	Companies attested much efficacy (small businesses did more to protect the climate) but failed to adequately employ it for climate matters Individual only deemed efficacious in relational terms Highest influence thought to lie with politics, had to regulate corporate actors where they did not meet their responsibility Celebrities also deemed highly influential, yet group weary of the media
Knowledge	Very well informed (due to occupational centrality of the issue) At times emphasis on factual knowledge, at times focus on practical relevance in the everyday, increasingly encompassing notion of knowledge (incl. emotional messages)
Denial tendencies	Little denial, much reflection

Responsibility

The self-perception presented by the members of this group was interesting, since they attributed a lot of responsibility for climate action to themselves as employees of an NGO that held the advancement of climate action as one of its core aims. One participant asked: *If WE don't consume responsibly, who else is going to?* This shows how important climate action is for the members of this group. Flying was seen as a deeply moral issue:

> **B2:** There is no right to travel by plane.
> [...]
> **B6:** I have stopped engaging when friends are speaking about where they went by plane. Because I could not stand it anymore when everyone goes: wow, cool! And I'm thinking, no, that's just not okay...

Or elsewhere:

> **B2:** I find it extremely ironic that precisely those people raise the argument of social fairness when it comes to taxing flights, [...] who perceive it as their exclusive right [...] and then at the same time they defend those who do not have this right that they should continue to be able to book charter flights. [...] that's also the case with consumption. Yes, we want to feel happy. But there are other ways to feel happy than through consumption and flying.

At the same time, one was deeply aware of one's own bubble and the fact that not all of society felt that way. Where there was attribution of personal responsibility for climate action in society, this was also often denied, this group believed. One member made an analogy to how kitchen duty unfolded within the NGO: as it was often unclear who was actually responsible and the responsibility rested upon so many shoulders, it was very easy to escape one's responsibility. This denying of responsibility sometimes even occurred deliberately, when people had other things to do or simply did not feel like cleaning the kitchen. This, in this respondent's eyes, could also be applied to the diffusion of responsibility that occurred in relation to climate action within society. Therefore, like the green startup, this group noticed that focusing on individual responsibility often resulted in such responsibility diffusion.

Hence, overall, the group had a quite nuanced concept of responsibility that did not only include the role of the individual as consumer but also responsibility in terms of political participation. One group member criticised that these two dimensions were still mainly being treated separately. Therefore, a different form of campaigning for elections was demanded that actually took into consideration the everyday realities of the population by pointing towards how the individual could actually meaningfully contribute to climate action in order to counter feelings of inadequate self-efficacy.

However, this group did not display as much aversion against 'pointing-the-finger' as the green startup did – here, some members were even in favour of responsibilising others. This group had internalised the imperative to protect the climate to the point of it serving as means for self-identification. One saw oneself responsible as an individual (on moral grounds), as employee of a climate NGO and also as voter. However, politics was also seen as responsible to implement the mandate given by voters and enforce regulations and prices to advance climate action. The group was convinced that voluntary action would not suffice as corporations who were also responsible for climate action did not meet this expectation. Further responsible agents were believed to be the media and the educational system. Public figures (like the YouTuber Rezo) also had a special responsibility in their function as role models:

> Icons should represent this new (climate-friendly) lifestyle [...] so that in movies [...] the hero is not the Porsche driver any more...

Lastly, the scientific community was seen as responsible for effectively communicating their insights to the public.

Everyday efficacy

This group saw one strength of their role as NGO to lie in the communication of climate change, thus they considered a potential future cooperation between scientific bodies and themselves to be a particularly fruitful avenue to advance climate action. For their NGO, they thought it was more helpful to point towards attractive and manageable alternatives to climate-harmful behaviour instead of arguing for prohibitions and regulations. However, most efficacy was ascribed to the political sphere, that was however still lacking clear direction:

> People don't believe in politics making a difference. What was meant to be a climate package was instead referred to as 'small parcel' by the press, which shows a certain amount of cynicism. Everybody knows this is not enough. And somehow, one just takes it as such.

Here for example, it was pointed to the kind of denial that subconsciously occured amongst the population. Social fairness was further seen as a political hurdle and reason for political inaction (referral to the *yellow vests protests* in France). Different politicians had a different standing in the group. The overall efficacy of politicians was however further reduced by the short-term nature of political processes, the group concluded. Politics was also thought to have failed in regulating corporations, which was seen as urgently necessary since the latter were not meeting their considerable amount of responsibility (that their efficacy afforded them). The group also thought that in theory, corporations had considerable potential to make a difference for climate action.

It was then pointed out that currently, social and environmental costs did not feature in economic considerations. If these were actually considered, it would become obvious that less consumption and extended product lifecycles would considerably advance climate action. Small firms were thought to do more for the climate than larger ones.

In terms of individual efficacy, the group was divided. In some instances, it was voiced that the individual did indeed have an influence, provided they were sufficiently informed about the consequences of their actions (information deficit thinking). On the other hand, the group also thought that people were often demoralised by their own lack of self-efficacy, which frequently resulted in the diffusion of responsibility. Therefore, the individual's relational efficacy was deemed more important as the group believed that feelings of belonging and one's social circle incorporated key roles for climate-relevant action. This group did not display such a clear aversion against 'pointing-the-finger' as the group of the green startup. Instead, this strategy was partially even endorsed. Thus, individual efficacy was here mainly conceived of in its relational form in terms of one's influence on others. Besides, as a single citizen, one could only achieve very little, which was thought to be further exacerbated through inconclusive information about how to best contribute to climate action. The moral imperative to adapt one's behaviour to climate change was however still unequivocally endorsed. The group believed that CO_2-compensation was not only morally objectionable but also inefficacious as the prices were thought to be far too low to really make a difference.

The *Fridays for Future* movement was believed to have significantly advanced climate action, as was the YouTuber Rezo. Celebrities were thought to have a lot of influence overall. Towards the media, the group was however rather sceptical.

Embodied information practices

This group was very well informed about climate change. Its notion of knowledge was however not uniform. At times, information deficit logics were endorsed:

> **B3:** To a large extent we don't only have a responsibility problem, we also actually have an information problem (overall agreement)…

On the other hand, the efficacy of information about the climate impact of everyday practices was questioned:

> I think, this is so far removed from the everyday reality of some people […]. I think people must be addressed directly in this respect. I don't know whether numbers on the packaging will make such a difference…

That knowledge also operates in less palpable forms had been internalised:

> At some point a critical mass became aware that smoking is harmful. Then, these things kind of rumble in public knowledge...

Thus, it was also stressed that factual knowledge by itself did not mobilise people and thus some connection to people's everyday realities had to be established. In the course of the interview, an increasingly wholesome notion of knowing developed, that also rested upon the role of emotional messages and cultural aspects:

> I think this is a really good example for information not being able to change everything. We all know how bad flying is and we still do it (as a society).

Extent of denial

At times this group employed information deficit thinking by demanding more information about the consequences of certain individual behaviour for the climate. However, as discussed, such apocalyptic rhetoric had in fact not resulted in more effective climate action (refer to chapter 2). As has been discussed, instead this often leads to resignation and denial as a kind of self-protection mechanism instead, which keeps people from experiencing negative emotions (cf. Norgaard, 2011). For example, one group member recounted a situation, where the NGO had held a workshop with children about climate-friendly nutrition that resulted in the children making fun of ingredients being wrapped in plastic. The group believed this ridiculing (humour as denial strategy) was an overreaction by the children to avoid having to feel the fear that would otherwise have resulted from the prior information input about the potential catastrophic consequences of climate change, especially for *their* lives. With respect to flying the group had also already noticed a certain tendency towards denial as some people were deluding themselves by habitually taking considerable effort for climate action in their everyday lives and then cancelling out all of this achievement by still taking some vacation flights.

Denial strategies

This group did not deny climate change, instead it had internalised the issue to the point where it served as means for self-identification. One group member even noticed in himself that he sometimes manipulated pieces of information so that they could more easily be denied:

> **B6:** ... every time I read about [...] the catastrophe, I think, I also still have so many blind spots. But I don't do anything about them. [...]
> **I:** Why not?
> **B6:** I don't know. Because I'm too lazy. [...] I am informed about the bigger picture.

> But then again, I wonder, what was the deal with upcycling? My jeans are ripped.
> **B4:** Where do you go?
> [...]
> **B2:** But that's precisely the aspect where politics has to do something. Because if the path of least resistance were the most environmentally friendly, then you'd take this laziest and at the same time most environmentally friendly [one].

Thus, this group displayed such a deep level of reflection that it was already making a conscious effort to become aware of these pitfalls in order to avoid such denial. Only the overemphasis of information deficits pointed towards some form of denial.

6.5 Climate just exists and cannot be changed – Farmers

Table 8: Overview: The focus group of farmers

Group: Dimension	**Farmers**
Responsibility	Diffusion of responsibility + pronounced externalisation (politics, corporations, media, science); trust in the steering ability of the market (e.g., price mechanism)
Efficacy	Little individual efficacy expectation, little trust in decision-makers, masking of the substantial influence of own interest group in Germany and the EU
Knowledge	Patchy climate knowledge, comparatively large extent of trivialisation or denial, emphasis on practical everyday competences + knowledge about nature. References to urban-rural gap with respect to knowing; training of young farmers criticised for being productivist and thus 'climate blind' vs. relativising of said training by focusing on positive developments;
Denial tendencies	Pronounced denial + blaming of other actors outside farming; much frustration that own professional group was being held responsible for climate change

The members of this group leant towards tradition and conservatism. The group unequivocally believed that the topic of climate action featured much too prominently in public debates and that the extent to which young people were responsibilising the public was hypocritical and overstated. Consequently, climate action was somewhat ridiculed rather than taken seriously. One participant had extensively prepared herself and presented a comprehensive conspiracy theory that was however largely passed over by the rest of the group. Overall, one was very critical of different elites (politicians, consultants, corporate figures as well as representatives of the *Fridays for Future* movement). One was also very suspicious of the media, especially because they were perceived to practice substantially exaggerated discourses of catastrophe in relation to climate change and because they were seen to habitually ascribe responsibility to the guild of farmers.

Responsibility

Even though it was initially stated that responsibility for climate action lay with the whole of society, in the course of the discussion it was however mainly attributed to societal elites (in those instances where it was deemed at all necessary to attribute it).

The group particularly emphasised that politicians had to lead with a good example instead of behaving hypocritically. In relation to this, it was criticised that political agents were still not taxing kerosene as this would certainly lead to less flying. It was then added that part of the problem was that the Bavarian state was an investor of Munich airport, which gave it the incentive to protect its business and jobs. The group was generally very sceptical towards political executives as they were thought to be governed by corporate interests and short-term election cycles. Experts and consultants that worked for the political sphere were also attested partial responsibility.

Consumers were deemed responsible for coming up with the right kind of demand. Overall, they were however thought to be uninformed, self-interested and irresponsible. Therefore, retail was attested responsibility for reconsidering its product range. Here, in the eyes of the participants, regional produce should play a much larger role, whilst organic farming was not deemed particularly important. It was then taken issue with consumers reportedly being oblivious to what grew in the region and in which season, which the group then ridiculed at length. This attested lack of knowledge was however only partially the consumers' fault as the group thought that they were also repeatedly mislead by (other) producers.

The following dilemma illustrates the group's struggle in straightforwardly attributing responsibility for climate action: the consumer was perceived to simply be reacting to supply and the producer was exposed to competition. Politics were also seen partially responsible for regulating retail as it was the whole system that was problematic because consumers had become so used to being offered so much of everything at extremely low prices.

Such low prices could however not be offered by the farmers in the region. Therefore, corporate agents (retailers) were deemed responsible for pointing out more clearly what was being produced in the region. Overall corporate agents were ascribed considerable responsibility for climate action, but the group was sceptical of them meeting this, especially when it came to large firms.

The group was also very critical towards the media, as they were thought to firstly endorse fatalistic and apocalyptic messages in relation to climate change and secondly holding farmers responsible for considerably contributing to climate change:

> Today people don't get this anymore. They believe every story and take it at face value and say, yes, the world is going to end and every farmer is off their head...

The scientific community was considered responsible for presenting the facts that would allow a clearer definition of the issue of climate change. Besides, researchers should finally come up with some technical solutions.

The group then vehemently complained that climate change was being debated much too emotionally, which to a large extent was thought to be due to the momentary momentum of the *Fridays for Future* movement. Here, it was stressed that going to school was actually compulsory. The protestors were then said to be only voicing demands whilst not presenting any concrete or constructive ideas.

> **B6:** [...] first of all, 'climate change', alone the word... Climate just exists and cannot be changed in that sense, you can only treat the resources that you have in a mindful way. And this I don't do by going somewhere to protest. [...] I then also have to change my own life. And then it doesn't make any difference if I have a vegetarian. Or if I subsist on nothing or something like that. Because humans themselves also emit CO_2. Are we supposed to lock them away as well?

In line with this, the group firmly refuted its own responsibility as the current 'green hype' was thought to firstly be ridiculously overrated and secondly, if at all, elites were the ones responsible.

Everyday efficacy

Initially, it was voiced that the individual could make a difference but since the issue was overall believed to be substantially exaggerated and responsibility was not attributed to the group of farmers themselves, in the course of the interview, it ceased to play a role if the individual could make a difference. Moreover, consumers were described as uninformed and lazy which also pointed to them having been perceived as inefficacious. Instead, people who were seen as role models were deemed influential. The group harboured a particularly negative attitude towards the *Fridays for Future* movement that was at the centre of public attention at the time of the interview, which also came with a profound questioning of its true efficacy as the farmers deeply judged the student protestors on the grounds of alleged hypocrisy.

One was further angry about the negative reputation and lack of regard for farming in general in relation to climate change since its contribution to emissions were in fact much smaller than generally perceived. Also, much more CO_2 was actually coming from elsewhere (diffusion of responsibility):

> **B6:** [...] this hype that this group is getting right now, I don't get it. They are being invited to see the Pope and I don't know what. For me that's something anyways, how politics is paying court to all these young people...

One was also annoyed that for instance the consequences of flying for the climate were not adequately publicly addressed as that industry could afford pervasive lobbying as opposed to one's own. Once again, politics was advantaging the elite and the group questioned why business managers needed to fly when they could simply be using video calls instead.

Further critique was addressed at the unquestioned growth imperative and increasing inequality within society. A consequent pricing strategy for climate action was believed to have the potential to make a difference:

> So I think nowadays it is not a question of transmitting knowledge any more. You can generally only educate people through their wallets [...] because they only buy what is cheapest, thus what is bad has to become more expensive [...] and then you don't have to explain stuff anymore...

Politics could influence educational institutions so that for example more climate-friendly farming was taught as part of professional training. Again, this did not point towards the farmers themselves being able to make a difference. Hence, they were also not considered responsible. At the same time, politicians' integrity was severely doubted (here in relation to the climate cabinet):

> **B6:** These are only people who want to shine a positive light onto themselves. Who want to be re-elected next year.
> **B7:** When I don't know what to do any more, I build a working group (laughing). That's how it is. It is just cosmetics.

Overall, politicians were deeply disliked since they were perceived as inconsistent and short-sighted. Besides, the behaviour of corporate agents was received as particularly harmful to the climate. Larger corporations were seen as behaving particularly irresponsibly, which was partially ascribed to the shareholder system. Above all, the group was dismissive of large firms that came to its region as this was argued to also have negative impacts on the climate (reference to area sealing). Thus, this should be politically prevented but instead politicians were vying for big companies to come to the area. One also questioned the efficacy of the media as they were only interested in gaining clicks and attention and also their reporting was deeply one-sided, sensational and apocalyptic:

> **B3:** ... We just have this one-sided reporting of the media. That's simply only one-sided. [...]
> **I:** Ok, so one-sided on which side? Which kind of knowledge do we have too much of and which-, we don't have enough everyday competency (you said)? And we have too much of what? We are inundated by-?
> **B?:** Advertising!
> **B3:** Catastrophes!
> **B?:** Advertising.
> **B3:** Catastrophes. Advertising.

Ultimately, this group doubted that much could be done about climate change at all since firstly, the challenge would have to be approached globally which was seen as outstandingly complicated. Secondly, it was thought to already be too late to mitigate climate change.

Embodied information practices

The concept of knowing was complex in this group. At one point the multidimensionality of the climate debate was recognised with it being a global challenge that several actors were responsible for. It was also acknowledged that the issue already lay in the definition of the problem. On the other hand, climate change was being outright denied in this group:

> So, climate action for me is a word, a word that doesn't actually really exist, because climate is actually everything around us, the atmosphere that comes in from outside, which cannot, I think, be protected.

The rest of the group thought that the imperative to act on climate change was at least severely overrated and there was already enough effort made for climate action. The climate movement was ridiculed and emotions were thought to be stirred by politics and the media who were over-reporting on the issue 'twenty-four-seven' although in Germany there were enough other issues that should gain political attention. Politics was instead practicing mere actionism with the only objective of gaining more votes.

> **B?:** So again we cause fear-. So through fear, we fuel something. Maybe it isn't as bad at all as it is being presented. I'm sure, when the studies-, it is not as bad as it is being pushed.

Such evoking of negative emotions, it was believed, also led to the occupational group of farmers being presented in a bad light.

> I generally always find it difficult to talk about climate action when you don't even have the criteria that you want to look at. What is the climate? What plays into that? What do I even have to protect? That, as I think, is still a very unanswered question in the whole discussion. And it is being discussed very emotionally, at the moment [...] only a certain section is being looked at in each instance. And this is being encapsulated from any, let's say, intercorrelations with other things. And I am finding it very concerning, when you are only looking at it like through a crystal ball, like right now with farming. As producer. As one point that plays into the whole debate.

Overall, one identified particularly strongly with one's own occupation and thus felt treated unfairly by decision makers in this respect. The group was very tightly knit, fixated on its own situation and perceived itself as rather separate from the rest of society. A picture was painted of us (the farmers) against those at the top (the elite) that were transporting inconclusive information about the issue (misinformation, conflicting information or e.g., lack of information about e-mobility and batteries). For this, discourses based on accusations of hypocrisy, distance to nature and a lack of everyday competency were employed, which rendered the climate debate *not an honest and truthful discussion*. In line with this, elite groups were made fun of due to their perceived distance to nature and it was agreed that their theoretical knowledge was often far removed from people's lives, useless and quixotic whilst the farmers themselves acted responsibly and actually preserved resources.

Consequently, the group unequivocally and vehemently demanded the transmission of 'everyday competency', that young people today were allegedly neither taught by their parents nor by educational institutions. By contrast, the group perceived itself as well informed and very practically competent due the focus of one's occupation and one's closeness to nature.

Due to its members disliking the emotional intensity with which the topic of climate change was being debated, the group believed more factual information was needed:

> **(?B4):** Because if you look, these talks of CO_2, that is thought to harm the climate. (then follows a discussion about air composition)
> **B7:** And only this aspect is being looked at. This cause.
> **(?B4):** Yes, indeed.
> **B7:** The CO_2 emissions
> **B2:** And the information is being debated very controversially. There is this camp and that camp. How am I as layperson supposed to trust that this really is the prob-

lem now. So I am convinced, even if we practice 100 percent climate action, this will also not change the climate.

Extent of denial

In this group there existed several strands of collective denial with the most obvious being the unequivocal relativisation of climate change that generally culminated in climate scepticism and at times even outright climate change denial, most notably through the endorsement of a climate-related conspiracy theory that was either accepted and then built upon or ignored by the rest of the group. Even the participant who had reported that he himself practiced organic farming did not elucidate to climate action playing an important role in his professional everyday life.

Denial strategies

Particularly telling was also that the issue of climate change was collectively taken very personally by the group, one almost saw it as direct affront towards one's own occupation. At this point, generational and class conflicts played into what was being said (resentment towards elites) which resulted in further hardening of the fronts.

B6: Recently there was this study, how many farmers travel by plane in comparison to, let's say, some office worker or something. There was this comparison, ...
B?: They have better lobbying. You never hear anything against air traffic.

6.6 I don't think flying per se is as bad as it is always made out to be – Mobility provider

This group was quite heterogeneous in terms of age (mid-twenties – late forties) and sex but its members had a similar educational level. Like the farmers, here the group members also collectively identified very strongly with their occupation. Climate change again (like with green startup and NGO) played a central role in their everyday working life, but in direct contrast to for example the group of the NGO, the moral aspect of the issue had not been internalised. Instead, personal freedom and the right to decide for oneself were underlined, which was reminiscent of statements made by those working for the green startup. Overall, one grappled intensely with the externally perceived contradiction between the particularly high emissions of the mobility sector on the one hand and the nature of the work of the sustainability department this group belonged to on the other. There was a lot of annoyance amongst the group members since they themselves had been accused of hypocrisy on numerous occasions.

Table 9: Overview: The focus group of the mobility provider (sustainability division)

Group: Dimension	**Mobility provider (sustainability division)**
Responsibility	Relatively complex notion of responsibility, however at times strong rejection of individual responsibility; responsibility recognised in all spheres of life (work, private consumption); mobility perceived as achievement – society had responsibility to conserve it (incl. flying); Corporations were already behaving responsibly, thus no need for further political intervention
Efficacy	Both individuals and corporations perceived as efficacious when they voluntarily strive to protect the climate Politics also efficacious but should largely keep out and instead focus on solving the perceived conflict of 'jobs versus the climate' Besides, there was already a lot of effort invested to protect the climate, for example by corporate initiatives; here deep trust in technological solutions and innovation
Knowing	Extensive and in some ways sector specific knowledge; explicit rejection of 'alarmist' and emotional climate messages and strong preference for factual and rational knowledge
Denial tendecies	Denial pronounced, e.g., through the narrative of *a lot is already being done for the climate* Particular frustration about the frequent attribution of responsibility towards own industry

Responsibility

Widespread diffusion of responsibility amongst societal actors was what first came to mind in this group discussion when prompted about the responsibility for climate action. The group thought this was mainly due to laziness. Common sense should however result in the individual taking responsibility for oneself and one's direct surroundings instead. The following statement also indicated that the group had deeply reflected upon the notion of responsibility:

> **G3w**: I believe, and it sounds so lapidary, but every individual is responsible and that is the case in every role one has at each moment; so I am responsible here as someone from sustainability management, but I am just as responsible if I work in engineering or IT. And this also doesn't stop when I leave work, I go home and there

> I also continue to carry responsibility. For me, climate change is actually too serious that the responsibility can be pushed into just one corner, I think this should be much more comprehensive, across all parties and all people (agreement).

It was easy for the members of this group to talk about responsibility for climate action in relation to mobility as it was obvious that this question had been playing a central role in their work. Initially, the individual was attributed considerable responsibility to reconsider mobility decisions due to climate change. When asked how the group itself approached flying, it was admitted that it was much appreciated by the members of this group and that one saw it as a technological attainment that one was not prepared to forego.

This was justified by seeking information on carbon offset options, which were however not used due to their alleged lack of transparency. Alternative mobility practices were in both cases, privately and professionally, deemed too time-consuming to be a viable alternative to flying. Here it was added that the employer had started to offset flying for work related reasons.

It was then reasoned that climate action had to be considered together with other matters and not everyone could afford to pay extra for climate action. One group member voiced that to her it seemed that in relation to mobility there was already a lot being done for climate action, also besides compensation, and those who could afford it were already *living their responsibility*.

Moreover, this group, similar to the green startup, was particularly offended by people 'pointing-the-finger', which they found presumptuous and had no time for. Furthermore, someone being told they had no right to drive an SUV by *Fridays for Future* protestors was vehemently rejected as *this was legally just not the case* the group thought. Accordingly, responsibility for climate action was thought to lie with the individual and should not be interfered with by others. Interestingly, at the same time, the importance of the relational was however recognised, which is quite a contradiction:

> **G4w:** Well, society only works as a community and I think these status symbols like SUVs are important for people because this way they can show what they have achieved, [...] yes, and it is their right of course to show it when they have achieved something.

One group member stated in relation to this: I am just not in favour of everything being completely overregulated.

Thus, this group did not believe that politics needed to endorse further legislation when it came to climate action. It was also said that there was already a lot of responsibility taken by the corporate sector and that it could not necessarily be expected that this would be expanded as companies were exposed to many economic pressures. In relation to the corporate sphere, the moral imperative to protect the climate was again not endorsed by this group (like in relation to individuals): greenwashing was deemed acceptable if the net effect was positive for the climate. One did not appreciate too much criticism in relation to corporate efforts for climate action as in the eyes of the group many were already pouring their heart into finding new ways to advance it.

So whilst the group had this quite nuanced concept of responsibility, it was at the same time still deemed a free and personal decision (like it was the case with the green startup). This allowed the respondents to deny the direct consequences of (their) mobility practices, which was necessary for reconciling the at first sight conflicting aspects of this group's occupation, namely the carbon-intensive mobility sector itself on the one hand and the sustainability focus of the department on the other (see chapter 2, Norgaard on cognitive dissonance):

> **I:** Flight shame, yes. What do you think of that?
> **G2w:** Yes... Sorry... (rolls eyes)
> (Talking over each other)
> **G3w:** If you feel shame for flying, you also have to feel shame for eating meat and buying at H&M and driving...

Beyond this, it is particularly telling how in this group this new phenomenon of flight shame was perceived to have originated:

> **G4w:** So I generally find it interesting, how this emerged and how it spread, this, this idea of shame, that is very much triggered externally. So it is not the case that people experienced this feeling of shame themselves and this was then discovered, or something, it is more that this is being imposed onto someone, societally, through a movement, [...]
> **G3w:** ... yeah, that is quite crazy.

This excerpt indicates that the members of this focus group experienced the imperative to protect the climate as something that was being imposed onto them from the outside and not as something they themselves had internalised.

Overall, the group seemed to struggle profoundly with this contradiction that it had also been repeatedly confronted with in several social situations. One was particularly disturbed by having repeatedly been accused quite aggressively of hypocrisy in relation to flying. Thus, the group wished that the debate were carried out less emotionally and that in one's private life one would not continuously be on the receiving end of such accusations. In relation to this, one group member commiserated that the employer's mobility sector was currently generally treated as scapegoat in relation to climate matters.

Everyday efficacy

The group reported that they were observing many people being overwhelmed by the sheer scope of the climate crisis. Accordingly, it was emphasised that feeling as if oneself could make a difference was a necessary precondition for climate action. People also needed to be given ideas and information regarding how to begin reducing CO_2. Besides, an individual's relational efficacy was recognised like in several of the previous group discussions:

> Many business executives are today being briefed by their children [...]. It doesn't matter where the impulse is coming from. [...] and if it is only that I have impinged on my Dad and said, You are the boss, do something! (laughter)

Corporate entities were generally perceived as efficacious, including the group's own employer. Here, it was believed that corporate efforts were neither adequately seen nor acknowledged by the public. It was voiced that the public was by and large unreceptive towards the climate efforts made by the group's company and that the population only wanted to be told sensational, negative messages in relation to the issue.

Politicians were also deemed efficacious. Deviating from the other group discussions, here the participants believed that politicians were serious about climate action and already doing what they could, given the many social and economic hurdles they faced.

> **I:** So why else are we failing (to adequately protect the climate)?
> **G3w:** I don't think we are failing.
> **I:** Okay.
> **G3w:** ... it just takes longer, there is a lot of impatience.
> **G2w:** Yes.
> **I:** Aha.
> **G2w:** Exactly, that's also what I think. I think this should not be looked at so one-sidedly. Yes, climate action, of course, and yes, something must be done, fast. But you also have to look at it from the other side, [...] and that's also the politician's job. [...] Nothing's won when I put billions into climate action but then five [...] million people lose their jobs.

Interestingly, at a different point in the discussion, more comprehensive and democratic ways of approaching things were questioned, as this was thought to decrease politicians' scope for advancing climate action.

> **G2w:** [...] certain things should simply be decided and then the discussion should only happen afterwards. This probably sounds really bad but if I need to push something through fast, I don't need to start with great transparency and much

> discussion and grassroots-democratic voting, I can skip that because nothing will ever be achieved that way.

It was also stated that politicians were habitually criticised because the climate debate was approached so negatively overall, but the critics themselves did not actually have better answers either. It was deemed unfair that they were calling politicians incompetent as they were in fact doing their own honest best for the climate.

Embodied information

Ultimately, one was fairly relaxed in the face of the climate crisis – the group thought that firstly, the issue was not necessarily as serious as it was being portrayed in some instances and secondly that there was already a lot being done to avert climate change. The group was in favour of discussing the issue less emotionally and more rationally and fact-based. This was mainly because due to the nature of their profession they repeatedly found themselves to be on the receiving end of emotional responsibilisation in society, which they vehemently rejected:

> **G4w**: I think many people who are not 100 % informed just very much feel like bashing and then they join into those protests and I think we need more education on both sides, also to have a bit less emotion in it (the debate). I'm personally not a fan of such entirely emotional discussions, I also don't find them that interesting in my private life, I much prefer it if it goes into a more fact-based direction, because it A) relaxes the situation and B) makes you grasp arguments more clearly and so you can objectively try to analyse the situation and arrive at a shared opinion.

The group also firmly believed in the value of technological innovation.

Extent of denial

The members of this group thought that flying for work presented a professional necessity. In the private sphere, flying was deemed the personal and free choice of each individual. One did not have a problem with a frequent flyer status embodying a status symbol. The group noticeably struggled to align its occupational focus on climate action with the climate impact of the mobility sector, which it tried to reconcile through the use of several denial strategies:

Denial strategies

Therefore, and very similarly to the group of the green startup, flying was ultimately still approached in a positive way, despite this pronounced elite dilemma. It was seen as admirable when someone had made it so far professionally that they managed to gain a frequent flyer status. Moreover, this group did absolutely not want to be attributed responsibility or be deemed hypocritical by others in relation to climate action.

> **G3w:** [...] (if you have a job) that brings a lot of flying with it and you can feed your family with it because it simply is your job, then, yes...
> **G4w:** These people also really work a lot. Such people, who have such cards (frequent flyer status)
> **G3w:** yes. (laughter)
> **G4w:** You don't get those for free just on the side...
> **G3w:** Yes.
> **G4w:** I'm not jealous here.
> **G3w:** And maybe this is somebody who offsets each and every single flight. And, erm, eats vegan the rest of the time, and, erm, would never buy fast fashion [...]. You don't know this, so...

Especially this last statement illustrates the efforts by this group to justify, relativise and defend flying.

> **G2w:** [...] I don't think flying per se is as bad as it is always made out to be. Because the question is, how do I fly, yes. Because you also have to consider, when I fly somewhere, then I have a four kilometre start- and landing strip, four kilometres sealed land. When I take the train, I have a sealed area of thousands of kilometres.
> **I:** Hm-mmh.
> **G2w:** I have thousands of kilometres of residents being impacted by the noise and the train also doesn't run completely without CO_2.

Another denial strategy was the underscoring of the harm other practices were doing to the climate.

6.7 I have not once heard the word 'sustainability' since working here – Industrial enterprise

The participants of this group were all students who were working part-time or doing an internship in different departments of the company whilst still studying at university. Therefore, the group was very homogenous in terms of age and educational level. In terms of cultural tendencies, the group was however not homogenous – different cultural orientations came together here (performance culture of an industrial enterprise, culture of a transformation division, green growth ideology, questioning of capitalism). One participant delineated that consumers were limited by diverging purchasing power, as you had to be able to afford climate action. In order to approach this dilemma, she herself often bought clothes 'second-hand'. Overall, the responsibility question's multidimensionality was recognised. Another group member described the current situation as one of radical change and thus tried to justify climate action not yet living up to what was needed. Someone else stated that this was mainly due to the current economic system. Thus, climate action played an (at times quite important) role for part of the group, whilst one participant clearly stated that she did not consider herself responsible. Thus, the attitudes towards matters related to the climate were comparatively heterogeneous. At the same time, the group members were well aware of being influenced by their own respective social circles. Like the two previous groups of the green startup and the mobility provider, this group did also consider it counterproductive to get involved in or voice one's opinion on other people's climate-relevant behaviour, since it was ultimately deemed a personal decision.

Table 10: Overview: The industrial enterprise focus group

Group: Dimension	Industrial enterprise
Responsibility	The whole of society carried responsibility, in particular corporate and political spheres; differing time scales of climate issues and solutions determined attribution of responsibility, individual responsibility at times rejected
Efficacy	High efficacy expectation of oneself, both individual and in relation to work sphere; here, in everyday work life conventional and climate-harmful behaviour not being questioned by other employees (although the working students themselves did so partially); large companies' potential efficacy thought to be substantial, but demand created by individual consumers also deemed influential
Knowing	Quite comprehensive knowledge concept, recognition of influence of social group; trust in innovation and technology pronounced; some statements critical of capitalism
Denial tendencies	Group very heterogeneous; responsibility outright denied by one member; trust in 'green growth' expressed by another, condoned emissions as a necessary relict of not having completed the transformation to a 'zero carbon future'; collectively, medium level of denial

Responsibility

This group believed that decision-makers in the political and corporate sphere were particularly responsible for climate action. At the same time, the respondents had a quite individualised concept of responsibility. Initially, it was directly stressed that responsibility for climate action should not be pushed away:

> **G1w:** [...] issues such as the phasing out of nuclear energy, ending coal, these are all things that are far, far away in the future, so I say, things that concern the individual right here and right now, they have to be carried by everyone themselves.

This individualist view was then extended to encompass the different roles the individual carried, e.g., as a private agent but also as an employee of a large corporation:

> **G4m:** I think it's important that you contribute in all possible spheres.

Then it was observed that climate action was a very polarising issue with some members of society simply declaring that it didn't concern them, whilst the group's consensus was that everybody had some responsibility to get involved. In relation to flying the group disagreed: one member said that the issue concerned her, another stated that she had flown twice that year[1], another stated she was indifferent and had taken several flights (8–10). The last participant also admitted to flying a lot (to visit his family in South America) while experiencing pronounced *flight shame* when doing so (also 8–10 flights). The group was annoyed that in Germany, travelling by train was often more expensive than flying so that as a student this more climate-friendly alternative was often out of reach. The description of the many perceived benefits of travelling to distant destinations by plane by one group member illustrated the extent to which flying played an important role in her life. She called flying her *biggest vice* which points towards her experienced ambivalence as she saw it as a means to bring people together and develop an understanding for other cultures.

In the end, both flying and driving an SUV (for 'long distances') were considered a necessity in people's professional everyday lives and the comforts they afforded were important means to be able to work productively the next day. At the same time, it was vehemently taken issue with for example influencers behaving inconsistently and dishonestly, for instance when they *preached climate action* but then also took many flights. Very similar to the group of the mobility provider, one member tried to justify certain climate-harmful practices:

---

1 Outbound and return flight = one flight; the interview was taken in October.

G1w: [...] on the other hand, maybe there are people who drive an SUV when they go long distance and then there are also just as many people who take their, I don't know, VW Up or whatever, to go each and any distance in the city. And those who have the SUV maybe say that they only drive it long distance and leave it at home the rest of the time. So I think either you extend this to driving in general or you...

Furthermore, the demands made by the *Fridays for Future* protestors were seen as problematic, immature, far removed from reality and at times hypocritical. It was not anybody else's business how one lived their life, which in turn pointed to an extremely individualised notion of responsibility.

G2w: Well, when you get older, other things become important. You think more about the future in the sense of that you have to make money, you have to maintain a certain standard of living, an apartment and a car, and all that was not an issue when I was 13, I didn't think about what kind of car I would drive one day either or which job I would do. So then I didn't really have a clear plan. But when you're about to graduate and you know: okay, I am going to have to enter my working life, then such things take a much more concrete form, and yes...
G1w (points to picture of the protest where a sign has been drawn on an amazon cardboard)**:** and this is also great, climate change on the one hand, and then the amazon logo next to it, that's the kind of thing, ..., this person still orders things there that were then driven through half of Germany, but still....

The group perceived responsibility as a multidimensional issue however:

G4m: I am convinced it is the individual, because a company consists of individuals. And politics (consists of individuals). And I believe everything starts with one's personal attitude.
G3w: Okay, that's hard because it is a bit of a chicken and egg situation, because of course the consumer determines what a company produces and at the same time the consumer cannot buy anything the company does not produce. So if the company says from the start, we only produce climate-friendly things, then the consumer has no other choice. So I think at the end, maybe the corporation has more influence.

Ultimately, the industrial sector was ascribed particular responsibility, which probably was related to the group members being employed by this company.

Everyday efficacy

The industrial company the group worked for did however not remain true to this responsibility the participants thought. The group reported that there was not very much budget attributed to climate-relevant matters when compared to for example measures for process optimisation. One group member, who worked for the transformation division, did then however emphasise that in his view the company was already doing a lot for climate action. It was concluded that the rest of the group worked more on the cost side of things and the transformation division was the only department in the company that actually had a budget for such matters:

> **G3w:** I have not once heard the word 'sustainability' in my department since I have worked here. [...] I mean, I remember one conversation where Greta was used as a positive example for all she has managed to achieve. [...] I do have the feeling that there is an awareness and that it is being talked very liberally about such matters and there are colleagues who drive electro-cars [...], although I have to say, when you meet some colleagues who are a little more distant (in the company structure), and recently there was this debate about Fridays for Future and many actually think, and I was a little surprised by that, that Greta is, that she is being instrumentalised and many think there is an agenda behind it, yes, that's definitely the purport to an extent.

When prompted, the group considered these theories ridiculous and absurd. One group member then went on to say that in her everyday work life conventional and climate-harmful behaviour was not being questioned at all. The colleague who worked for the transformation division did however believe that the company cared about climate action but that it could only get so far and then it was on politics to set the concrete regulatory frameworks. Here the group member who was least involved with climate action objected that large industrial entities like their company even often had the means to escape regulations.

> **G1w:** So I think there is always this kind of gap between what our climate cabinets decide on the one hand and what is actually being implemented by industry in the end. [...]
> **G2w:** And I mean, politics almost always complies with what industry wants. I mean, how successful a government is is being measured by how well the economy is doing and so of course governments do what large corporations want.

Where companies made efforts towards climate action, they often actually only wanted to upgrade their image. Nevertheless, the efficacy large companies could potentially have was thought to be substantial. Here, demand created by individual consumers was also deemed influential and one participant said that consumers did have the responsibility to actually fulfil this role. In terms of the efficacy of the political sphere the group did not agree: on the one hand, politics was deemed to have particularly large influence, on the other side one did not trust that politicians were that serious about climate action since not much had been achieved so far.

Politics was perceived to have been going back on its promises and delaying its own deadlines instead of making true progress. This was due to too many people propagating too many different interests and lobbyism being too powerful.

Ultimately it was concluded that the individual carried the highest responsibility whilst the most efficacy lay with industrial entities. At the end of the day, politics was attested the principal responsibility to become active for the climate, but the group did by and large severely doubt that this would happen given that politicians were mostly inefficacious due to their alleged incompetence. Only one member of the group disagreed by emphasising that she believed in some green politicians' authenticity and competence. She then said that politics had the biggest potential to make a difference as it could influence the individual and the corporate sphere, but then she also agreed that this was happening too slowly and unsatisfactorily.

It was generally believed that it was counterproductive to get involved in or voice one's opinion on other people's climate-relevant behaviour, since it was ultimately deemed, again, a personal decision. Despite being known for precisely such pointing-the-finger the group detested, *Fridays for Future* protestors were still deemed influential and believed to have legitimacy in society.

Embodied information practices

The members of this group were well aware of the influence their respective social environments had on their decision-making:

> **I:** Other opinions on the climate cabinet? Is it going to make a difference?
> **G1w:** I think definitely not, but my thinking is of course always impacted by the kind of thinking that is being conveyed here (in the company).

The group thought that innovation could certainly be a potential solution for the issue of climate change. The media was thought to be the main source of information about climate change, which the group looked down upon since true scientific knowledge was what was considered truly necessary instead. *Fridays for Future* were then criticised as the group doubted they were supplied with sufficient scientific information that was initially seen as the only trustworthy source of knowledge. It was however then admitted that this kind of information was often too dry to reach people, therefore movies could have more of an impact. So emotional messages were definitely also seen as efficacious whilst at the same time, the role of factual knowledge was being stressed. Overall, the group considered itself much better informed than the average population:

> **G1w:** The average person who works in production [...], also here in our company, those production workers will talk to each other, but, ... [...]

> **G4m:** And there is also going to be a lot of 'fake news' being spread.
> **G1w:** Definitely, yes. Definitely.

The group displayed cultural leanings that were both for and against more climate action.

> **G3w**: [...] So I do think that it is more hip and cool than weak and laughable (to be pro climate action).
> **I**: Yes?
> **G2w**: So I think, this completely and entirely depends on in which social circle one moves about in.

Extent of denial

This group combined several cultural tendencies and climate action played an (at times quite important) role for the majority of the group, whilst one participant clearly stated that she did not consider herself responsible since her concept of responsibility did simply not include climate rationales.

Denial strategies

One group member considered the current situation a state of exception because of the transformation that society needed to go through and in this way attempted to justify where climate action was so far not going far enough:

> **G4m:** So we are going through this radical change. There are initiatives that aim for a better future but right now we are still very dirty. And I think these contrasts are not rare to find. [...] They are already part of the transformation, these contrasts.

He then argued that the government had to play an important role in instigating such transformative change, but not thereafter (then it should not interfere any longer), which the recent example of France had shown (*yellow vest protests*).

> **G4m:** When the government declares such an aim that has to be achieved and then the population says "no, no, no, that's too expensive, [...] stop!" I think that's what happens when you only count on the power of the government. But for the transition I do think that taxes... and that the ground can be evened a bit for climate-friendly alternatives and conventional technologies that are harmful to the environment.

Here, one participant said that there simply reigned other priorities in the industrial sphere which was mainly due to the current economic system as a third group member pointed out. She went on to say that some studies had shown that continued economic growth would always remain unsustainable and in order to really achieve change, there would have to be *negative growth*. She was however the only one in the group who thought this would be sensible and present many advantages such as more time for private matters. The rest of the group did however not deem this desirable or realistic. One participant was convinced of green growth being the solution to reach the transformation towards a *zero-carbon future*.

6.8 Flying is indeed something that I don't prohibit for myself – Teachers

Table 11: Overview: The focus group of teachers

Group: Dimension	**Teachers**
Responsibility	Climate action seen as task for the whole of society (state, corporations, individuals); own occupational group carried special responsibility due to its role in education; thus responsible for leading with a good example, being a role model for younger generations; students took responsibility (e.g., *Fridays for Future*) – but a lot of them also just follow along (to get out of school)
Efficacy	Relatively pronounced expectation of individual efficacy, at the same time moderate trust in collective action for meaningful climate action (e.g., this accusation of following along within *Fridays for Future*)
Knowing	Very well informed and reflected, focus on factual knowledge, value agency gap raised (in relation to own person but also *Fridays for Future*); consideration of the practice of travelling long distance, its educational effect as opposed to its consequences for the climate
Denial tendencies	Little denial, overall reflected and strong emphasis on own responsibility

The male-female ratio in this group was balanced and the educational level was homogeneous. Some participants stood at the beginning of their professional lives, some were middle-aged. Climate responsibility was practiced only to an extent in these teachers' everyday lives. Members of the group were for instance willing to pay extra for climate-friendly clothes, but found the supply that was being offered to be very limited up to this point. Textile production in countries with low labour costs was criticised due to there being poor labour conditions – climate reasons were not raised, however. One group member stated that flying was still more important to her than protecting the climate. Yet her tone was quite defensive. Overall, the group detected a lot of conflicting information in relation to climate action, rendering climate action a much more difficult endeavour.

Responsibility

Initially the group thought that everybody was responsible for climate action, so in a first instance the individual was mentioned. It was thought to also be the job of individuals to form groups that could then have a larger impact. From this interview it emerged that the participants practiced climate action only rudimentarily in their everyday lives:

> **G?w:** Flying is indeed something that I don't prohibit for myself, somehow. That's something that I have to admit I do myself. And I love travelling and seeing the world. And I am actually not willing to stop doing so. I would be ok with paying more, but then...

In relation to this, some members of the group said that they paid to carbon-offset their journeys, for example when travelling by coach and that this was not expensive at all. At the same time, they thought that this was morally objectionable to an extent as one was simply buying oneself a clear conscience. Here it was emphasised that one should generally travel with more consciousness. The group also discussed feeling guilty when flying but thought that the majority of society did not experience this. Especially young people were increasingly taking flying for granted and believed they had an intrinsic right to have been to exciting places. Here one group member heatedly expressed that when she was growing up, flying used to be a luxury that one had to save up for and young people had shed all modesty when it came to this topic, which she was very angry about. Someone else then said that it was problematic that those who could not afford to fly would end up being the only ones responsible if flying was made more expensive. It was deeply unfair for those people to miss out on flying (also on the learning experience afforded by travelling).

> **G?m:** I think everybody being able to afford flying is actually very democratic and anti-capitalist. [...] that this now goes into the direction of everybody being able to emit, that is a problem. But I don't think that this democratic equality should be forgotten.

The group then said that at the end it was however mainly the responsibility of corporate- and political decision-makers who had to be role models in relation to climate action. Teachers too were seen as role models and thus endowed with a special responsibility, also to be consistent when it came to climate matters. Yet not everyone in the group was willing to invest extra time to support the *Fridays for Future* protests, for example. Here, the teachers were annoyed that the school headmaster simply expected them to do so. Then the group questioned whether the student protestors were actually taking responsibility for climate action in their everyday lives as they themselves were demanding during their demonstrations. Instead, the teachers thought that many students simply followed along in the protests.

The responsibility initially attributed to the corporate sphere was then relativised as companies were exposed to European and international competition which left the largest share of responsibility with politicians. The global nature of economic practices nowadays made this much more complex, however. One group member voiced that German corporations actually had the potential to be pioneers but it would help if they were nudged into the right direction by political players. It was also politics that was responsible to regulate free returns in e-commerce or (particularly cheap) flying for more climate action. Politics should also finally subsidise going by train as this was currently so expensive that it had become an 'elite practice' to take the train within Europe. This was debated in a quite heated and emotional manner.

Everyday efficacy

Initially, the group disagreed with respect to individual efficacy: on the one hand, it was stated that the individual foregoing consumption hardly made a difference, even if more than a couple of idealists did so. Politics had much larger levers as this participant believed. On the other hand, it was said that consumption decisions did indeed have a substantial impact. Ultimately, the individual was expected to have a certain limited efficacy in their own small social environment (relational efficacy) whilst political and corporate agents were thought to be the ones that could truly make a difference. Here it was pointed out that there had been considerable change in terms of how people in society now thought about vegan diets or plastic bags for example.

The group members also thought that their role as teachers endowed them with particular efficacy:

> **G?m**: I do indeed tell my students that I don't own a car. I leave it at that but then they at least have a role model, negative or positive, does not matter, but at least they know someone who has no car. And is kind of normal (laughter).
> **G?w**: At least you think that they think so.

The group did not unequivocally deem the student protests efficacious and at times their authenticity was questioned. However, the point at which scientists endorsed the statements made by the students was thought to have made a big difference for the legitimacy of *Fridays for Future*.

The group also questioned the efficacy of politicians as they were problematically influenced by lobbying. The German environmental minister arguing that people had to be rationally convinced of the necessity to protect the climate indicated that politics still relied much too heavily on voluntary measures (and a knowledge concept resting on information deficits), which had failed as experience had shown. What was needed instead was concrete political legislation although one was unsure how the public would then receive having to pay more for climate action. Therefore, the group expected politics to water down its legislation once again leaving it very long-term and vague. Overall, the group was very dissatisfied with political decisions related to climate action.

Corporate actors were also criticised for not doing enough to protect the climate. For example, Germany was far behind other countries in the e-mobility sector. Corporations also often practiced *greenwashing* that they tailored to their respective target group. Sustainable fashion was still deemed a niche-product, which showed the limited efficacy the group attributed to the corporate sphere. Here, it was thought to also be the task of educational institutions to train economists so that they were not exclusively presented mainstream economic rationales as these conflicted with meaningful climate action. One group member replied to this by saying that companies had to act in terms of shareholder interests and thus their efficacy was curtailed. Therefore, only politics could initiate actual progress in this respect.

Embodied information practices

The extent of the negative impact of flying for the climate had been internalised by this group only to a limited extent. Meaningful climate action was thought to be made much more difficult by conflicting information. For example, both batteries and energy provision for e-mobility were perceived to be unresolved issues, which made it much less straight-forward to switch to it. Besides, there often existed practices in people's professional everyday lives that were so counterproductive that they left people demoralised with regard to making an effort for the climate as private individuals. For example, people had reported that retail used that much plastic behind the scenes that any effort to avoid it by people in their private lives seemed completely pointless. This was also the case for organic produce that one would initially assume to be superior. At other times, there was too little information in the group's perception as it did for example not know what best to do with used clothes. The notion of knowing in this group was quite encompassing, however. The group appreciated both, factual and emotional information and proposed *a mixture of both*. It was seen to also make a sizable difference how somebody had grown up and been socialised.

Extent of denial

This group denied the imperative to protect the climate only to an extent. The group members reported that in some areas, they were not acting according to what was best for the climate, for example with respect to flying. Overall, they had however extensively reflected on the issue, including its complexity and multi-dimensionality. There was very strong emphasis of one's own responsibility, both as an individual and as a teacher.

Denial strategies

At times, this group kept information, for example about the extent of the climate impact of flying, at arm's length for not having to feel so guilty about still practicing it. Here, awareness existed, however, of the possibility to offset emissions, which some group members already practiced. One second denial strategy consisted in questioning the authenticity of the *Fridays for Future* student protestors, yet this was certainly also related to other reasons within the occupational field of school education. Overall, the group was quite aware of the need to protect the climate, its members did however not substantially integrate climate action into their own everyday lives.

6.9 Conclusion

The groups analysed each displayed specific denial patterns that were sometimes dependent on whether or not climate action played a role in the participants' everyday work sphere. Here, it is thus particularly relevant how members of a professional field define themselves collectively. Consequently, the necessity and urgency of acting on climate change and integrating this into one's everyday life is interpreted differently, depending on societal location. Climate-cultural leanings identified in these group discussions also displayed varying patterns of climate-relevant material and discursive practices and differing interpretations of media reporting on climate change. Further, the analysis shows that not only the constellations of this study's three key concepts, responsibility, efficacy and knowing differ along climate-cultural location but also the specific climate-cultural interpretations what each of these notions mean. Thus, each group displays its own particular logic of climate action, i.e., a specific climate habitus, which makes visible diverse inter- and intra-group power constellations. Emerging alliances between groups hitherto perceived as substantially different that however (and somewhat surprisingly) did show similar climate-cultural propensities to deny proved to be particularly telling.

Part IV – Discussion, recommendations and outlook

7 Discussion

7.1 Introduction

The following discussion of my findings is structured around three core insights that emerged from the in-depth analysis and interpretation of the empirical material introduced in the previous three chapters:

First, in German society, 'elite' notions of a public consensus regarding climate change and the need for action are challenged by an in fact profound climate-cultural diversity. My empirical evidence revealed a substantial gap between those climate (sub)cultures within the population whose members receive, acknowledge, and internalise 'official' messages regarding climate change and -action, and those with whom these messages do not (at all) resonate. It shows that mainstream calls for climate action generally reflect the language and mind-set of groups who are endowed with larger shares of capital (cultural capital types here being particularly indicative), thereby eclipsing the everyday realities of large parts of the population. These profound climate-cultural differences are not yet reflected in research or policy. This is deeply problematic as it renders climate action largely irrelevant to less privileged sections of society, perpetuating their sense of marginality and inefficacy.

Second, the observed climate-cultural diversity is rooted in distinct constellations of responsibility, efficacy, and ways of knowing. Importantly, it was uncovered that incongruences between responsibility attributions and efficacy expectations often lead to climate inaction. Furthermore, it must be differentiated between official attributions of responsibility and efficacy, and the lived responsibility and efficacy that people experience in their everyday realities. These discrepancies are currently almost entirely unacknowledged in both research and policy. Accordingly, making them visible first and handling them thereafter currently presents a key challenge.

Third, specific constellations of responsibility, efficacy, and ways of knowing that characterise particular climate cultures can result in different forms of *denial*. This denial was found to be either explicit or implicit. Explicit denial is performed by those sceptical of climate change even occurring whilst implicit denial refers to people who acknowledge the issue but diffuse their responsibility and deny the imperative to act accordingly. However, there is no clear link between societal status and engagement in climate action, with members of 'elite' climate cultures being similarly prone to climate inaction than their less well-off counterparts. This is all the more worrying given that these sections of society tend to experience high levels of efficacy that reflect their above-average educational, cultural and financial capital.

7.2 Climate action as 'elite project' obscures climate-cultural diversity

Germany's climate-cultural diversity turned out to be much higher than is generally assumed in both, academic literature and public debate. However, this only became apparent when the investigation moved beyond 'elite perceptions' expressed through expert interviews and 'official' media messages. As Beck has poignantly pointed out (refer to section 2.4), climate policy will only ever cease to be an "elite cloud-cuckoo-land" if a majority of very different people agree to vote and act accordingly, and do so, in many ways, against their own personal interest.

Views expressed by members of elite climate cultures were thus surprisingly homogenous, given the apparent diversity of actors involved (ranging from elected politicians to YouTubers). Here, prevalent discourses by and large reflected the climate-cultural orientations of the socio-political establishment that implicitly accept the IPCC-consensus, the necessity for rapid climate action and the need to consider related questions of responsibility and efficacy. This confirms that official calls to (climate) action are mainly noticed and internalised by those in society who speak the same language as the originators of these messages. Elites from political, scientific and some corporate and social spheres form 'discourse coalitions' (Hajer, 1993, 2004) that also dominate the debates around climate action, for instance in conventional media formats (e.g., television, prestige print media). Those who are not part of these particular elite discourse coalitions often accuse the media of being complicit with these narratives, as several social media statements indicated (see chapter 5.3). Similarly, craftsmen and farmers interviewed for this study also believed that the media were generally biased towards the climate movement (see sections 6.2 and 6.5).

Experts interviewed by and large participated in these particular elite discourse coalitions (see chapter 4). For example, they stated (nearly) unequivocally that climate action needed to be undertaken by the whole of society – mirroring political calls that ask everyone to contribute. However, the question remains how this can be achieved when such official political calls for action address only some sections of society (endowed with the relevant types of capital). Predominantly speaking to the public as if it were one uniform entity completely overlooks the everyday realities of large sections of society that have less capital at their disposal (cf. section 2.5, Norgaard, 2011) and thus do not belong to such elite climate cultures.

In contrast to this 'elite consensus', climate cultures of the less capital-rich parts of the population were found to vary considerably, ranging from radical pro-climate action perspectives to climate change scepticism and even denial. The detected extent of both radicalism and expressiveness of these sceptical narratives was especially surprising. These discourses were particularly loud, yet it is granted that they may not actually be practiced by as many people as their pronounced presence suggests. Nevertheless, it is vital to acknowledge their manifestation in German society as it points to the existence of deep cultural disagreement over how the challenge of climate change ought to be handled. More so, for climate action to actually become an inclusive, society-wide project, social and cultural diversity must be recognised as an integral part of it. Instead, current approaches focus on concepts or buzzwords like individual *carbon footprints* or *zero waste initiatives* which runs the risk of continuing to approach society with unequivocal messages.

'Avoiding CO_2 has never been easier' versus 'Rise against Left-green incitement'[1]

Thus, in reality, perspectives on climate change often diverge substantially, as indicated by this subheading. This becomes particularly evident in debates on social media (see chapter 5). Here, a pronounced propensity of people to seek out spaces that are frequented by like-minded others has been observed (cf. Bourdieu, section 2.4). Social media providers' notorious algorithms further propagate the entrenchment of such 'echo chambers' (cf. Walter et al., 2018). This is quite problematic from a democratic perspective: when one does not have to fear opposition and rejection, one may dare to raise points in a much less self-censored, more un-reflected and radical manner. This 'cultural cocooning' creates an atmosphere of unawareness or even ignorance of alternative standpoints within society.

An eclectic mix of views linked to climate action was also found in the focus group discussions (see chapter 6), linking climate-cultural diversity and occupational context. Here, divergences in opinion did not result in the same level of contestation that characterised many social media debates. Instead, focus group exchanges were less heated, as members *shared* this particular social space. Yet, looking at these group discussions at a whole, disagreement began already regarding the significance and urgency ascribed to the challenge of climate change, and measures needed to address it. For instance, and paradoxically, members of the strategic sustainability division of the mobility provider were comparatively relaxed

---

1 Two social media statements (see section 5.3).

about the threat posed by climate change. They believed that a lot was being done already for the climate in political and corporate spheres. This stood in sharp contrast to the statements made by members of the NGO and (to an extent also) the green startup whose work was also closely related to the issue, but who seemed much more alarmed. This shows that the way discourses typically unfold in conversation more or less directly points to the cultural regularities that shape people's climate-related everyday practices and experiences, including those in the workplace.

Figure 3: Climate activists of the group 'Extinction Rebellion' occupy office of Bavarian economic committee in Munich[2][3]

Thus far, dominant climate debates entirely overlook these discrepancies between regular discourses in (cultural) capital-rich settings, and debates and views expressed by the rest of the public (i.e., 'non-elite' climate cultures). The media analysis (and to an extent also the focus groups) revealed a significant (and potentially widening) gap between elite climate cultures and those attributed to other parts of the public. The remarkable unawareness in research and policy of the existence of some of these (non-elite) climate cultures, as well as the growing distance between them, represents one of the key findings presented in this study. This is especially the case regarding the scepticism that sometimes even cumulated in climate change

2 © Robert Haas, Süddeutsche Zeitung, 14/07/2021: https://www.sueddeutsche.de/muenchen/muenchen-extinction-rebellion-wirtschaftsbeirat-buero-1.5351464 (accessed 16/09/2022).

3 The picture reads: *occupied – now the climate protection lobby sits here* and *your motto: at full speed into the crisis.*

denial and repeatedly manifested in the presentation of elaborate conspiracy theories: here, the IPCC-consensus and the societal imperative to deal with impending climate change were not only second guessed but in fact severely doubted or even denied. This was unexpected insofar as German society is not usually described in the literature as particularly climate-sceptical (cf. Grundmann, 2007; Tranter and Booth, 2015; Walter et al., 2018).

The extent of disagreement over how to react to climate change is illustrated by the following two visual examples that serve as a kind of summary of the insights presented. Here, the contrast becomes so pronounced that one must wonder how these perceptions can possibly coexist *in one society*: in Germany, activists of the group *Extinction Rebellion* and people following this AfD politician on Facebook seem to live in completely different realities as people following the AfD member of the Bundestag Stephan Brandner on Facebook.

This scene (refer to figure 3) shows *Extinction Rebellion* activists occupying the office of an economic body in Munich. The group criticises the economic committee's alleged inaction regarding climate change and accuses it to practice lobbying that further inhibits existing efforts.

Figure 4: Facebook post by AfD member of the Bundestag Stephan Brandner[4]

4 The post reads: climate hysteria is not a good advisor – the bill of the CO_2 ideology is being paid by the small man.

By contrast, this posting (see figure 4) by the AfD member of the Bundestag Stephan Brandner[5] illustrates particularly well how the topic of climate change is being instrumentalised in populist discourses that supposedly side with the 'small man'.

That these two entirely opposing standpoints exist in Germany exemplifies how easy it is for representatives of each to talk at cross purposes. While the members of *Extinction Rebellion* express fear for the future, claiming not at all enough is being done for the climate, other climate cultures outright reject the priorisation of climate matters. In this view, the 'small man', as it is phrased in this Facebook post, is being asked to forego what is personally and subjectively deemed important for the benefit of the climate, whilst the privileged instigators of these same messages are perceived not to contribute themselves. Here, the critique in form of underscoring the lack of climate initiatives' relevance to people's lives functions as an outlet for the experienced irritation with elitist perspectives and the pronounced privileges they reflect. The point here is not to argue for radical revolution but for the inclusion of the majority of the German population that thus far has simply not been reached by the way climate action is propagated today. As shown, privileged people live profoundly different lives in terms of both, cultural meanings and financial means. Their experiences thus show little or no resemblance to the everyday realities and practices of those who have less capital at their disposal. When this gap between attribution and experienced reality is not considered, this leads to some groups already feeling excluded by the way these calls to action are even sent out. This is extremely problematic as feelings of not belonging or being excluded encourage a tendency to look and listen the other way whenever climate change is raised as an issue. Here, a clear link exists between more rightist/populist political orientations and hostility towards environmentalism in general, and climate policy in particular (see chapter 5, denial subculture). This position regularly coincides with nativist and anti-immigrant views, this aforementioned hostility towards all elites and strong support for individual choice and autonomy.

Relatedly, *Fridays for Future* is often viewed as a group of particularly privileged young people. For instance, German comedian Felix Lobrecht calls the movement "something only for grammar school kids" in a recent episode of climate activist Luisa Neubauer's podcast *1.5 degrees*[6]. He bemoans that the movement only addresses the white middle class, thereby excluding many people and their realities from the very beginning.

---

5 Facebook post by Stephan Brandner: https://www.facebook.com/stBrandner/photos/a.1769206119967250/2587552268132627/ (retrieved on 28/12/2023)

6 See *Redaktionsnetzwerk Deutschland*, 27/01/2022: https://www.rnd.de/medien/felix-lobrecht-im-podcast-mit-luisa-neubauer-fridays-for-future-ist-so-ein-gymnasiastending-HIBGHC6FXBFPDIYZ7JNBAE3TXA.html (accessed 16/09/2022).

This is confirmed by insights from this study, as members of non-elite climate cultures also rejected any attribution of responsibility to themselves for the living conditions of future generations. They do so by discrediting climate activism among young(er) people through practices of ridicule and ascriptions of limited life-experience and immaturity. Climate activists' calls to assist those most threatened by climate change (now and in the future, here and elsewhere) are interpreted simply as attempts to further limit people's freedom. Young climate activists and influencers as well as the *Fridays for Future* movement are currently running the risk of being engulfed by such elite discourse coalitions. This might result in only certain capital-rich sections heeding the demands of the movement to further their own interests, spurring even more aversion and resentment in the process. One farmer complaining that the protestors are being courted by politics and even invited to speak to the Pope (see chapter 6) confirms this.

One main reason why it is so hard to forego climate-harming practices is because they serve a host of social purposes. For instance, forms of conspicuous consumption associated with mobility practices are being used as a means to display one's status. In this way, capital-rich groups further remove themselves from the rest of the population's practical realities and necessities by the luxury of being able to afford their 'pure gaze' (cf. Bourdieu, section 2.4). By contrast, 'common people' are more likely to engage in 'functional consumption', as Bourdieu writes. Here, an environmentally sustainable but notoriously erratic *fairphone* will never become a crowd pleaser, whilst in elite circles the social- and climate friendly USP serves as a means for identification. This implies that taste is not naturally given or individually chosen but derives from the social conditions people find themselves in. Largely freed from many financial and social constraints, those at the top can develop their tastes, setting consumption standards for the rest of society.

Besides, at the current conjuncture, climate action is only deemed feasible if measures are perceived as tolerable, not limiting, and realistic to implement. The following debate about organic supermarkets took place in the author's social surroundings:

> **A:** This can never be profitable, when each individual walks up with their own container and they first have to each press the tare button. You end up with endless lines at the check-out. If only five people go to the self-filling unit, this will take forever. It will take forever because these processes are just so fundamentally unworldly that you cannot supply the public through them. These supermarkets take it as their right to have these processes for a small elitist group of people who can then say they are morally superior. [...] besides, so much falls through from these filling stations that it makes the shop seem pretty mucky.
>
> **B:** You know what is missing? The shopping experience, the colourful product assortment ('bunte Warenwelt'). When I go to my usual supermarket, I have every-

> thing under one roof. That's just really convenient. I go there with my grandson and he loves it and it is a real item on our agenda of the day to go shopping [...]. And I think a lot of people feel that way.

This example illustrates that powerful corporate and political decision-makers asking consumers to buy *organic* fails to acknowledge obstacles that depend on one's social position. Here, reasons for not wanting to buy organic products had nothing to do with affordability but with the desire to enjoy the 'shopping experience' offered by conventional stores. Messages that aim to rationally convince people of organic foods' climate benefits fail to reach people who value this shopping experience, with far-reaching consequences for planetary health. It is vital to understand these markedly different reasons why both elite and non-elite groups are not (yet) engaging in climate action. This study made a clear contribution to knowledge on this important issue.

7.3 Differentiating climate cultures: Responsibility, efficacy and knowing

Specific combinations of responsibility, efficacy and knowing are what characterises the different climate cultures. As outlined in chapter 2, climate cultures are defined according to these three aspects and how they potentially translate into different forms of collective climate-related denial.

Members of elite climate cultures (see chapter 5) regularly indicated that it remains unresolved who in society should initiate climate action. At times, responsibility was ping-ponged from the political to the corporate, then back to the individual sphere, then again onto civil society. To an extent, this diffusion of responsibility (cf. section, 2.5, Norgaard, 2011) served to deflect attention away from the requirement to involve the whole of society, and especially one's own social sphere. Yet the need for climate action to become a society-wide effort was also recognised by some of the capital-richer participants: a clear tension emerged between political and individual responsibility, with more collectively oriented politicians acknowledging that all social spheres should contribute. In this view, society needs to come together and act responsibly under the lead of the political sphere. In contrast, more conservative politicians emphasised choice and autonomy and thus individual responsibility.

Within the realm of public climate cultures, opinions regarding climate responsibility also varied markedly, with two broad trends emerging: members of the public were either radically pro-climate action, strongly endorsing individual responsibility. They did think they themselves were influential (belief in consumer power internalised), setting them apart from the collectivist elite (sub)culture. Yet members of other public climate cultures rejected personal responsibility to varying degrees, sometimes radically so: here, an outright questioning of any anthropogenic causes of climate change eclipsed one's own responsibility and efficacy. Where climate change is at least acknowledged as a problem, if anything, politics is held responsible.

Figure 5: Different constellations of responsibility, efficacy and knowing displayed by the focus groups, own presentation

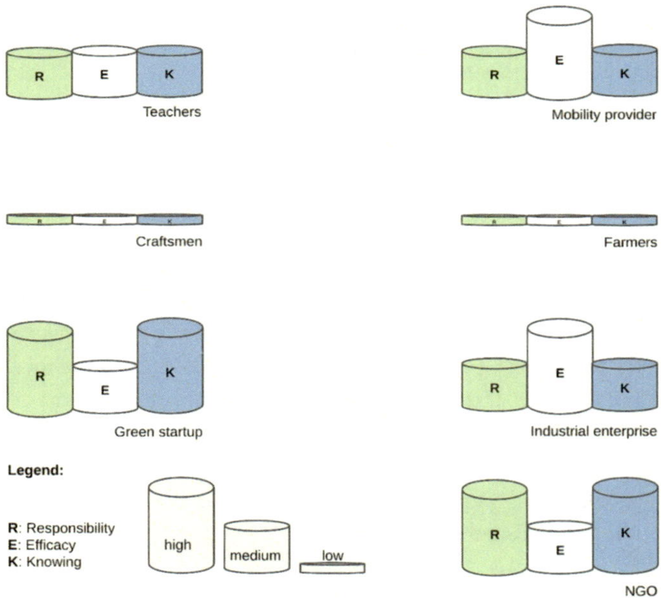

As figure 5 depicts, different focus groups (see chapter 6) also occupied different positions regarding climate-related responsibility, -efficacy and -ways of knowing. Barrel sizes indicate the relative importance (in qualitative terms) ascribed to each concept by each group (but are not to be understood as quantitative indicators).

For instance, members of the NGO believed that it was morally out of question to travel by airplane. They had internalised individual climate responsibility to the point where it played an important role in their lives and even served as a means for self-identification. At the same time, within the industrial enterprise, flying was deemed to be a professional necessity that allowed one to work productively again the next day. In the latter case, climate action played an (at times quite important) role for a part of the group, whilst one participant plainly stated that she did not consider herself responsible. Her concept of responsibility simply did not include any climate-related rationales. For her, responsibility was mainly related to the corporate structures that to her were particularly meaningful since she aspired to having a successful career in the company. The rest of this group, as well as the teachers and the green startup, were largely defensive about flying, indicating to varying degrees that they felt guilty about flying for private enjoyment. Yet, they all regularly continued to do so. By contrast, the mobility provider's employees were rather annoyed about the bad reputation flying was getting. What had become to be known as flight shame (*flygskam*) was thus only experienced by some of the more capital-rich focus groups, whereas those less privileged strongly rejected being responsibilised in this way. For instance, the craftsmen fundamentally externalised responsibility. They were not at all willing to forego private flying, stating that they simply did not care enough about climate change for doing so.

Efficacy expectations also varied considerably: members of more privileged focus groups generally viewed themselves as well-equipped to make a difference in society. For example, employees of the industrial enterprise considered their employer to be very efficacious, so much so that with the right amount of lobbying they could even escape political regulations (but that their company could also make a real difference if chosen to do so). This stood in stark contrast to less privileged members of the public who saw themselves as severely limited in their choices. The inefficacy climate subculture that emerged from the media analysis shows this particularly well (chapter 5), mirroring observations regarding the less privileged focus groups. Farmers, and to some lesser extent craftsmen, generally felt unheard and underappreciated in society, sparking resentment and distrust towards groups richer in (particularly cultural) capital. Farmers had extremely low efficacy expectations as individuals but also as a group which is particularly telling as the agricultural lobby's influence is in fact quite substantial.

'Like spiderman: With a lot of power comes a lot of responsibility'[7]

What stood out when initially speaking to the experts (see chapter 4) was their rather unanimous and implicit assumption that societal responsibility for climate action must be contemplated in terms of the actual power an agent holds. From the outset of undertaking this research, it became clear that the link between responsibility attributions and efficacy expectations is crucial for effective climate action.

Several experts also remarked that responsibility was originally conceptualised *in terms of* efficacy: the more power and resources someone held, the more responsible (s)he was to act accordingly. Even German basic law (Article 14) states: ownership is an obligation. Yet one of the experts (academic sociology and sustainability) observed a deep divide in society today between the two notions (refer to section 4.3).

7 Statement from one of the experts interviewed.

This study confirms this: discursive variations highlight a clear decoupling of responsibility and efficacy across a number of climate cultures. For instance, individual consumers are routinely blamed for not doing enough for the climate, including by climate activists (see chapter 5), which places the burden of responsibility on the shoulders of those actually least able to act. Yet others reject the idea that their individual efficacy is marginal, believing that 'green' consumption can be an essential part of successful climate action.

Decisive discrepancies

In the following, these discrepancies between responsibility and efficacy found in the data are delineated in some more detail as they characterise the different climate cultures: conservative politicians, for instance, display such a discrepancy: they generally attribute considerable efficacy to themselves, yet they do not necessarily see it as politics' responsibility to advance climate action through regulations or prohibitions[8]. Such refusal to expand climate action from these political directions often rests upon the argument that the market is better equipped to solve the issue (see chapter 4). References to the disagreeability and alleged unpopularity of regulations amongst voters (as made by one of the experts, politician Freie Wähler) allow the diffusion of responsibility (cf. Fox and Rau, 2017). This goes hand in hand with an ever more entrenched individualism that unsurprisingly meanders into less sense of community and collective fate. This is exacerbated by less capital-rich groups also being weary of any kind of authority, thus often being politically disenchanted. Politicians are frequently perceived as inefficacious, presenting again a large discrepancy between responsibility and efficacy that is likely to impact on climate action: "There is a growing erosion of trust in the social institutions that undergird democracy, as many citizens feel that their visibility and voice are losing political impact" (Dahlgren, 2012, p. 3). Dahlgren also observes "a growing literature on how citizens are apparently disengaging from the political system, coupled with feelings of powerlessness and cynicism towards the power elites" (ibid.). It is then particularly harmful if decision-makers who are openly engaged in responsibilisation are publicly perceived as hypocritical. In fact, accusations of hypocrisy surfaced repeatedly in this study, particularly regarding public statements by members of elite climate cultures. Although these politicians potentially take an interest in climate matters and express this in their political participation, in many cases they fail to foreground the 'big points' (Bilharz, 2007) like flying. Yet this also shows

8 This is illustrated, for instance, by the conservative party's (CDU) public outcry over German financial minister Christian Lindner (FDP) announcing his plans to reallocate 60 billion Euros to climate action (cf. Kubina, 2022). These funds had originally been assigned to relieving the Corona pandemic, yet they had not been retrieved at the end of 2021.

that the political offloading of responsibility onto the consumer has worked, at least to some extent, as the responsibility is then again demanded back from some individual politicians or other societal agents. This occurs instead of questioning the system itself or interpreting the issue as a structural problem. In fact, accusations of hypocrisy reflect the need to attribute responsibility.

Political calls to climate action thus still responsibilise the public in questionable ways (see for instance chapter 2, Julia Klöckner's campaign Echt kuh-l![9]), which significantly contributes to the current lack of progress in this regard. This diffusion of responsibility from a politician with obvious influence over outcomes onto not only individuals but in fact *children* (of all people) is deeply problematic: can children in Germany really personally decide to switch their diets from one day to another and spend their 'considerable disposable income' on plant-based food that is often more expensive than meat from mass production[10]? Or will they face considerable headwind from their families that have been eating a certain way for decades? As Norgaard argues, this "focus on individuals is more than a theoretical choice, it has the political function of leaving government and corporations unaccountable" (2018, p. 4).

Two of the experts interviewed for this study were politicians (with individualist outlooks) that were part of the government at the time of the interviews: one held a ministerial position in the Bavarian government, the other one was part of the Bundestag (federal government). They both attempted to justify in the interviews why they did not prioritise the topic of climate change more by elaborating on the many hurdles they reportedly saw themselves confronted with.

The analysed media material also showed that powerful political actors were repeatedly being portrayed as too self-interested or dependent on election outcomes to act decisively on climate change, despite their actual capacity to do so. Besides, participants who actually held considerable influence themselves repeatedly emphasised that climate change was a global challenge. This (perceived or professed) inefficacy of established actors, besides the pronounced levels of responsibility they are endowed with by the voter, results again in a marked divergence between responsibility and efficacy. This is similar to what Norgaard observed in the Norwegian community she studied (refer to section 2.5). Other political and civil society actors then often utilise this to challenge dominant scientific and 'official' climate cultures and to advance counterarguments, thereby rendering the successful implementation of climate action ever more unlikely.

9 Questionable ways beyond merely the name "Echt kuh-l!" (this is a wordplay on the words 'cool' and 'cow'; the German word 'Kuh' [spoken'*ku*] means 'cow').

10 Side note: as a vegan myself, I could fill this entire chapter with reports on the real obstacles one faces in familial and social settings where such diet switches can cause real opposition, tension and power struggles.

Policymakers are not as limited in their efficacy as they often claim when stating that 'their hands are tied' (as they did in the interviews, see chapter 4). As Lewis Akenji writes, they treat "individual consumption as a sovereign domain, which is beyond the reach of public intervention" (2013, p. 3, cited in Kenner, 2015, p. 10). At the same time, they do not shy away from restricting other harmful practices such as smoking and drinking, citing health reasons. Seemingly unpopular measures having been decisively implemented during the course of the Covid-19 pandemic further proves that politicians can indeed act in a determined manner. Besides, as Akenji confers further, "there is little logic in individual freedom that consumes away the livelihood of an entire planet!" (2013, p. 3, cited in Kenner, 2015, p. 10). Politicians' stance towards efficacy is interesting here as in this study it was found that they still managed to diffuse their own responsibility even though they often perceived their efficacy levels to be high. This occurred either by downplaying of efficacy as decision-makers or by blending out that the public at large has a completely different efficacy at its disposal.

However, not all the politicians' statements analysed indicate such deflection of responsibility. In contrast to the conservative politicians, the politicians who advocated for more collectivist approaches perceived themselves as both responsible and influential regarding climate action. At the same time, they were also more inclined to recognise the real obstacles many members of the population experienced in daily life that reduced individuals' efficacy (cf. Ford and Norgaard, 2020; Kessler and Rau, 2022). Therefore, these political circles tended to only hold the population responsible on a moral basis.

This, in turn, was often strongly rejected by some other (anti-climate action) groups within the population. Generally, in those instances where responsibility and efficacy levels were more congruent (e.g., NGO focus group, chapter 6; pro-action public climate culture, chapter 5), people reported to engage in climate action. This professed correspondence between responsibility and efficacy was then also often mentioned by members of these climate cultures (e.g., in social media postings), studded with arguments based on moral obligation. This reflects moral responsibility attributions from political directions. Again, this presented an ideal target for attacks on the grounds of perceived conformity or naivety from opposing segments of the population. Yet situations were also recounted where there would have been room for personal choice in higher income groups, but efficacy was then frequently hampered by political action, impracticability (see example above, organic shopping), social reasons or inconclusive information (see chapter 5, inaction subculture II).

Overall and in accordance with the conceptual work presented in chapter 2, there was a growing recognition among the majority of the experts interviewed (see chapter 4) that too much responsibility was being put on individuals. Recognising this lessens the gap between responsibility and efficacy, paving the way for future progress towards climate action. Some experts for instance focused on *strategic* individual action in the sense of *avoiding the worst excesses*, indicating that responsibility was already being considered in concordance with efficacy. This recognition was confirmed by what was said in some elite climate cultures, for instance by the collectively oriented climate cultures identified in the media analysis.

As the actual divergence between responsibility and efficacy is low for the political and pronounced for the private sphere, it makes sense that focus should be placed on the political realm. If the legislative landscape actually only permitted low carbon behaviours, or at least punished the most carbon intensive practices (like flying), it would be much harder to offload so much of the responsibility for climate action onto the consumer. Climate action thus urgently needs to become the path of least resistance.

Saving the world with non-plastic straws?[11]

Yet, conventional ways of communicating appeals to climate action usually provide information on products' climate impacts and the comparative benefits of voluntarily shopping for green alternatives (e.g., labelling of sustainable products, green shopping guides). Calls to actually reduce consumption feature much less, however. Here, some say that if inequality were reduced, environmental impact would also decrease as sustainable consumption would then become more accessible to more of the public (cf. Laurent, 2014; Wilkinson and Pickett, 2010, cit. in Kenner, 2015, p. 03). Yet this still neglects that 'green' consumption, besides generally being more expensive, brings significant extra effort as alternatives must be researched and labels must be read while shopping. Being able to expend such efforts would translate into higher efficacy (influence over outcomes) for consumers, which however remains unrealistic given that most of the population is either time- or resource poor. Furthermore, climate-friendly alternatives are not always readily available, for example in sub-, peri-urban or rural areas. Online shopping is no viable alternative either as it means long transport distances (and also problematic working conditions for delivery personnel, among other things).

Understandings of responsibility and efficacy transported into society therefore also primarily reflect privileged people's views and experiences. Here it is necessary and helpful to distinguish between 'lived' responsibility and 'everyday' efficacy versus *official* responsibility attributions and efficacy expectations: those rich in (cultural) capital responsibilising other segments of the public by pointing out how 'dirty' their diesels are, together with all the other climate harmful practices they perform on a daily basis, is not a particularly motivating discourse, especially when it is so hard to forego them. This is therefore often not received well by those groups

11 Joke made by one of the craftsmen.

within the public. These political calls to action being repeatedly mocked by some parts of the population indicates how ill-fated this strategy truly is (refer to e.g., chapter 5, and chapter 6). Here, the lack of consideration of the population's everyday realities within elite messages becomes particularly apparent. Perceived limitations in self-efficacy due to financial problems, time pressure (cf. Rau and Edmondson, 2013), or a(n apparent) lack of competencies in dealing with the complexity of climate change present real obstacles. This is further exacerbated through elite's privileged demeanour (cf. Fox and Rau, 2017; Ford and Norgaard, 2020).

Climate-cultural variations also surfaced with regard to different ways of knowing: trust in different ways of knowing varied among members of the public. many of them fiercely rejected the role of emotional messages. For instance, some respondents emphasised that they did not want to be 'framed' (craftsman) by the originators of official messages, and that the subject of climate change was being discussed 'way too emotionally' (farmer). Yet again, the farmers but also the NGO employees underlined the need for practical information that would match people's needs and daily lives more closely. Beyond this, it was important to some participants less rich in cultural capital to prove that they were sufficiently scientifically literate to participate in the debate. At the same time, these less privileged groups were more likely to embrace conspiracy theories, which shows, first, that emotions do play a decisive role in these discourses, and second, that one was not actually endorsing the current scientific consensus. Therefore, in this case the conveying of knowledge operates not only through the transmission of information but crucially also through affective, emotional and embodied messages.

Elite knowledge concepts also varied in their degree of reflection: some experts mentioned information deficits and deemed them problematic for advancing climate action. Yet other statements indicated that participants were moving beyond counting on factual information only. Still, the value of evidence-based scientific knowledge and rationality remain central among more privileged groups. In fact, a deep faith in science and information provision as 'silver bullet' was discernible.

Yet, the question remains why effective climate action stays so elusive given the comparative affluence of German society and the existence of sufficient information about climate change, at least since the Brundtland Report of 1987. Some (social media) statements from non-elite climate cultures confirm that trust in precisely these scientific types of information is not necessarily present in parts of the population. This fact alone points to the inadequacy of relying (more or less) exclusively on closing the public's information deficits. Besides, sustainable alternatives are almost always more expensive because of the structural conditions decision-makers who frequent exclusive elite circles have set in place. That climate-harmful practices are 'mostly those that are the most fun', as one green startup employee poignantly stated, further makes it unlikely that people will be rationally convinced to voluntarily forego them. Yet, the conservative politicians interviewed still attributed responsibility to consumers and expected them, due to their alleged power over market demand, to actually be able to make a difference. Some members of elite climate cultures tended to use a more encompassing notion of knowledge that included emotional messages. Such recognition of other types of knowledge was however mainly displayed by more progressively oriented speakers.

'Knowing' is more than just 'knowing'

From this emerges that what ultimately counts most is actually the acceptance of different types of knowing and facts (see chapter 2) within each climate culture. Here, a traditional focus on the cognitive dimensions of knowledge contrasts with public climate debates that are interspersed with references to embodied knowledge, everyday practices and emotions. This lends support to the use of emotional appeals in climate action initiatives.

Some experts interviewed (see chapter 4) also noticed widespread resignation among members of the public in an attempt to avoid experiences of fear and hopelessness. This points to the paradoxical situation where increasing levels of (threatening) information may prove counterproductive because they actually defer or prevent effective action. Numerous studies have shown that particularly alarming messages in catastrophic or apocalyptic discourses have not helped advance climate action (cf. Norgaard, 2011 and 2018; Ford and Norgaard, 2019; Kundzewicz et al., 2020). According to Norgaard (2011), these often result in resignation and denial for self-protection as this saves actors from experiencing negative emotions. "Cognitions related to climate change are avoided because they create [cognitive] dissonance and are thus troubling" (Norgaard, 2011, p. 217). The statement about cooking workshops with children in one of the focus group discussions (NGO, see section 6.4) confirms this. This suggests that less alarmist and catastrophic messages might help to remove emotional barriers to climate action.

What does, however, cause people to behave in certain ways is the principal and primal human desire to belong. Belonging to a certain group of people, a family unit, a group of friends, a work team, a particular culture, represents a true necessity for humans as social beings. Human action is to a large extent driven by this need to belong and express one's affiliation to particular social circles. Taking this into account is vital for attaining successful climate action in the future. Being presented with factual information on why meat consumption is particularly harmful to the climate will not make people sell their barbecue, especially if their circle of friends consists of steak connoisseurs. In this case, emotion trumps information, as feelings of belonging are often much more powerful than any information campaign can ever be. Social circles offer emotional ties, a fact that climate communication approaches have fatefully neglected thus far.

7.4 Differences in denial

Lastly, specific observed climate-cultural combinations of responsibility, efficacy and knowing each translate into different forms of collective denial (cf. Norgaard, 2011, section 2.5). In terms of the focus groups' overall tendencies to deny, the farmers and the craftsmen showed the highest levels and also the only outright denial of climate change, with both presenting elaborate conspiracy theories. In both groups, responsibility was almost entirely externalised, efficacy was expected to be particularly low, and the concept of knowing was very narrow. But these two groups were not the only ones with pronounced levels of denial. The groups of the mobility provider and the green startup (and to an extent also the industrial enterprise), which all consisted of highly educated individuals, showed more implicit denial (e.g., by justifying continued flying through presenting it as deeply personal choice), especially in the sense that Norgaard conceptualises (refer to section 2.5). This reflects Ford and Norgaard's view that "[e]mphases on apathy and scepticism foreground the responses of the most privileged communities" (2020, p. 44). The following diagram illustrates the key features of both types of group specific denial patterns:

Figure 6: Types of Denial, own presentation, adapted from Sutton and Norgaard, 2013, p. 520

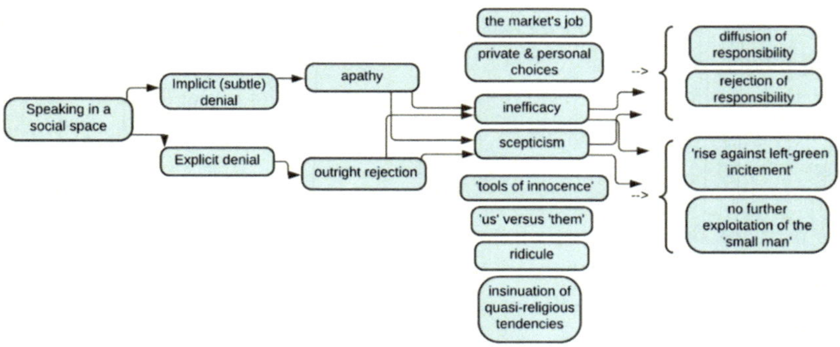

This study thus adds to Norgaard's work on the social organisation of denial by presenting instances where groups consider their responsibility and efficacy to be significant, yet they still manage to push this away. As has been discussed in chapter 2, in relation to climate matters, there occurs wide-spread diffusion of responsibility. This is also the case even when agents ascribe responsibility for climate action to themselves. Stoll-Kleemann and O'Riordan have found this kind of moral decoupling or implicit denial to be on the rise, whilst they saw explicit denial decrease: "This means, compared to [our] 2001 study, that denial is not so much observable in terms of pronouncing it with words, but that it continues to be existent in terms of instigating climate-change mitigation action" (2020, p. 11).

Culture functions in part by providing frameworks of meaning that shape what its adherents habitually and collectively notice and what, by contrast, is deemed irrelevant (cf. Norgaard, 2011, section 2.5). Expressions embodied in popular culture such as art and music play a key role here. Politics does not exclusively take place in parliamentary debate, it also unfolds elsewhere, for example through satire on TV (e.g., shows such as *extra3* or *Die heute show*) or fiction writing. "Thus, while the coherent articulation of ideas still remains central to political life, political sentiments in the form of dominant and oppositional social imaginaries are increasingly embedded in various modes of cultural expression and resonate in the subjective realm of affect" (Dahlgren, 2012, p. 9). Whilst people who explicitly deny climate change are largely aware of themselves rejecting climate action, those practicing the more implicit denial may actually paradoxically consider themselves quite climate conscious (e.g., mobility provider). They may find climate action important, yet their actual behaviour does not reflect this. Their denial operates more on subconscious levels. Denial by elite figures may also serve the purpose of maintaining existing power relations and securing one's own position of privilege. As Norgaard writes, elites do not only profit financially from practicing denial when not paying extra for the climate-friendly alternative, they also save themselves from troubling cognitive dissonance (cf. chapter 2).

To shed more light onto climate-culturally specific denial patterns, the analysis of the focus groups yielded new insight into whether (and how) the occupational field influenced collective interpretation and handling of the current societal imperative to protect the climate (refer to figure 7). Results reveal that this was especially dependent on how the members of a particular professional field defined themselves.

For instance, the climate habitus of the craftsmen rested upon practicality, as various statements about products being equally strictly monitored and thus enjoyable (mass-produced or not) indicated. Norgaard points to people practicing diffusion of responsibility by employing what she calls "cultural tools of innocence" (2011, p. 146, cf. section 2.5) that are often based on referrals to simplicity as this connotes innocence (ibid. p. 161). This allows participants to deny their own responsibility to escape the negative feelings of, for example, being held accountable or feeling guilty.

Both the farmers and the craftsmen employed a similar strategy. Here, they created an imagination of 'us' and 'them' and thereby implicitly deflected responsibility to those they were setting themselves apart from. The farmers did this by juxtaposing the embodied information at their own disposal in what they called practical 'everyday competency' against those with high cultural capital who in their eyes were not advancing matters for the better. Such knowledge elites' allegedly extremely abstract and theoretical types of knowledge were pestered by irrelevance in these farmers' eyes. Similarly, the craftsmen juxtaposed their own closeness to nature and the countryside against people living in the city, who they referred to dismissively. The employment of such imaginative geographies (refer to section 2.5) served as an avenue for diffusing responsibility. The craftsmen further displayed ambivalence towards people working in corporate or managerial positions. Whilst they expressed a certain level of admiration for attaining such positions, they also dismissed them for snobbishly *needing a jour-fixe for everything* (statement craftsman) and opting to take flights to attain them. This sort of ridicule was also used to deflect attention away from one's own responsibility (in cases where responsibility was acknowledged). As described in section 2.5, humour is often used as a strategy to keep an otherwise threatening conversation light-hearted and maintain control. The craftsmen repeatedly employed this strategy (cf. section 6.2). Overall, they displayed the highest level of denial, followed by the farmers, practising both explicit and implicit denial by rejecting climate change and the need to act and also by endorsing conspiracy theories.

Figure 7: Focus groups' levels of attributions of (own) responsibility and (own) efficacy, comprehensiveness of knowledge concept and tendency to deny (own presentation)

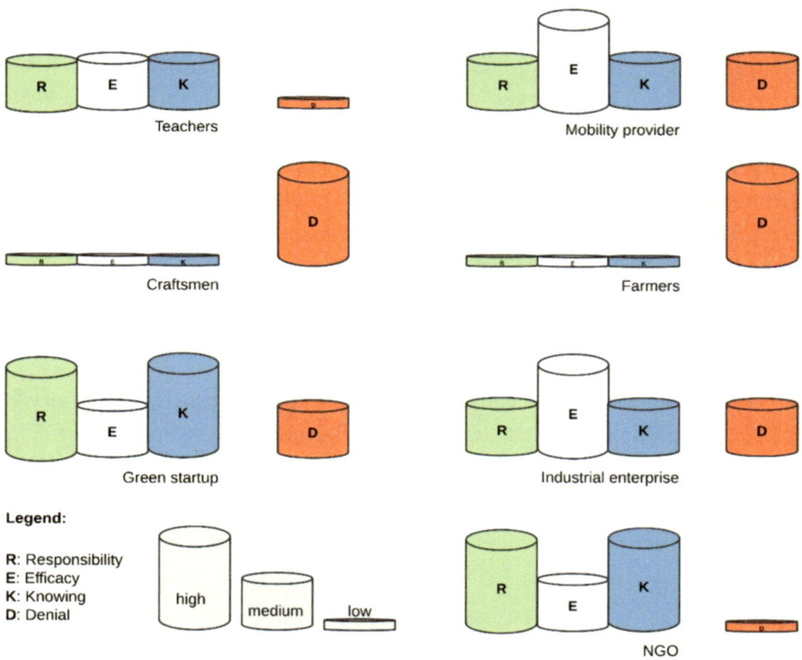

The groups of the green startup and the mobility provider each displayed relatively pronounced levels of implicit denial, which was particularly unexpected insofar as both groups' professional fields and work content were directly concerned with climate matters. One strategy utilised consisted in pointing to others' climate-harmful practices to relativise those undertaken by oneself. This reflects what Norgaard (refer to chapter 2) observed in her study where Norwegians emphasised that the US contributed considerably more to global emissions. Those climate cultures that displayed this type of looking the other way attributed more or less significant amounts of responsibility to themselves (mobility provider medium level, green startup high level) and both had comparatively high efficacy expectations. The knowledge concept of the green startup was also amongst the most comprehensive, yet this still did not result in them escaping denial. Ultimately, each focus group exhibited a certain *climate habitus* (see section 2.4) that also uncovers diverse manifestations of power relations between and within groups.

Climate action and privilege: The fading of conventional socio-economics and the rise of intersectionality

Climate-cultural differences do not surface according to conventional logics of class or socio-economic status alone. Socio-economic status was not related to groups' responsibility attributions (to themselves). Information deficit logic would insinuate that the more educated a group is, i.e., the more knowledge members have about the urgency of acting on climate change, the more responsibly they will act. Yet for instance, the work teams of the mobility provider, the green startup, the industrial enterprise, the teachers and the craftsmen all habitually continued to fly for private enjoyment. With the exception of the craftsmen (and to some extent the industrial enterprise and also the mobility provider), they all struggled to forego flying because of its connection with identity formation. We feel guilty when our different motives collide with each other in cognitive dissonance, showing "how profoundly difficult it can be to be both aware and informed at this point in human history" (Norgaard, 2011, p. 217f.).[12]

This study hence offers a radically different conceptual approach from somewhat outdated conceptions based on lifestyles or milieu models developed by, for example, the German Sinus Institute.[13] Although the concept of the milieu itself is useful, empirical approaches to capture milieu-specific aspects tend to be rather crude: traditional "social milieu or lifestyle theory is mostly descriptive and lacks a strong

12 It must be noted, however, that Norgaard is also very careful not to condone the denial she observes in privileged parts of society.

13 The SINUS Markt- und Sozialforschung GmbH is a market- and social research institute located in Heidelberg.

sociological mechanism" (Rössel, 2007, cited in Lutz, 2016, p. 3). Moreover, lifestyle approaches in particular rest on the assumption that people can more or less freely *choose* a lifestyle, an idea that this study seeked to refute by emphasising the oftentimes hidden but substantial influence of the social. This said, conventional lifestyle or milieu models that are built upon such socio-economic variables have been helpful insofar as they at least acknowledge profound diversity in society.

Some group members of the teachers, the industrial enterprise and the green startup were however each quite defensive about their flying habits, which indicates that they felt at least some responsibility for contributing to high carbon emissions, despite occupying different socio-economic locations – a clear climate-*cultural* similarity. The employees of the NGO were the only ones who displayed a level of responsibility pronounced enough to give up flying. Socio-economic differences alone cannot explain why members of the NGO displayed the highest levels of responsibility while teachers who earn substantially more only displayed medium levels. Clearly, cultural factors make the difference here.

The farmers did not habitually travel by plane, potentially because they could not leave their work for extended periods of time. Their complaint that air traffic was rarely seen as negative (section 6.5) directly contrasts the view of members of the group of the mobility provider who felt that air travel has become the scapegoat of the climate movement. Interestingly, farmers, in turn, also felt repeatedly being made the scapegoat when it came to climate change, as they had recently received much criticism in relation to animal welfare in the realm of the growing vegetarian/vegan movement.

Socio-economic position was, however, closely linked to the efficacy expectations of different groups: financial means and strong networks tend to translate into high power over outcomes. Norgaard points to this in relation to toxic waste, but the same could be said for climate change. "As a result of the forces of distanciation and denial, the environmental problem of toxic waste is invisible to those who do not live near hazardous sites or who can move, hire lawyers, and effectively make a fuss if they do" (2011, p. 219f.). Opportunities to overcome the invisibility of a pressing environmental problem and to show its impact are also clearly not at everybody's disposal.

Regarding information provision and ways of knowing, some links between lower cultural capital and a certain tendency to reject science and scientific information were observed, whilst in these groups there was also vehement (conscious) rejection of any type of emotional debating and framing. By contrast, the capital-richer groups show a fair amount of trust in science. Only occasionally, the benefit of going beyond the exclusively cognitive is recognised here (refer e.g., to statement by Ulf Poschardt, section 5.2).

Ultimately, higher capital stocks did not necessarily lead to lower levels of denial. While those with less cultural capital (farmers and craftsmen) featured aspects of outright climate denial and conspiracy theories, the more implicit denial was very present in some of the more capital-rich groups (mobility provider, green startup). Socio-economic approaches alone fail to account for why these climate-cultural differences each result in denial, albeit via different routes, i.e., different combinations and connotations of responsibility, efficacy and knowing. Thinking of the resulting climate cultures instead as manifestations of climate habitus integrates socio-economic with cultural aspects, which represents a promising avenue for future research. This furthers understanding why climate action is not yet adequately practiced in more disadvantaged societal groups (as official calls to action are simply often irrelevant to their realities), nor even in capital-rich circles that could theoretically (at least financially) afford to do so. That conventional socio-economic variables have become somewhat obsolete in straightforwardly predicting climate-relevant behaviour is also confirmed by the most recent nation-wide study about environmental awareness in Germany[14].

Perhaps most interestingly, this study's results reveal the formation of unexpected climate-cultural coalitions currently forming in society, which is similar to what has also been observed in the context of the recent Corona pandemic. For example, the views of members of the non-elite pro-climate action culture showed considerable overlap with those held by the collective elite climate (sub)cultures. Employees of the mobility provider and craftsmen were equally annoyed about the idea of flight shame, albeit for different reasons. Thirdly and by contrast, the farmers agreed that one should feel guilty about flying (which was probably due to them not habitually doing so), which in this respect is most similar to the responses from the NGO.

In sum, traditional socio-economic variables are being complemented or even replaced by other aspects such as cultural influences related to education and socialisation. Elite climate cultures in Germany have been found to also overlook or ignore calls for climate action. Insights generated in in this study that have emerged by triangulating expert interview-, media analysis- and focus group data are therefore in many ways profound and path-breaking. Perhaps most importantly, they show that elite views that dominate public debates around climate change and -action tend to be rather narrow and homogeneous, which clearly contrasts with evidence of significant climate-cultural diversity in the wider population. The latter range from being

14 Environmental awareness study, 2020 (UBA, 2021, p. 45): identifies six different environmental awareness 'personas' or 'types', none of which could be clearly related to a particular lifestyle. Although there are certain sociodemographic particularities for each type, these were not pronounced enough to produce homogenous groups. In fact, the six environmental awareness types can be found in all age groups and segments of society. Environmental awareness types are further to be understood as dynamic concept. The relation amongst the groups can change as much over time as individuals belonging to one of the groups.

radically pro-climate action to climate change scepticism and even denial. The implications of these findings for climate policy and practice are also wide-ranging, pointing towards the urgent need to take seriously diverse views and practices that impact on people's collective engagement in climate action. The following section will now attend to this challenge.

7.5 Policy recommendations

7.5.1 Difference

Evidence of profound climate-cultural difference in German society clearly presents a number of challenges to policymakers engaged in climate action. Reflecting diverging power relations, different social groups reveal markedly varied, if not truly opposing propensities to act on climate change. If corporate culture rewards frequent flying, messages that inform about the climate impact of flying tend to clash with these workplace-based practices. Therefore, both less privileged and elite groups must be considered and addressed differently for climate initiatives to be relevant and effective.

At the same time, societal conflicts around climate (in)action present a real challenge for climate politics. This has so far received far too little attention. A culture- and context-sensitive social-scientific analysis is uniquely suited to present different options for addressing different climate cultures, by better grasping, analysing and presenting their idiosyncrasies. As such, it can contribute to the meaningful and, crucially, differentiated[15] integration of these insights into German climate policy (cf. Norgaard, 2011; Bulkeley, 2019). Research efforts in this direction should be better resourced in the future.

This observed diversity however also harbours significant conflict potential that points to the limitations of conventional democratic and political processes and decision-making. High levels of climate-cultural diversity identified in this study help explain why official assumptions about information provision have so far proven rather un- or even counterproductive, as a public imagined as uniform entity simply does not exist (cf. section 2.5). The assumption that the majority of the population will internalise the imperative for climate action as soon as provided information is just precise enough, catchy enough or alarming enough has proven false. This also indicates the need to develop new forms of participation, for instance by perceiving of science communication as a two-way street between the scientific community and the public(s), instead of mere information transfer from former to latter.

15 group-specific.

7.5.2 Responsibility, Efficacy, Knowing

Most types of climate-friendly consumption (e-mobility, vegan diets, slow fashion) are still niche phenomena. A lot of insecurity exists in the German population regarding individual contribution to climate action. In fact, people are acutely aware that the effects of their efforts are comparatively miniscule. It must finally be acknowledged that individual efficacy, and therefore individual responsibility, are severely limited.

What individuals can actually do for the climate, however, is refocusing on their role as political agents and contributing to climate action in their different social spheres and on local levels so this can grow into more collective change and re-install faith in democratic processes. What they can also do is behaving and talking as if climate change matters, thereby activating their relational efficacy and declaring war on socially organised denial (cf. Norgaard, 2018, p. 4, section 2.5).

Yet, importantly, it is not individual responsibility that political efforts should focus on. One must consider societal groups' climate-cultural standpoints and practices (that rest upon the concatenation between responsibility, efficacy and knowing) and address them accordingly. Different societal groups have different concepts of, for instance, what is 'the right thing to do' in the way they go about their everyday. To establish a connection to the different living realities within society, one must address this 'lived responsibility'. Only through considering how people actually defray their everyday and make meaning while doing so, climate action can be integrated into people's realities. Here, it is generally neglected that climate-friendly consumption means significant extra effort. Conceiving of consumption as a form of work (Rau, 2015; Hobson et al., 2021) would advance political approaches as this helps explain refusal of time-poor individuals to contribute to climate action and other environmental measures. Instead of focusing on information and its provision, it is vital to consider the social functions of consumption, not just on an individual level but, importantly, also in the collective – for example at the work place. This differentiation is essential for including less visible sections of society and eventually rendering climate action relevant to more people.

Here, it is particularly useful to ask where exactly these discrepancies between responsibility and efficacy lie, and how they may be reduced. This also grants opportunities for broader inclusion of different climate cultures into projects for climate action. Considering decision-makers' particular takes on responsibility and efficacy and the ways these are anchored in their own privileged realities can also ameliorate observed disengagement. Although the capital-richest people[16] represent only a small section of society, their practices are outstandingly detrimental to the climate (cf. UBA, 2021; Di Muzio, 2015, section 1.1, p. 14f.). For this reason alone, they

16 Here: in terms of *economic* capital.

urgently have to be included in climate action. Yet they may have the financial means to simply pay for both mitigation (climate-related taxes) and adaptation. These idiosyncrasies, also of the most privileged, must be considered when drafting policy measures.

Given that corporate and political agents display high levels of actual efficacy or power over societal outcomes, they should also be ascribed significant responsibility to ameliorate climate change. For this it must be differentiated between actual everyday efficacy and expected efficacy. For example, conservative politicians downplaying their own efficacy departs from the actual comparative influence they have.

By contrast, corporate agents often acknowledge their own influence, thus a promising future strategy may be to actually address them from this angle, by pointing out their power and potential for climate action. This is a much more motivating angle than addressing corporations through messages that attest them culpability for past emissions. Taking this avenue of addressing elite figures' efficacy expectations to hold them responsible whilst preventing diffusion of this responsibility has the potential to yield future progress.

The analysis of diverse climate cultures also reveals the need for dominant notions of knowledge to evolve by fusing cognitive, emotional and affective elements rooted in everyday practices and routine conduct. Knowledge itself should be thought of as less cerebral and more emotional and embodied. One avenue that productively engages people emotionally is the presentation of art. Art is also particularly suited to gain people's attention through visual means. As opposed to information provision, art is much closer to bilateral communication between artist and viewer, as here interpretation of the work is particularly salient. Ultimately, the necessity to link both cognitive and emotional aspects of knowing in the context of climate debates emerges as a key challenge to those interested in advancing climate action. Undifferentiated emotional appeals to the public (as well as efforts that focus solely on closing knowledge gaps) appear counterproductive, however.

Also, when drafting climate policy, one must consider "that often decisions are influenced by group identity" (Jackson, 2005, cited in Kenner, 2015, p. 09). When promoting climate action, these social functions are habitually overlooked: in certain social circles, possessing a private car still embodies a status symbol. For many, giving up their cars would entail precisely the kind of costly and uncomfortable retooling that Swidler and Norgaard point towards (see 2.5). Social norms and everyday practices' relative resistance as part of people's habit architecture (mobility, diet, shopping) render appeals to consume differently largely non-effective.

So far, structural conditions like experienced socialisation and practical everyday demands have inadequately been considered in research and policy – a void this study has tackled. Political decision-makers receive valuable impulses regarding how climate action can be developed into a project that is more relevant to people's lives and addresses more of society, which both significantly raises the potential for successful implementation. It is politicians' responsibility to instigate and drive structural change towards private and, arguably much more importantly corporate (high efficacy), climate action. This should entail symbolic and financial incentives but also politically legitimised regulations and targeted prohibiting of what (most) significantly contributes to climate change.

7.5.3 Denial

The explicit recognition of climate-cultural diversity can open up new avenues for climate policy that, for the first time, is also equipped to deal with different forms of climate denial. Denial based on fear of further future financial strain through climate policy and carbon taxation must be addressed markedly differently from denial primarily linked to conservative worldviews, for instance. Justified hesitation towards the feasibility of some climate action measures also has to be approached differently than explicit denial that endorses conspiracy discourses.

Here, the identified climate cultures can be placed into three broad categories: first, climate cultures whose members are already radically pro-climate action (no/low denial), second, climate cultures whose members are undecided and may thus potentially be motivated (or deterred) to contribute, and third, climate cultures whose members reject climate change and the need to act (explicit denial).

The second type accommodates the vast majority of the population, including those that exhibit implicit denial that operates partially on subconscious levels. As shown, the third type consists of a surprisingly sizable and in any case particularly visible group of climate sceptics, some of which even explicitly deny climate science. From a policy perspective, it is urgently necessary to make sense of and address these different types of denial. From this follow a number of key insights:

groups already convinced of climate action can actually be further motivated by new information and scientific insights. Here it is vital to also engage them emotionally as well and point towards their political and relational efficacy.

Climate cultures whose members are not particularly committed to either endorsing or rejecting climate action represent the largest fraction of the public. These people are generally open to science and information, yet they are often preoccupied with demanding everyday lives.

As discussed, many from this unconvinced majority turn a blind eye to calls for climate action (implicit denial), especially when confronted with particularly threatening information. Here, increasing informational bases may prove counterproductive. Climate communicators must deliberate when this may be the case, consider people's specific living situations and ask how climate action could be meaningfully integrated therein. Existing hurdles must also be eliminated. For instance, making opt-out (of climate action) the default instead of current general opt-ins would certainly help. This could concern several contexts, like energy provision, mobility and nutrition.

Caution must be taken when designing research, however: doing so based on what is considered climate-friendly within the 'ivory tower' of scientific institutions pre-empts that this is also perceived as such by all of society. One example is academic literature's and policy's current emphases of green growth and sustainable consumption instead of questioning growth-fetishism (Hamilton, 2004) itself. The frequent surfacing of the 'system question' (as called in this study) in the material confirms this. More inclusive, 'participatory' or 'transformative' approaches may present a step into the right direction here. Yet, Alfred Eberhardt bemoans that "processes that accord participants some form of true participation are still hard to find" (2000, cited in Böde and Gruber, 2000, p. 9). Moreover, Annika-Kathrin Musch emphasises in this respect that practitioners must critically evaluate participatory approaches as they should by no means be seen as a sure-fire success: "'Better' participation, in my understanding, refers to a reflexive, responsible, inclusive and diverse participation, that factors in long-term societal efficacy" (2021, p. 165). Measures springing from such a 'diverse participation' that considers both, responsibility and long-term efficacy could indeed be tailored to the needs and specifics of diverse climate cultures. This then has true potential to substantially advance societal treatment of climate change.

Lastly, much potential lies in engaging people emotionally by stressing that it is not too late for climate action and providing concrete and practicable options, as this will appeal to self-efficacy.

The question of if and how to engage with those rejecting climate action remains most controversial, however. Some say that it is entirely futile to even address these social groups as this will only cause so-called boomerang or backfire effects (cf. e.g., Lewandowsky, 2021; Hornsey et al., 2018, see chapter 2). This springs from the theory that when new information challenges people's core beliefs, this threatens their identity and leads to the incorporation of new material into the already existing belief system. In other words, people will not cease to passionately defend their position (cf. Rosenberg, 1990; Norgaard, 2011, see section 2.5). However, the answer cannot be to simply give up trying to involve these groups in climate debates and actions. It is in fact essential to engage with them and make sense of their life realities and the corresponding specific sources of their explicit denial. If these particularly fervent groups remain excluded, they are left to boil in their (somewhat understandable)[17] resentment which can then easily exacerbate their radicalisation. As their dis-

17 As they are in fact being actively excluded. Yet, one could argue that once people propose the exclusion of others, they thereby disqualify (exclude) themselves, an argument that I find increasingly convincing.

courses often reject science whilst being emotionally engaging instead, they may actually outpace climate communicators in swaying the undecided majority. This is why it is so dangerous to exclude these groups from public discourse.

Several factors let them appear to represent a larger share of the public than they actually are: sceptics often think that much more people share their conviction than is actually the case ('false consensus effect'; Ross et al., 1977). An Australian survey found this effect in all the groups they questioned (cf. Leviston et al., 2013). Believing they have much support, sceptics will less likely reconsider their views. This also makes this small but loud minority seem disproportionately large to the rest of society, which can in turn induce doubt on the scientific establishment of anthropogenic climate change. In combination with so-called 'balance of bias' (Boykoff and Boykoff, 2004) – the media's tendency to give equal attention to both sides of the human cause question (even despite the IPCC-consensus) – this becomes particularly problematic.

How to engage with sceptical and denialist groups then? As Sauer et al. have found in their research aptly titled: "People, not facts, alter students' perceptions on climate change" (2021), employing well-established public figures who certain groups identify with may help: "Our data suggest that [this] may allow for a broadening of cultural identity to include acceptance of climate change" (p. 5800). This strategy was especially effective in increasing more sceptical conservatives' willingness to engage in climate action. Focusing on the local instead of communicating abstract and distant consequences of climate change also furthers engagement of these groups in particular (cf. Hart and Nisbet, 2012).

Inoculation or *prebunking*[18] can also be beneficial: this "involves two elements: first, an explicit warning of an impending disinformation attempt and, second, a refutation of an anticipated argument that exposes its fallacy" (Lewandowsky, 2021)[19]. Inoculation rests upon increasing the addressees' defences or 'immune system' vis-à-vis misinformation by presenting an 'example fallacy' and subsequently explaining how this can easily be debunked. This then stops misinformation from spreading – like a vaccine.

The human tendency to rely on anecdotal and immediately perceivable local evidence (instead of representative results) also plays a role here: challenging 'fake experts' with questionable credentials or credentials relating to a completely different

18 It is granted that this strategy also relies on the provision of (factual) information, which in this particular instance may however prove a useful strategy.

19 To illustrate, one study "applied inoculation to climate change by presenting participants with (a) a warning that political operatives often attempt to cast doubt on the scientific consensus and (b) a detailed explanation of the dissenting fake experts technique that is used to feign a lack of scientific consensus" (Lewandowsky, 2021, p. 11).

field can also be conducive to inoculation (cf. e.g., Van Der Linden, 2020). Questioning frequent employment of so-called ad-hominem argumentation (accusing opponents imperfectly practicing climate action of *hypocrisy*) could serve as such pre-emption. However, exposing cases of ecological fallacy and other limitations to sound scientific argumentation must always be done in a particularly rigorous and reliable manner to avoid equipping sceptics with any further ammunition.

Moreso, particularly resilient myths should be debunked with science communication that is equally, if not more, 'sticky' as Chip Heath and Dan Heath have argued (2007). Ideas that resonate particularly well are those that are surprisingly counter-intuitive (as this engages people) and employ emotional messages, stories, metaphors or analogies.

Measures to effectively address and engage more sceptical societal segments are urgently needed to advance climate action, particularly as these groups have hitherto been notoriously difficult to reach. Communication that does not threaten their worldview may also help through mitigating aforementioned backfire effects (see section 2.4). Promoting climate action by concomitantly endorsing health motivations (encouraging cycling or eating fresh produce) may also work when climate action is an unpopular subject. Similarly, the conversations with the craftsmen and farmers uncovered their respective appreciation of regional produce. This was not based on climate motives but on their connections to their occupation or to the countryside. Besides, principal reasons for scepticism may not actually be climate-related, people may instead hold at their core other rationales like for instance a free-market ideology. Here Dixon et al. (2017) have found that when measures focused on the market's role, conservative groups were more inclined to accept climate science.

This relates to the question of how inherently individualistic information-centrist economic theories (e.g., nudging) have become so hegemonic in modern life. To answer this, it must be asked where power is concentrated and where decisions are made. Here, Norgaard refers to Brulle and Dunlap: "Social science disciplines such as economics and psychology are better able to fit into the scientific models not only because they use individuals as the unit of analysis, but more importantly because they are compatible with existing political and economic paradigms" (2015, cited in Norgaard 2018, p. 4). Recognising this is a necessary precondition to understand phenomena like socially organised denial and how it manifests differently, depending on climate-cultural location.

In response to the hegemony of market economics as bases for policy making, it thus pays to consider the question of *economic literacy*. This came up in two of the focus group discussions (farmers and teachers). One of the teachers stated for instance that it lies in educators' responsibility to teach economics in ways that are more conducive to the collective common good instead of solely those that are based on self-interest. This points to the problematic that in modern society, current performance- and competition-based economic logics have deeply infiltrated almost all areas of daily life, forming the basis of people's sense-making of their socio-economic world surroundings. This facilitates denial of one's own responsibility to protect the climate (professionally and privately), when one is repeatedly told that the market will fix things.

Policymakers, economic scientists, and corporate agents should consider alternative economic theories that go beyond, firstly, the self-interested individual, and secondly, the premises of growth, profit maximisation, efficiency, consumption, and the invisible hand. These unquestioned ideas about how to navigate current economic systems are being communicated already to school children, rendering profound structural change unlikely. When so much emphasis is put on the individual, as shown in this study, and market efficiency, it becomes increasingly improbable that people perceive of themselves as part of a collective they want and need to take responsibility for. This maintains the status quo of "growth-fetishism" (Hamilton, 2004), putting even more strain on the climate in the future.

7.6 Outlook

Future research that therefore looks into the effects of orthodox economic theories within education and their effects on students' worldviews and the resulting (in)compatibility with successful future climate action could bring some much-needed answers.

Research that endorses a new, more encompassing concept of knowledge would also be extremely valuable to the social advancement of climate action. Knowledge itself should be thought of as less cerebral or cognitive and instead as more emotional and embodied. Such a knowledge concept would need to fuse cognitive, emotional, and affective elements and should be rooted in everyday practices and routine conduct.

As shown in this study, thinking of climate cultures as manifestations of climate habitus integrates socio-economic with cultural aspects, which represents a promising avenue for future research. Therefore, investigating climate-cultural leanings in other contemporary societies and how they resemble or depart from the findings gained in this study would also afford further valuable insights.

8 Conclusion

If climate action is to be successful in the future, it has to be planned and implemented as inclusive project involving the whole of society. However, mobilisation of large sections of society has thus far remained behind expectations because official responses to climate change are generally blind to the substantial climate-cultural differences that exist between social groups. Calls to action sent out by political decision-makers (e.g., in political talk shows) are received markedly differently by different societal segments. Thus, first and foremost, this study established profound climate-cultural difference existing in Germany. It set out to shed light on the reasons why some people's passion is lit when confronted with climate change, whilst others are substantially paralysed by the threat and still others reject it outright.

The initially observed homogeneity in outlooks amongst elite groups shows that official calls for more climate action in Germany generally use the language of those privileged segments of society that have had the means to attain the roles of decision-makers or knowledge providers (like politicians, scientists or journalists). In these statements, not much objection to or deviation from official climate-related narratives was found. Yet a sharp contrast was then observed between these elite interpretations that take aspects (anthropogenic component, need to act) on the matter of climate change for granted (elite discourse coalition) and the rest of the public that still debates these aspects as if it were living on a completely different planet.

In direct opposition to this elite discourse coalition stand the eclectic and multifaceted statements made by the focus groups and the non-elite climate cultures 'from below' identified in the media analysis. What particularly stood out in this respect was the widespread climate scepticism and even outright climate change denial that exists, somewhat surprisingly, in Germany. However, this has hitherto remained almost completely invisible in (elite) climate debates, including in academic research, proving that vital insights are missed when one does not look beyond elite discourses. Only certain segments of society hold the privilege, in terms of financial means and time, to contribute to climate action as it is officially being conceived of thus far. This results in the danger that only certain elites will take part and that they will then promote their own interests. Acknowledging and investigating these climate-cultural differences, as done by this study, presents a vital prerequisite for implementing more meaningful climate action that finally engages all of society. One key insight from this study is therefore that climate action does not stand a chance to become an inclusive project involving the whole of society if it keeps being presented only in such elite terms.

For considering these climate-cultural differences, it especially pays to do so in relation to responsibility, efficacy and knowing. Here, it makes particular sense to approach responsibility together with efficacy: for instance, a clearly discernible readiness to lead and shape climate action in the more elite climate cultures often comes with a pronounced self-efficacy expectation. Yet, at the same time there is some variety regarding the attribution of responsibility (either to oneself or others). By contrast, the statements regarding responsibility and efficacy that emerge from the rest of the public's different climate cultures indicate experiences of financial and time-related limitations and perceived or actual impotence. With this comes a more or less deeply rooted scepticism towards the willingness of political and social elites to actually practice climate action. Here, the perceived lack of accountability and distance to the everyday experience of 'common people' attributed to such elites are repeatedly stressed. This irrelevance might lead to even less engagement, as not being addressed and included steers up reactions of anger and opposition, potentially even as an act of defiance. In all this, the divergence between responsibility and efficacy plays a central role. This gap widens (and with it the scepticism becomes further entrenched) when responsibility is repeatedly attributed to individual citizens, for example by means of publicly orchestrated and ministerially endorsed medial calls for climate-friendly food consumption. When this overresponsibilisation collides with the actual limited self-efficacy that defines many people's everyday experiences in a highly complex and bureaucratically operated society, this becomes particularly discouraging. Ultimately, responsibility for climate action can no longer be offloaded onto uniformly imagined standard consumers. Such discrepancies between responsibility and efficacy and also between attributed and self-perceived responsibility or efficacy affect different segments of society in different ways. Steps towards the inclusion of larger segments of the public could therefore lie in thinking responsibility together with efficacy and differentiating between official attributions of responsibility and efficacy and the real lived responsibility and efficacy that people experience in their everyday lives.

Furthermore, information provision alone is not sufficient to spark meaningful climate action. Commonly instigated official information campaigns that aim to motivate consumers to act climate-responsibly must therefore remain below expectations and so they have. Such narrow messages can simply not be equally relevant to different social groups with diverging climate cultures. Besides, unidirectional information deficit logics must be deemed insufficient due to the complexity of human behaviour alone. People have numerous motives that must be prioritised and integrated to surmount crushing ambivalences. Again, this becomes particularly apparent with respect to the startling difference in life-realities of elite and non-elite climate cultures. Both research and policy have thus far neglected the importance of social environments and practical demands that substantially play into people's climate-related everyday behaviour.

This study's findings further show that there is widespread denial present in relation to climate action in Germany. In each instance, different manifestations of such denial reflect different combinations of responsibility, efficacy and knowing. Denial surfaces both explicitly (in the form of resistance movements) and implicitly and is more or less pronounced depending on groups' different social and cultural positions. Clearly, to successfully decarbonise society, this differently manifesting denial must be taken into consideration. However, most approaches so far do not do justice to this diversity – in fact they are entirely blind to it, as they are to social disadvantage. They also completely overlook that current forms of communication also often fail to reach even those privileged parts of society that would actually (at least financially) be equipped to contribute. Climate action can be considered important but the concurrent desire to be perceived as cosmopolitan and worldly can still cause one to take a plane to the southern hemisphere each summer, thereby practicing implicit denial.

Therefore, what constitutes different social imaginaries should by no means be conceived of only as consisting of cognitive ideas and conscious convictions. The necessity to link both cognitive and emotional aspects of knowing in the context of climate debates and action thus emerges as a key challenge to those interested in advancing climate action. New forms of multi-directional, dialogic knowledge exchange like those that surface in the societal dialogues investigated could help alert different actors to their respective responsibilities for climate action. Pointing to people's actual capacities to act could also further the goal of effective climate action.

If such insights were integrated into policy, this would finally render it more applicable, feasible and relevant for people's lives. Here, it is the politicians' responsibility to provide the necessary structural framework conditions to enable climate-friendly consumption and, arguably much more importantly (due to corporate efficacy being profound), also production. This should entail symbolic and financial incentives but also politically legitimised regulations and targeted prohibiting of what is particularly significantly contributing to climate change. The discrepancy between responsibility and efficacy shrinks the moment political decision-makers act climate-responsibly, according to the mandate they were given by the voter. Differentiated and targeted addressing of diverse social groups and establishing links to their lived everyday realities present possible first steps.

The meaning of climate change does not simply exist out there waiting to be unveiled by science and subsequently transmitted to the public. Instead, meaning must be made in ways that can be integrated consistently and, in turn, *meaningfully* with what already matters in people's lives. This type of sense making is thoroughly shaped by the different socialities people are surrounded by on a daily basis. This study's data on climate-related debates that occur across different media formats and occupational fields clearly reiterates this lack of attunement that exists in German society regarding who should take the lead in climate action or who can actually make a true difference. Its results thus underscore the need for a markedly more culture-sensitive and therefore inclusive societal engagement with climate change as a precondition for successfully implementing current and future climate action targets and measures.

References

ADAM, B. and GROVES, C. 2007. *Future matters: Action, knowledge, ethics,* Leiden, the Netherlands: Brill.

ADAMS, J. 2007. Risk management: It's not rocket science...... It's much more complicated. *Risk Management,* 54, 36.

AKENJI, L. N/A. *Sustainable Consumption or Consumer Scapegoatism?.* Institute for Global Environmental Strategies. Part of the discussion on "Sustainable consumption – whose responsibility is it?

ALKEMEYER, T. 2018. Verantwortung als Komplizenschaft oder als gesellschaftskritischer Gegen-Entwurf? *In:* HENKEL, A., LÜDTKE, N., BUSCHMANN, N. and HOCHMANN, L. (eds.) *Reflexive Responsibilisierung. Verantwortung für nachhaltige Entwicklung.* Bielefeld, Germany: transcript Verlag.

ANDERSON, B. 1983. *Imagined Communities,* New York, New York, USA: Knopf Doubleday Publishing Group.

ANNE WILL. 2019. *Streit um CO_2-Steuer – wer zahlt für den Klimaschutz?* Berlin, Germany.

AßLÄNDER, M. S. 2011. Unternehmerische Verantwortung und die Rolle der Konsumenten. *In:* HEIDBRINK, L., SCHMIDT, I. and AHAUS, B. (eds.) *Die Verantwortung des Konsumenten. Über das Verhältnis von Markt, Moral und Konsum.* Frankfurt a.M., Germany/New York, USA: Campus Verlag.

BACKES, L., BECKER, T., GORRIS, L., HORCHERT, J., JAENSCH, A.-L., KÜHN, A., MÜLLER, A.-K., OLBRISCH, M., POPP, M., ROSENBACH, M., SCHEUERMANN, C. and THIMM, K. 2019. Kinder der Apokalypse. *Der Spiegel.* 23/2019. Hamburg.

BANDURA, A. 1977. Self-efficacy: Toward a unifying theory of behavior change. *Psychological Review,* 84, pp. 191–21.

BANDURA, A. 1982. Self-efficacy mechanism in human agency. *American Psychologist,* 37, p. 122.

BANDURA, A. 1994. Social cognitive theory and exercise of control over HIV infection. *Preventing AIDS.* Berlin, Germany: Springer Verlag GmbH.

BANDURA, A. 1995. *Self-efficacy in changing societies,* Cambridge, UK: Cambridge University Press.

BANDURA, A. 1997. *Self-efficacy: The exercise of control*. New York, New York, USA: Freeman.

BAUMAN, Z. 1995. *Life in fragments: Essays in postmodern morality,* Oxford, UK: Blackwell.

BAUMAN, Z. 2001. *The individualised society,* Cambridge, UK: Polity Press.

BECK, U. 1986. *Risikogesellschaft: Auf dem Weg in eine andere Moderne,* Frankfurt a.M., Germany: Suhrkamp Verlag.

BECK, U. 1992. *Risk society: Towards a new modernity,* London, UK: Sage Publications.

BECK, U. 1997. *The Reinvention of Politics,* Cambridge, UK: Polity Press.

BECK, U. 1998. *Wie wird Demokratie im Zeitalter der Globalisierung möglich)? – Eine Einleitung,* in (ibid.) (ed.), Politik der Globalisierung, Frankfurt a. M., Germany: Suhrkamp.

BECK, U. 2009. *World at risk,* Cambridge, UK: Polity Press.

BECK, U. 2010. Klima des Wandels oder Wie wird die Grüne Moderne möglich? In: WELZER, H., SOEFFNER, H.-G. and GIESECKE, D. (eds.) *KlimaKulturen: Soziale Wirklichkeiten im Klimawandel*. Frankfurt a.M./New York, New York, USA: Campus Verlag.

BEDER, S. 2001. Global spin. *In:* STARKEY, R. and WELFORD, R. (eds.) *Earthscan Reader in Business and Sustainable Development.* London, UK: Earthscan.

BICKMAN, L. and ROG, D. J. 2008. *The SAGE handbook of applied social research methods,* London, UK: Sage Publications.

BIELING, H.-J. 2014. Neogramscianismus. *Theorien der Internationalen Politischen Ökonomie.* Berlin, Germany: Springer VS.

BILHARZ, M. 2007. Key Points nachhaltigen Konsums. *Nachhaltiger Konsum und Verbraucherpolitik,* 21, pp. 105–138.

BLAKE, J. 1999. Overcoming the 'value-action gap' in environmental policy: Tensions between national policy and local experience. *Local Environment,* 4, pp. 257–278.

BMEL. 2019. Klima. Wandel. Landwirtschaft. – Du entscheidest! *Start des Schulwettbewerbs "Echt kuh-l!".* Nr. 225/2019 ed. Berlin, Germany: Bundesministerium für Ernährung und Landwirtschaft.

BÖDE, U. and GRUBER, E. 2000. *Klimaschutz als sozialer Prozess,* Heidelberg, Germany: Pysica.

BOSTRÖM, M. and DAVIDSON, D. J. 2018. *Environment and Society: Concepts and Challenges,* Berlin, Germany: Springer-Verlag GmbH.

BOURDIEU, P. 1984. *Distinction: A social critique of the judgement of taste,* Boston, Massachusetts, USA: Harvard University Press.

BOURDIEU, P. [1977] 1990. *The logic of practice,* Stanford, California, USA: Stanford University Press.

BOURDIEU, P. 1990. *In other words: Essays towards a reflexive sociology*. Stanford, California, USA: Stanford University Press.

BOURDIEU, P. 1997. Die männliche Herrschaft. *In:* DÖLLING, I. and KRAIS, B. (eds.) *Ein alltägliches Spiel. Geschlechterkonstruktion in der sozialen Praxis.* Frankfurt a.M., Germany: Suhrkamp.

BOURDIEU, P. 1998. *Practical reason: On the theory of action,* Stanford, California, USA: Stanford University Press.

BOURDIEU, P., PASSERON, J.-C. and MOLDENHAUER, E. 1973. *Grundlagen einer Theorie der symbolischen Gewalt,* Frankfurt a.M., Germany: Suhrkamp.

BOYKOFF, M. T. and BOYKOFF, J. M. 2004. Balance as bias: Global warming and the US prestige press. *Global Environmental Change,* 14, pp. 125–136.

BREMER, H. 2004. *Von der Gruppendiskussion zur Gruppenwerkstatt: Ein Beitrag zur Methodenentwicklung in der typenbildenden Mentalitäts-, Habitus-und Milieuanalyse,* Münster, Germany: LIT Verlag Münster.

BROWN, C. C. 1979. *Beyond the bottom line,* New York, New York, USA: MacMillan Publishing Company.

BRANDNER, S. 2019. Facebook post, https://www.facebook.com/stBrandner/photos/a.1769206119967250/2587552268132627/, [Accessed 28/12/2023].

BRULLE, R. J., CARMICHAEL, J. and JENKINS, J. C. 2012. Shifting public opinion on climate change: an empirical assessment of factors influencing concern over climate change in the US, 2002–2010. *Climatic Change,* 114, pp. 169–188.

BRYMAN, A. 2008. *Social Research Methods,* Oxford, UK: Oxford University Press.

BULKELEY, H. 2019. Navigating climate's human geographies: Exploring the whereabouts of climate politics. *Dialogues in Human Geography,* 9, pp. 3–17.

BUNDESAMT FÜR NATURSCHUTZ. 2014. *Naturbewusstsein 2013: Bevölkerungsumfrage zu Natur und biologischer Vielfalt.* Berlin, Germany: Bundesministerium für Umwelt, Naturschutz, Bau und Reaktorsicherheit (BMUB/BfN).

BUNDESMINISTERIUM FÜR WIRTSCHAFT UND KLIMASCHUTZ. 2022. *Nationale Klimaschutzinitiative.* https://www.klimaschutz.de/de, [Accessed 31/10/2023].

BUNDESTAG, D. 1949. Deutsches Grundgesetz. Berlin, Germany: Deutscher Bundestag.

BURKE, N. J., JOSEPH, G., PASICK, R. J. and BARKER, J. C. 2009. Theorizing social context: Rethinking behavioral theory. *Health Education and Behavior,* 36, pp. 55–70.

BUSCHMANN, N. and SULMOWSKI, J. 2011. Von "Verantwortung" zu "doing Verantwortung". Subjektivierungstheoretische Aspekte nachhaltigkeitsbezogener Responsibilisierung. *In:* HEIDBRINK, L., SCHMIDT, I. and AHAUS, B. (eds.) *Die Verantwortung des Konsumenten. Zum Verhältnis von Markt, Moral und Konsum.* Frankfurt a.M., Germany/New York, USA: Campus.

BUTLER, C. 2010. Morality and climate change: Is leaving your TV on standby a risky behaviour? *Environmental Values,* 19/2, pp. 169–192.

BUTTERWEGGE, C., 2020. *Ungleichheit in der Klassengesellschaft.* Kologne, Germany: PapyRossa Verlag.

CALLAGHAN, G. 2005. Accessing habitus: Relating structure and agency through focus group research. *Sociological Research Online,* 10, pp. 33–44.

CIALDINI, R. B., WOSINSKA, W., BARRETT, D. W., BUTNER, J. and GORNIK-DUROSE, M. 1999. Compliance with a request in two cultures: The differential influence of social proof and commitment/consistency on collectivists and individualists. *Personality and Social Psychology Bulletin,* 25, pp. 1242–1253.

CIALDINI, R. B., WOSINSKA, W. B., DANIEL W., BUTNER, J. and GORNIK-DUROSE, M. 1993. *Influence: Science and practice,* Boston, Massachusetts, USA: Pearson Education Boston.

COHEN, S. 2001. *States of denial: Knowing about atrocities and suffering.* Cambridge, UK: Polity Press.

COLEMAN, J. S. 1958. Relational analysis: the Study of social organizations with survey methods. *Human Organization,* 17, pp. 28–36.

COOK, J., NUCCITELLI, D., GREEN, S.A., RICHARDSON, M., WINKLER, B., PAINTING, R., WAY, R., JACOBS, P. AND SKUCE, A. 2013. Quantifying the consensus on anthropogenic global warming in the scientific literature. *Environmental research letters*, 8/2, p. 024024.

DAHLGREN, P. 2012. *Social media and counter-democracy: The contingences of participation. International Conference on Electronic Participation*, Kristiansand, Norway. Berlin/Heidelberg, Germany: Springer, pp. 1–12.

DAVIDSON, D. 2012. Analysing responses to climate change through the lens of reflexivity. *The British journal of sociology*, 63/4, pp. 616–640.

DAVIES, P. 2012. The limits of science: Paul Davies, Theoretical physicist. *New Statesman.* London, UK.

DI MUZIO, T. 2015. *The 1 % and the rest of us: A political economy of dominant ownership,* London, UK: Bloomsbury Publishing.

DIERIG, C. 2019. Das schmutzige 1442-Kilometer-Problem der Milch in Glasflaschen. *Die Welt*, 23/07/2019.

DIXON, G., HMIELOWSKI, J. and MA, Y. 2017. Improving climate change acceptance among US conservatives through value-based message targeting. *Science Communication,* 39, pp. 520–534.

DRYZEK, J. S., DOWNES, D., HUNOLD, C., SCHLOSBERG, D., HERNES, H.-K. 2003. *Green states and social movements: environmentalism in the United States, United Kingdom, Germany, and Norway*. Oxford, UK: Oxford University Press.

DUBOIS, G., SOVACOOL, B., AALL, C., NILSSON, M., BARBIER, C., HERRMANN, A., BRUYÈRE, S., ANDERSSON, C., SKOLD, B. and NADAUD, F. 2019. It starts at home? Climate policies targeting household consumption and behavioral decisions are key to low-carbon futures. *Energy Research and Social Science,* 52, pp. 144–158.

DUNLAP, R. E. and BRULLE, R. J. 2015. *Climate Change and Society: Sociological Perspectives,* Oxford, UK: Oxford University Press.

EBERHARDT, A. 2000. Partizipationsmodelle zur breiten Einbindung gesellschaftlicher Akteure in Prozesse der Nachhaltigkeit. *Klimaschutz als sozialer Prozess.* Heidelberg, Germany: Springer.

ECO, U. 2021. *Verschwörungen: Eine Suche nach Mustern,* Munich, Germany: Hanser

EHRHARDT-MARTINEZ, K., RUDEL, T. K., NORGAARD, K. M. and BROADBENT, J. 2015. Mitigating climate change. *Climate change and society: Sociological perspectives*, pp. 199–234.

ELIASOPH, N. 1998. *Avoiding politics: How Americans produce apathy in everyday life,* Cambridge, UK: Cambridge University Press.

EMIRBAYER, M. 1997. Manifesto for a relational sociology. *American journal of sociology,* 103, pp. 281–317.

ERNST, A. 2010. Individuelles Umweltverhalten – Probleme, Chancen, Vielfalt. In: WELZER, H., SOEFFNER, H.-G. and GIESECKE, D. (eds.) *KlimaKulturen. Soziale Wirklichkeiten im Klimawandel.* Frankfurt a.M., Germany/New York, USA: Campus.

EUROSTAT. 2023. *Deutschland: Entwicklung der Einkommensungleichheit auf Basis des Gini-Index im Zeitraum 2010 bis 2022.* Statista GmbH. https://de.statista.com/statistik/daten/studie/1184266/umfrage/einkommensungleichheit-in-deutschland-nach-dem-gini-index/ [Accessed 31/10/2023].

FELL, D., AUSTIN, A., KIVINEN, E. and WILKINS, C. 2009. *The diffusion of environmental behaviours; the role of influential individuals in social networks.* In: LYNDHURST, B. (ed.). London, UK: Defra.

FINCH, J. 1987. The vignette technique in survey research. *Sociology,* 21, pp. 105–114.

FINCH, J. and MASON, J. 2003. *Negotiating family responsibilities,* Milton Park, Abingdon-on-Thames, UK: Routledge.

FISHER, D. R. 2006. Bringing the material back in: Understanding the US position on climate change. *Sociological Forum*. Heidelberg, Germany: Springer, pp. 467–494.

FORD, A. 2019. The Self-sufficient Citizen: Ecological Habitus and Changing Environmental Practices. *Sociological Perspectives,* 62, pp. 627–645.

FORD, A. and NORGAARD, K. M. 2019. From Denial to Resistance: How Emotions and Culture Shape our Response to Climate Change. *In* Feola, G., Geoghegan, H., & Arnall, A. (Eds.). *Climate and culture: Multidisciplinary perspectives on a warming world*. Cambridge, UK: Cambridge University Press, pp. 219f.

FORD, A. and NORGAARD, K. M. 2020. Whose everyday climate cultures? Environmental subjectivities and invisibility in climate change discourse. *Climatic Change,* 163, pp. 1–20.

FOUCAULT, M. 1977. *The History of Sexuality: 1: The Will to Knowledge,* London, UK: Penguin UK.

FOX, E. 2014. *Society, Power and Climate Change: A social critique of public climate change receptivity in Ireland.* Doctor of Philosophy, National University of Ireland, Galway.

FOX, E. and RAU, H. 2017. Disengaging citizens? Climate change communication and public receptivity. *Irish Political Studies,* 32, pp. 224–246.

FOX KELLER, E. 1985. *Reflections on gender and science*. New Haven, Connecticut, USA: Yale University Press.

FRANTZ, C. M. and MAYER, F. S. 2009. The emergency of climate change: Why are we failing to take action? *Analyses of Social Issues and Public policy,* 9, pp. 205–222.

GARDINER, S. M. 2001. The real tragedy of the commons. *Philosophy and Public Affairs,* 30, pp. 387–416.

GEO MAGAZIN. 2000. *Grüner Punkt für Grünes Gewissen*. Geo Magazin, July. Hamburg, Germany: G+J Medien GmbH.

GHERARDI, S. 2008. *Introduction: The critical power of the practice lens*. London, England, UK: SAGE Publications.

GIDDENS, A. 1979. *Central problems in social theory: Action, structure, and contradiction in social analysis*, Berkely, California, USA: University of California Press.

GIDDENS, A. 2009. *Politics of climate change,* Cambridge, UK: Polity Press.

GLANTZ, M. 1999. *Creeping environmental problems and sustainable development in the Aral Sea basin*, Cambridge, UK: Cambridge University Press.

GOFFMAN, E. 1959. *Regions and region behaviour. The presentation of self in everyday life*. London, UK: Penguin Books.

GOLDBLATT, D. 2004. *Knowledge and the social sciences: Theory, method, practice,* Milton Park, Abingdon-on-Thames, UK: Routledge.

GRAMSCI, A. 1971. *Selections from the prison notebooks*. New York, USA: International Publishers.

GREENE, J. 2016. Do emotions and morality mix?. Interview by Lauren Cassani Davis. *The Atlantic Monthly Group*. Boston, Massachusetts, USA.

GRUNDMANN, R. 2007. Climate change and knowledge politics. *Environmental politics,* 16, pp. 414–432.

GRUNWALD, A. 1999. Verantwortungsbegriff und Verantwortungsethik. *In:* GRUNDWALD, A. (ed.) *Rationale Technikfolgenbeurteilung. Konzepte und methodische Grundlagen*. Berlin, Germany: Springer.

GRUNWALD, A. 2018. Warum Konsumentenverantwortung allein die Umwelt nicht rettet. Ein Beispiel fehllaufender Responsibilisierung. *In:* HENKEL, A., LÜDTKE, N., BUSCHMANN, N. and HOCHMANN, L. (eds.) *Reflexive Responsibilisierung. Verantwortung für nachhaltige Entwicklung*. Bielefeld, Germany: transcript.

GUHA, R. 2000. *Environmentalism. A global history*. New York, New York, USA: Longman.

HAAS, R. 2021. Süddeutsche Zeitung, 14/07/2021, München, Deutschland: https://www.sueddeutsche.de/muenchen/muenchen-extinction-rebellion-wirtschaftsbeirat-buero-1.5351464 [Accessed 16/09/2022].

HABERMAS, J. 1984. *Reason and the rationalisation of society. Vol. I. The theory of communicative action,* Boston, Massachusetts, USA: Beacon Press.

HAJER, M. A. 1993. *Discourse coalitions,* Durham, North Carolina, USA: Duke University Press.

HAJER, M. A. 2004. Coalitions, Practices, and Meaning in Environmental Politics: From Acid Rain to BSE. *In:* HOWARTH, D. and TORFING, J. (eds.) *Discourse Theory in European Politics: Identity, Policy and Governance.* London, UK: Palgrave Macmillan.

HAMILTON, C. 2004. *Growth fetish,* London, UK: Pluto Press.

BROCKHAGEN, D. 2019. Atmosfair-Chef Brockhagen: Für seinen Mallorca-Flug ist jeder selbst verantwortlich. Interview by Lea Hampel and Vivien Timmler. *Süddeutsche Zeitung*, 10/11/2019.

HARDIN, G. 1968. The tragedy of the commons: The population problem has no technical solution; it requires a fundamental extension in morality. *Science,* 162.

HARDTKE, A. and KLEINFELD, A. 2010. *Gesellschaftliche Verantwortung von Unternehmen,* Wiesbaden, Germany: Betriebswirtschaftlicher Verlag Gabler.

HARES, A., DICKINSON, J. and WILKES, K. 2010. Climate change and the air travel decisions of UK tourists. *Journal of Transport Geography,* 18, pp. 466–473.

HARGREAVES, T. 2011. Practice-ing behaviour change: Applying social practice theory to pro-environmental behaviour change. *Journal of Consumer Culture,* 11, pp. 79–99.

HART ABER FAIR. 2019. *Die Erde schwitzt, das Eis schmilzt: Wie radikal müssen wir uns ändern?* Cologne/Berlin, Germany.

HART, P. S. and NISBET, E. C. 2012. Boomerang effects in science communication: How motivated reasoning and identity cues amplify opinion polarization about climate mitigation policies. *Communication Research,* 39, pp. 701–723.

HAYTHORNTHWAITE, C. 1996. Social network analysis: An approach and technique for the study of information exchange. *Library and Information Science Research,* 18, pp. 323–342.

HEATH, C. and HEATH, D. 2007. *Made to stick: Why some ideas survive and others die,* New York, New York, USA: Random House.

HEIDBRINK, L. 2003. *Kritik der Verantwortung,* Weilerswist, Germany: Velbrück Wissenschaft.

HEIDBRINK, L. and HIRSCH, A. 2006. *Verantwortung in der Zivilgesellschaft: Zur Konjunktur eines widersprüchlichen Prinzips,* Frankfurt a.M., Germany/New York, New York, USA: Campus Verlag.

HEIMANN, T. 2016. *Klimakulturen und Raum: Umgangsweisen mit Klimawandel an europäischen Küsten,* Wiesbaden, Germany: Springer-VS.

HEIMANN, T. and MALLICK, B. 2016. Understanding climate adaptation cultures in global context: Proposal for an explanatory framework. *Climate,* 4, pp. 59f.

HEISSERER, B. and RAU, H. 2017. Capturing the consumption of distance? A practice-theoretical investigation of everyday travel. *Journal of Consumer Culture,* 17, pp. 579–599.

HENKEL, A. and LINDEMANN, G. 2018. Reflexion der Beiträge: Individuum und Gesellschaft. *In:* HENKEL, A., LÜDTKE, N., BUSCHMANN, N. and HOCHMANN, L. (eds.) *Reflexive Responsibilisierung. Verantwortung für Nachhaltige Entwicklung.* Bielefeld, Germany: transcript Verlag.

HENKEL, A., LÜDTKE, N., BUSCHMANN, N. and HOCHMANN, L. 2018. *Reflexive Responsibilisierung: Verantwortung für nachhaltige Entwicklung,* Bielefeld, Germany: transcript Verlag.

HOBSON, K., HOLMES, H., WELCH, D., WHEELER, K., & WIESER, H. 2021. Consumption Work in the circular economy: A research agenda. *Journal of Cleaner Production*, 321, 128969.

HORNSEY, M. J., HARRIS, E. A. and FIELDING, K. S. 2018. Relationships among conspiratorial beliefs, conservatism and climate scepticism across nations. *Nature Climate Change,* 8, pp. 614–620.

HOVDEN, E. and LINDSETH, G. 2002. Norwegian climate policy 1989–2002. *Realizing Rio in Norway: Evaluative Studies of Sustainable Development,* pp. 143–68.

HUDDART KENNEDY, E., PARKINS, J. R. and JOHNSTON, J. 2018. Food activists, consumer strategies, and the democratic imagination: Insights from eat-local movements. *Journal of Consumer Culture,* 18, pp. 149–168.

HULME, M. 2009/10. Why we disagree about climate change: Understanding controversy, inaction and opportunity. *The Carbon Yearbook. The Annual Review of Business and Climate Change* [Accessed 24.09.2022 Online].

HULME, M. 2015. Climate and its changes: A cultural appraisal. *Geo: Geography and Environment,* 2, pp. 1–11.

HULME, M. 2016. *Weathered: Cultures of climate,* Thousand Oaks, California, USA: Sage.

HUME, D. 1738. *A treatise of human nature,* Oxford, UK: Clarendon Press.

IKERD, J. 2005. *Sustainable capitalism: A Matter of Common Sense,* West Hartford, Connecticut, USA: Kumarian Press.

JAEGER-ERBEN, M. 2017. Zwischen kommuniziertem und routiniertem Sinn – Alternative Perspektiven auf die Rolle von Umwelt-und Naturbewusstsein für umweltrelevante soziale Praktiken. *Gesellschaftliche Naturkonzeptionen.* Berlin, Germany: Springer Verlag GmbH.

JAMISON, A. 2001. *The making of green knowledge: Environmental politics and cultural transformation,* Cambridge, UK: Cambridge University Press.

JENKINS, R. 2002. *Pierre Bourdieu, Revised Edition,* Milton Park, Abingdon-on-Thames, UK: Routledge.

JONAS, H. 1979. *Das Prinzip Verantwortung. Versuch einer Ethik für die technologische Zivilisation*, Frankfurt a.M./Germany: Suhrkamp-Taschenbuch-Verlag.

JONAS, H. 1985. *The imperative of responsibility: In search of an ethics for the technological age (English Edition)*, Chicago, Ilinois, USA: University of Chicago Press.

JONAS, M. 2018. Moralisierung der Marktsphäre? – Verantwortungszuschreibungen in der Inszenierung von Fairtrade. *In:* HENKEL, A., LÜDTKE, N., BUSCHMANN, N. and HOCHMANN, L. (eds.) *Reflexive Responsibilisierung. Verantwortung für nachhaltige Entwicklung*. Bielefeld, Germany: transcript Verlag.

JURT, J. 2010. Die Habitus-Theorie von Pierre Bourdieu. *Lithes Zeitschrift für Literatur und Theatersoziologie*, 3, pp. 5–17.

KALLIS, G., KOSTAKIS, V., LANGE, S., MURACA, B., PAULSON, S. & SCHMELZER, M. 2018. Research on degrowth. *Annual Review of Environment and Resources*, 43, pp. 291–316.

KAUERTZ, B., BRICK, C., SCHLECHT, S., BUSCH, M., MARKWARDT, S. and WELLENREUTHER, F. 2018. FKN Ökobilanz 2018 *Ökobilanzieller Vergleich von Getränkeverbundkartons mit PET-Einweg-und Glas-Mehrwegflaschen in den Getränkesegmenten Saft/Nektar, H-Milch und Frischmilch*. Heidelberg, Germany: IFEU (Institute for Energy and Environmental Research).

KELLSTEDT, P. M., ZAHRAN, S. and VEDLITZ, A. 2008. Personal efficacy, the information environment, and attitudes toward global warming and climate change in the United States. *Risk Analysis: An International Journal*, 28, pp. 113–126.

KEMPER, T. D. 1990. *Research Agendas in the Sociology of Emotions*, Albany, New York, USA: SUNY Press.

KEMPF, H. 2008. *How the rich are destroying the earth*, Hartford, Vermont, USA: Chelsea Green Publishing Company.

KENNER, D. 2015. Inequality of overconsumption: The ecological footprint of the richest. Global Sustainability Institute, pp.1-18.

KENT, J. 2009. *Individual responsibility and voluntary action on climate change*. Amsterdam Conference on the Human Dimensions of Global Environmental Change. Earth System Governance: *People, Places and the Planet*. Institute for Environmental Studies, Vrije Universiteit Amsterdam.

KESSLER, S. and RAU, H. 2022. *Capturing climate-cultural diversity: A comparison of climate change debates in Germany*. In: HEIMANN, T., SOMMER, J., KUSENBACH, M. and GABRIELA, C. (eds.) *Climate Cultures in Europe and North America*. Milton Park, Abingdon-on-Thames: UK, Routledge.

KEYNES, J. M. 1937. The general theory of employment. *The Quarterly Journal of Economics*, 51, pp. 209–223.

KLEIN, N. 2015. *This changes everything: Capitalism vs. the climate (kindle edition)*, London, UK: Penguin Books.

KRASMANN, S. 2003. Die Kriminalität der Gesellschaft. Zur Gouvernementalität der Gegenwart. *Kriminologisches Journal* 36, pp. 229–230.

KROESEN, M. 2013. Exploring people's viewpoints on air travel and climate change: Understanding inconsistencies. *Journal of Sustainable Tourism*, 21, pp. 271–290.

KROSNICK, J. A., HOLBROOK, A. L., LOWE, L. and VISSER, P. S. 2006. The origins and consequences of democratic citizens' policy agendas: A study of popular concern about global warming. *Climatic Change*, 77, pp. 7–43.

KUBINA, M. 2022. Nachtragshaushalt: Lindners Sinneswandel [Online]. Berlin, Germany: ARD-Hauptstadtstudio. Available: https://www.tagesschau.de/inland/innenpolitik/lindner-nachtragshaushalt-103.html [Accessed 23/03/2022].

KUCKARTZ, U. 2010. Nicht hier, nicht jetzt, nicht ich. *In:* WELZER, H., SOEFFNER, H.-G. and GIESECKE, D. (eds.) *KlimaKulturen – Soziale Wirklichkeiten im Klimawandel.* Frankfurt a.M., Germany: Campus.

KUCKARTZ, U. 2012. *Qualitative Inhaltsanalyse: Methoden, Praxis, Computerunterstützung*, Weinheim, Germany/Basel, Switzerland: Beltz Juventa.

KUHN, T. S. 1962. *The structure of scientific revolutions*, Chicago, Illinois, USA: University of Chicago Press.

KUNDZEWICZ, Z. W., MATCZAK, P., OTTO, I. M. and OTTO, P. E. 2020. From "atmosfear" to climate action. *Environmental Science and Policy*, 105, pp. 75–83.

LATOUCHE, S. 2014. *La scommessa della decrescita*, Feltrinelli Editore.

LAURENT, É. 2014. *Inequality as pollution, pollution as inequality: The social-ecological nexus*. Paris, France, Sciences Po.

LEGGEWIE, C., WELZER, H. and HEIDBRINK, L. 2009. Klimakultur – ein transdisziplinärer Projektverbund. *Zwei Grad. Das Wetter, der Mensch und sein Klima.* Göttingen, Germany: Wallstein Verlag.

LEISEROWITZ, A., MAIBACH, E., & ROSER-RENOUF, C. 2009. Global warming's six Americas 2009: An audience segmentation analysis. Yale, Connecticut, USA: *Yale Project on Climate Change*.

LENK, H. 2006. What is Responsibility? *Philosophy Now.* London, UK: Anja Publications.

LEVISTON, Z., WALKER, I. and MORWINSKI, S. 2013. Your opinion on climate change might not be as common as you think. *Nature Climate Change*, 3, pp. 334–337.

LEWANDOWSKY, S. 2021. Climate change disinformation and how to combat it. *Annual Review of Public Health*, 42, pp. 1–21.

LIDSKOG, R. and WATERTON, C. 2018. The Anthropocene: A narrative in the making. *Environment and Society.* Berlin, Germany: Springer-Verlag GmbH.

LIEBOLD, R. and TRINCZEK, R. 2002. Experteninterview. *Handbuch Methoden der Organisationsforschung.* Berlin, Germany: Springer Verlag GmbH.

LIFTON, R. J. and FALK, R. 1982. *Indefensible weapons: The political and psychological case against nuclearism*, USA, N/A.

LINDNER, C. 2019. Klimatag statt Klimademos während der Schulzeit. *ZEIT ONLINE GmbH*, 15/03/2019.

LOOS, P. and SCHÄFFER, B. 2001. *Das Gruppendiskussionsverfahren,* Wiesbaden, Germany: VS Verlag für Sozialwissenschaften.

LORDE, A. 1984. *Age, race, class, and sex: Women redefining difference,* Berkely, California, USA: The Crossing Press, (A Division of Ten Speed Press).

LÜDKE, S. 2015. *#OursToLose: YouTuber sammeln Klicks gegen Klimawandel* [Online]. Hamburg, Germany: DER SPIEGEL GmbH and Co. KG Available: https://www.spiegel.de/panorama/ourstolose-youtube-kaempft-gegen-den-klimawandel-a-00000000-0003-0001-0000-000000139329 [Accessed 04.12.2019.]

LÜDTKE, N. 2018. Transdisziplinarität und Verantwortung: Wissenschaftssoziologische Perspektiven auf projektförmig organisierte Forschung. *In:* HENKEL, A., LÜDTKE, N., BUSCHMANN, N. and HOCHMANN, L. (eds.) *Reflexive Responsibilisierung. Verantwortung für Nachhaltige Entwicklung.* Bielefeld, Germany: transcript Verlag.

LÜTJEN, T. 2016. *Die Politik der Echokammer: Wisconsin und die ideologische Polarisierung der USA.* Bielefeld, Germany: transcript Verlag.

LUKE, T. W. 2005. The death of environmentalism or the advent of public ecology? *Organization and Environment,* 18, pp. 489–494.

LUTZ, C. 2016. A Social Milieu Approach to the Online Participation Divides in Germany. *Social Media and Society,* 2.

MANIATES, M. 2001. Individualization: Plant a Tree, Buy a Bike, Save the World? Confronting Consumption, *Global Environmental Politics,* 1(3), 31–52, Cambridge, Massachusetts, USA.

MARKUS LANZ. 2019. *Sendung vom 27. Juni 2019.* Hamburg, Germany.

MARR, A. 2008. *Parallel Mind, the Art of Creativity,* N/A, Aliyah Marr.

MARWELL, G. and AMES, R. E. 1981. Economists free ride, does anyone else?: Experiments on the provision of public goods, IV. *Journal of Public Economics,* 15, pp. 295–310.

MACARTHUR, H. J., & SHIELDS, S. A. 2015. There's No Crying in Baseball, or Is There? Male Athletes, Tears, and Masculinity in North America. *Emotion Review,* 7(1), 39–46. https://doi.org/10.1177/1754073914544476.

MEADOWS, D. H. 1998. Indicators and information systems for sustainable development. *The Sustainability Institute,* Stellenbosch, South Africa.

MERRIAM-WEBSTER. (N/D). *Ad hominem.* In Merriam-Webster.com dictionary. Retrieved from https://www.merriam-webster.com/dictionary/ad%20hominem [Accessed 05/11/2023].

MEUSER, M. and NAGEL, U. 1991. ExpertInneninterviews – vielfach erprobt, wenig bedacht. *Das Experteninterview.* Berlin, Germany: Springer Verlag GmbH.

METAG, Julia; FÜCHSLIN, Tobias; SCHÄFER, Mike S. 2015. Global warming's five Germanys: A typology of Germans' views on climate change and patterns of media use and information. *Public Understanding of Science,* 26/4, pp. 434–451.

MILÉŘ, T., HOLLAN, J., VÁLEK, J. and SLÁDEK, P. 2012. Teachers' understanding of climate change. *Procedia – Social and Behavioral Sciences,* 69, pp. 1437–1442.

MILLS, C. Wright. 2016. *Soziologische Phantasie*. Berlin, Germay: Springer-Verlag

MOSER, S. C. 2006. Talk of the city: engaging urbanites on climate change. *Environmental Research Letters,* 1, 014006.

MOTESHARREI, S., RIVAS, J. and KALNAY, E. 2014. *Modeling Inequality and Use of Resources in the Collapse or Sustainability of Societies*. Houston, Texas, USA: NASA, Goddard Space Center.

MURACA, B. & SCHMELZER, M. 2017. *Sustainable degrowth: Historical roots of the search for alternatives to growth in three regions. History of the Future of Economic Growth*. Milton Park, Abingdon-on-Thames, UK: Routledge.

MUSCH, A.-K. 2021. *Transformation oder Stagnation?: Partizipation in der Nachhaltigkeitsforschung-eine vergleichende Fallstudie.* Munich, Germany: Universitätsbibliothek Ludwig-Maximilians-Universität.

NERLICH, B., KOTEYKO, N. and BROWN, B. 2010. Theory and language of climate change communication. *Wiley Interdisciplinary Reviews: Climate Change,* 1, pp. 97–110.

NEUBAUER, L. 2022. Felix Lobrecht – was machen wir falsch? *1,5 Grad – der Klima-Podcast mit Luisa Neubauer.* Germany: Spotify Original.

NEVERLA, I., TADDICKEN, M., LÖRCHER, I. and HOPPE, I. 2019. *Klimawandel im Kopf*. Wiesbaden, Germany: Springer Fachmedien.

NGUYEN-KIM/MAILAB, M. T. 2018. *Die Klimawandel-Therapie*. Germany.

NGUYEN-KIM/MAILAB, M. T. 2019. *Klimawandel: Das ist jetzt zu tun! (feat. Rezo)*.Germany.

NIDA-RÜMELIN, J. 2011. *Verantwortung,* Ditzingen, Germany: Reclam.

NORGAARD, K. M. 2006. "We don't really want to know" environmental justice and socially organized denial of global warming in Norway. *Organization and Environment,* 19, pp. 347–370.

NORGAARD, K. M. 2011. *Living in denial: Climate change, emotions, and everyday life,* Cambridge, Massachusetts, USA: MIT Press.

NORGAARD, K. M. 2018. The sociological imagination in a time of climate change. *Global and Planetary Change,* 163, pp. 171–176.

OEHLMANN, M., KLAAS, K., NUNES-HEINZMANN, A.-C., KAHLENBORN, W. and CIROTH, A. 2021. *Keine Wende in Sicht: Einkommen and Umweltbelastung gehen weiter Hand in Hand.* In: (UBA), U. (ed.). Berlin, Germany.

OLSSON, M. and LLOYD, A. 2017. Being in place: embodied information practices. *Information Research, CoLIS paper 1601, published by the University of Borås, Sweden,* 22.

ORRELL, D. 2017. *Economyths: 11 Ways Economics Gets it Wrong,* London, UK: Icon Books.

OVERLAND, I. and SOVACOOL, B. K. 2020. The misallocation of climate research funding. *Energy Research and Social Science*, 62, 101349.

OXFORD GEOENGINEERING PROGRAMME. 2018. Oxford, UK: Oxford Martin School, University of Oxford. Available: https://www.geoengineering.ox.ac.uk / https://www.geoengineering.ox.ac.uk/what-is-geoengineering/what-is-geoengineering/ [Accessed 13/02/2022].

PAECH, N. 2012. *Befreiung vom Überfluss: Auf dem Weg in die Postwachstumsökonomie*, Munich, Germany: oekom Verlag.

PAECH, N. 2018. Überforderte Politik – warum nur individuelle Verantwortungsübernahme die Ökosphäre rettet. *In:* HENKEL, A., LÜDTKE, N., BUSCHMANN, N. and HOCHMANN, L. (eds.) *Reflexive Responsibilisierung. Verantwortung für nachhaltige Entwicklung*. Bielefeld, Germany: transcript Verlag.

PIRGMAIER, M. 2020. Consumption corridors, capitalism and social change, *Sustainability: Science, Practice and Policy*, 16:1, 274–285, DOI: 10.1080/15487733.2020.1829846.

PÖTTER, B. 2019. Ökobilanz: "Bei der Umweltpolitik ist Deutschland Entwicklungsland" https://www.spiegel.de/wissenschaft/natur/umweltpolitik-was-deutschland-von-anderen-laendern-lernen-kann-a-1259518.html, spiegelonline.de 26/03/2019.

POPPER, K. 1980. *Die offene Gesellschaft und ihre Feinde II: Falsche Propheten: Hegel, Marx und die Folgen*, Munich, Germany: Francke Verlag.

RAU, H. 2008. Environmental Arguing at a Crossroads? Cultural Diversity in Irish Transport Planning, in R. Edmondson and H. Rau (eds.) *Environmental Argument and Cultural Difference: Locations, Fractures and Deliberations*. Oxford, UK: Peter Lang, pp. 95–124.

RAU, H. 2015. Time use and resource consumption, in M. Fischer-Kowalski, H. Rau and K. Zimmerer (eds.) *International Encyclopedia of the Social and Behavioural Sciences*, 2nd ed., Area 9/1e – Ecological and Environmental Sciences. Oxford: Elsevier, pp. 373–378.

RAU, H. 2018. Minding the Mundane: Everyday Practices as Central Pillar of Sustainability Thinking and Research. *Environment and Society*. London, UK: Palgrave Macmillan.

RAU, H., DAVIES, A. R. and FAHY, F. 2014. Moving on – Promising pathways to more sustainable futures. *In:* RAU, H., DAVIES, A. R. and FAHY, F. (eds.) *Challenging Consumption: Pathways to a More Sustainable Future.* Milton Park, Abingdon-on-Thames, UK: Routledge.

RAU, H. and EDMONDSON, R. 2013. Time and sustainability. *Methods of Sustainability Research in the Social Sciences*, pp. 173–190.

RECKWITZ, A. 2002. Toward a theory of social practices: A development in culturalist theorizing. *European Journal of Social Theory*, 5, pp. 243–263.

RECKWITZ, A. 2003. Grundelemente einer Theorie sozialer Praktiken. *Zeitschrift für Soziologie*, 32, p. 282.

REDAKTIONSNETZWERK DEUTSCHLAND. 2022. Felix Lobrecht bei Luisa Neubauer: *Fridays for Future ist so ein Gymnasiastending*, Verlagsgesellschaft Madsack GmbH & Co. KG, Hannover, Germany.

REZO/REZO JA LOL EY. 2019a. *Die Zerstörung der CDU.* Aachen, Germany.

REZO/REZO JA LOL EY. 2019b. *Offener Brief-Video: Ein Statement von 90+ YouTubern.* Aachen, Germany.

ROBERTS, J. T. and PARKS, B. 2006. *A climate of injustice: Global inequality, north-south politics, and climate policy,* Cambridge, Massachusetts, USA: MIT press.

ROSA, E. A., RUDEL, T. K., YORK, R., JORGENSON, A. K. and DIETZ, T. 2015. The human (anthropogenic) driving forces of global climate change. *Climate Change and Society: Sociological Perspectives,* 2, pp. 32–60.

ROSA, H. 2007. Wir wissen nicht mehr, was wir alles haben. *In:* RADISCH, I. (ed.). Hamburg, Germany: Die Zeit.

ROSENBERG, M. 1990. Reflexivity and emotions. *Social Psychology Quarterly,* 53, pp. 3–12.

ROSS, L., GREENE, D. and HOUSE, P. 1977. The "false consensus effect": An egocentric bias in social perception and attribution processes. *Journal of Experimental Social Psychology,* 13, pp. 279–301.

RÖSSEL, J. 2007. Conditions for the Explanatory Power of Life Styles. *European Sociological Review,* 24, pp. 231–241.

ROWELL, A. 1996. *Green backlash: Global subversion of the environment movement,* Milton Park, Abingdon-on-Thames, UK: Routledge.

RUHR NACHRICHTEN. 2021. *Fahrradfahren: Nordkirchen macht auch 2021 wieder mit bei der Aktion Stadtradeln* [Online] https://www.ruhrnachrichten.de/nordkirchen/nordkirchen-macht-auch-2021-wieder-mit-bei-der-aktion-stadtradeln-w1625025-2000217608/ [Accessed 17/09/2022].

SAHAKIAN, M. and WILHITE, H. 2014. Making practice theory practicable: Towards more sustainable forms of consumption. *Journal of Consumer Culture,* 14, pp. 25–44.

SAHAKIAN, M. R., HENRIKE, GREALIS, E., GODIN, L., WALLENBORN, G., BACKHAUS, J., FRIIS, F., GENUS, A. T., GOGGINS, G., HEASLIP, E., HEISKANEN, E., ISKANDAROVA, M., JENSEN, C. L., LAAKSO, S., MUSCH, A.-K., SCHOLL, C., VADOVICS, E., VADOVICS, K., VASSEUR, V. and FAHY, F. 2021. Challenging social norms to recraft practices: A Living Lab approach to reducing household energy use in eight European countries. *Energy Research and Social Science,* 72.

SAUER, K. A., CAPPS, D. K., JACKSON, D. F. and CAPPS, K. A. 2021. Six minutes to promote change: People, not facts, alter students' perceptions on climate change. *Ecology and Evolution,* 11, pp. 5790–5802.

SAVOLAINEN, R. 2007. Information behavior and information practice: reviewing the "umbrella concepts" of information-seeking studies. *The Library Quarterly*, 77, pp. 109–132.

SCHÄFER, M. S. 2012. Online communication on climate change and climate politics: a literature review. *Wiley Interdisciplinary Reviews: Climate Change*, 3, pp. 527–543.

SCHÄFER, M. S. and BONFADELLI, H. 2017. Umwelt-und Klimawandelkommunikation. *Forschungsfeld* Wissenschaftskommunikation. Wiesbaden, Germany: Springer VS.

SCHATZKI, T. 2016. Practice theory as flat ontology. In: SPAARGAREN, G., WEENICK, D. and LAMERS, M. (eds.) *Practice theory and research: Exploring the dynamics of social life*. Milton Park, Abingdon-on-Thames, UK: Routledge.

SCHILLY, J. 2013. Der Standard, Wien, Österreich: Nachhaltig Einkaufen: Der Einkaufszettel als Stimmzettel; Zwei neue Einkaufsführer wollen den Konsumenten den umweltfreundlichen und fairen Einkauf erleichtern: Rezension, https://www.derstandard.at/story/1385169710727/der-einkaufszettel-als-stimmzettel/ [Accessed 02/11/2023].

SCHIRMER, D. 2009. *Empirische Methoden der Sozialforschung: Grundlagen und Techniken*. Stuttgart, Germany, UTB GmbH.

SCHMIDT, A., IVANOVA, A. and SCHÄFER, M. S. 2013. Media attention for climate change around the world: A comparative analysis of newspaper coverage in 27 countries. *Global Environmental Change*, 23, pp. 1233–1248.

SHOVE, E. 2010. Beyond the ABC: Climate Change Policy and Theories of Social Change. *Environment and Planning A*, 42, pp. 1273–1285.

SHOVE, E., PANTZAR, M. and WATSON, M. 2012. *The dynamics of social practice: Everyday life and how it changes*, Thousand Oaks, California, USA: Sage.

SHOVE, E. and WALKER, G. 2010. Governing transitions in the sustainability of everyday life. *Research Policy*, 39, pp. 471–476.

SINUS INSTITUT. 2022. *SINUS-Milieus Deutschland* [Online]. Heidelberg, Germany. Available: https://www.sinus-institut.de/en [Accessed 17/03/2022].

SÖRLIN, S. 2013. Reconfiguring environmental expertise. *Environmental Science and Policy*, 28, pp. 14–24.

SPIELHAGEN, J. 2009–2022. BEEF! MÄNNER KOCHEN ANDERS. Hamburg, Germany: G+J Medien GmbH.

SPURLING, N., MCMEEKIN, A., SHOVE, E., SOUTHERTON, D. and WELCH, D. 2013. Interventions in practice: Re-framing policy approaches to consumer behaviour. *University of Manchester, Sustainable Practices Research Group*.

STATISTA RESEARCH DEPARTMENT. 2021. *Statista Trend-Report: Retrospektive zu den ersten 20 Monaten COVID-19 in Deutschland* [Online]. https://de.statista.com/statistik/studie/id/101811/dokument/die-corona-pandemie/ [Accessed 31/10/2023].

STERN, P. C. 2020. A reexamination on how behavioral interventions can promote household action to limit climate change. *Nature Communications,* 11, pp. 1–3.

STEWART, D. W. and SHAMDASANI, P. N. 1998. Focus group research: Exploration and discovery. *In:* BICKMAN, L. R., D. J. (ed.) *Handbook of applied social research methods*. Thousand Oaks, California, USA: Sage Publications, Inc.

STOLL-KLEEMANN, S. and O'RIORDAN, T. 2020. Revisiting the Psychology of Denial Concerning Low-Carbon Behaviors: From Moral Disengagement to Generating Social Change. *Sustainability,* 12, 935.

SULDOVSKY, B. 2017. The information deficit model and climate change communication. *Oxford research encyclopedia of climate science.*

SUTTIE, J. 2015. *Is Morality Based on Emotions or Reason?* Berkeley, California, USA: The Greater Good Science Center at the University of California, Berkeley.

SUTTON, B. and NORGAARD, K. M. 2013. Cultures of denial: avoiding knowledge of state violations of human rights in Argentina and the United States. *Sociological Forum*. Hoboken, New Jersey, USA: Wiley Online Library, pp. 495–524.

SZERSZYNSKI, B. 2007. The post-ecologist condition: Irony as symptom and cure. *Environmental Politics,* 16, pp. 337–355.

TAMMER, T. 2009. *Unwissen macht nichts? Das Prinzip Verantwortung wird 30. TABVLA RASA*. Jena, Germany: TABVLA-RASA-Verlag.

THALER, R. H. and SUNSTEIN, C. R. 2008. *Nudge: Improving decisions about health, wealth, and happiness,* New Haven, Connecticut, USA: Yale University Press.

TRANTER, B. and BOOTH, K. 2015. Scepticism in a changing climate: A cross-national study. *Global Environmental Change,* 33, pp. 154–164.

UMWELTBUNDESAMT (UBA) 2016. *Higher income earners usually have higher climate-impact lifestyles: "Blind spots" in mobility and living are common.* In: POETSCHKE, F. P. O. (ed.) 26/2016 ed. Berlin, Germany: Umweltbundesamt (UBA).

UMWELTBUNDESAMT (UBA). 2021. Umweltbewusstsein und Umweltverhalten in Deutschland 2020: Vertiefungsstudie: Trends und Tendenzen im Umweltbewusstsein. *In:* WILLIAMS, H. B., REFERAT G II 1) and GELLRICH, A. U., FACHGEBIET I 1.4) (eds.) *Umweltbewusstsein und Umweltverhalten in Deutschland.* Berlin, Germany: Umweltbundesamt (UBA).

UN ENVIRONMENT PROGRAMME. 2015. Sustainable lifestyles and education. Nairobi, Kenya.

VALENTE, T. W. and PUMPUANG, P. 2007. Identifying opinion leaders to promote behavior change. *Health Education and Behavior,* 34, pp. 881–896.

VANDERHEIDEN, S. 2016. Climate change and free riding. *Journal of Moral Philosophy,* 13, p. 1–27.

VAN DER LINDEN, S., ROOZENBEEK, J. and COMPTON, J. 2020. Inoculating against fake news about COVID-19. *Frontiers in psychology*, 11, p. 2928.

VEBLEN, T. 1899. Conspicuous Leisure and Conspicuous Consumption. *The Theory of the Leisure Class: An Economic Study of Institutions.* New York, New York, USA: Macmillan.

WAGNER, G. and WEITZMAN, M. L. 2015. *Climate shock: The economic consequences of a hotter planet,* Princeton, New Jersey, USA: Princeton University Press.

WAHNBAECK, C. 2018. Das können Sie persönlich gegen den Klimawandel tun. *Spiegel Online.* Hamburg, Germany: SPIEGEL-Gruppe.

WALTER, S., BRÜGGEMANN, M. and ENGESSER, S. 2018. Echo chambers of denial: Explaining user comments on climate change. *Environmental Communication,* 12, pp. 204–217.

WDR WISSEN N/A. Nitrat Stickstoff, Westdeutscher Rundfunk Cologne, Germany: https://www1.wdr.de/wissen/natur/nitrat-stickstoff-100.html [Accessed 16/09/2022].

WELZER, H., SOEFFNER, H.-G. and GIESECKE, D. (eds.) 2010. *KlimaKulturen: Soziale Wirklichkeiten im Klimawandel,* Frankfurt a.M./New York, New York, USA: Campus Verlag.

WENDT, B. and GÖRGEN, B. 2018. Macht und soziale Ungleichheit als vernachlässigte Dimensionen der Nachhaltigkeitsforschung. Überlegungen zum Verhältnis von Nachhaltigkeit und Verantwor tung. *In:* HENKEL, A., LÜDTKE, N., BUSCHMANN, N. and HOCHMANN, L. (eds.) *Reflexive Responsibilisierung. Verantwortung für Nachhaltige Entwicklung.* Bielefeld: Sozialtheorie.

WESTLAKE, S. 2017. *A Counter-Narrative to Carbon Supremacy: Do Leaders Who Give Up Flying Because of Climate Change Influence the Attitudes and Behaviour of Others?* MSc Climate Change Management Master Thesis, Birkbeck University.

WETZEL, J. 2021. Extinction Rebellion: Klimaaktivisten dringen in Münchner Büro ein. *Süddeutsche Zeitung,* 14/07/2021.

WILKINSON, R. and PICKETT, K. 2010. *The spirit level: Why equality is better for everyone (kindle edition),* London, UK: Penguin Books.

WITTGENSTEIN, L. and ANSCOMBE, G. E. M. 1953. *Philosophical Investigations,* Oxford, UK: Blackwell Publishing.

WORLD COMMISSION ON ENVIRONMENT AND DEVELOPMENT. 1987. The Brundtland report: Our common future. *United Nations Documents.* New York, New York, USA.

ZERUBAVEL, E. 1997. *Social mindscapes: An invitation to cognitive sociology,* Boston, Massachusetts, USA: Harvard University Press.

ZERUBAVEL, E. 2010. The social sound of silence: Toward a sociology of denial. In Ben-Ze'ev, E. Ginio, R. and Winter, J. (eds.), *Shadows of War: A Social History of Silence in the Twentieth Century.* Cambridge, UK, Cambridge University Press. pp. 32–44.